D1189911

Reading
North Korea

An
Ethnological
Inquiry

Harvard East Asian Monographs 341

Reading
North Korea

An
Ethnological
Inquiry

Sonia Ryang

Published by the Harvard University Asia Center
and distributed by Harvard University Press
Cambridge (Massachusetts) and London, 2012

Printed in the United States of America

The Harvard University Asia Center publishes a monograph series and, in coordination with the Fairbank Center for Chinese Studies, the Korea Institute, the Reischauer Institute of Japanese Studies, and other faculties and institutes, administers research projects designed to further scholarly understanding of China, Japan, Vietnam, Korea, and other Asian countries. The Center also sponsors projects addressing multidisciplinary and regional issues in Asia.

Publication of this book was partially underwritten by the Academy of Korean Studies Institutional Grant at the Korea Institute, Harvard University.

Library of Congress Cataloging-in-Publication Data

Ryang, Sonia.
    Reading North Korea : an ethnological inquiry / Sonia Ryang.
       p. cm. -- (Harvard East Asian monographs ; 341)
    Includes bibliographical references and index.
    ISBN 978-0-674-06247-4 (hardcover : acid-free paper) 1. Korean literature--
Korea (North)--History and criticism. 2. Literature and society--Korea (North)
3. Ethnography--Korea (North) 4. Korea (North)--Social life and customs.
I. Title.
    PL997.A25R93 2011
    895.7'09--dc23

                                                 2011046702

Index by Mary Mortensen

♾ Printed on acid-free paper

Last figure below indicates year of this printing

22 21 20 19 18 17 16 15 14 13 12

Acknowledgments

As with the birth of any book, this one is derived from a series of moments, each containing a mixture of hesitation, uncertainty, and increasing momentum. At each of these moments, certain key individuals have been there to offer me help, support, and constructive criticism. First of all, I would like to thank William Hammell, director of the Harvard University Asia Center publications program. Without Will's sustained faith in my work, I would not have been able to complete this book in the current form. I also wish to thank Charles Armstrong and Robert Oppenheim, who, as anonymous reviewers, have given me a wealth of constructive suggestions and encouragement. I also wish to thank the members of the Asia Center publications committee, who not only unanimously voted to support this book's publication, but also provided me with valuable feedback for the final revision of the manuscript. In particular, Carter Eckert's positive reaction to my work was a tremendous source of encouragement.

I thank my father, Ryang Nam In, for having granted me access to his extensive collection of North Korean books, published from the mid-1940s up to the present day. Without such access, this book could not have been written. Sidney Mintz, the main party responsible for encouraging me to delve into the world of Ruth Benedict, helped me to clarify my thoughts, as always. I thank also my copyeditor, Donald Cameron, whose editorial eye immensely improved my text so as to help me better convey my thoughts. Portions of research for this book were carried out in the George H. W. Bush Presidential Library at Texas A&M University. I wish to thank the Bush School of Government and Public Service at Texas A&M University for awarding me a Korea Grant for this research. I wish also to thank the Department of Anthropology and Institute for Comparative Culture at Seoul National University for inviting me to their seminar, where I was able to test out my ideas contained in this book. Faculty and students there gave me helpful feedback. The day of my seminar happened to be the day of North Korea's Yeongpyeong Island bombing (November 2010). Yet, the audience was thoughtful and measured in their approach to North Korea. It was a memorable experience that I feel ought to be acknowledged along with the publication of this book.

The bulk of this manuscript was written while my family was staying in temporary rental accommodations in the aftermath of the serious flooding in the Midwest in June 2008. After our home disappeared under more than six feet of water, we experienced many days of uncertainty, and my husband, Bradley Kaldahl, heroically helped our family sustain its spirit and my focus. I am writing these acknowledgments back in our home on the Iowa River, newly rebuilt nine feet above the ground. It is fortuitous that this book is reaching my readers just as our family resumes its normal routine. Above all, my children, Samantha and Thomas, their every smile and every loving hug, are behind the birth of this book. I am truly grateful.

Iowa City
October 2011

Contents

Figures viii

Preface ix

INTRODUCTION
A Journey into the Abyss 1

ONE
Love 40

TWO
War 85

THREE
Self 140

CONCLUSION
On the Social and the Political 190

Reference Matter

References 213

Index 221

Figures

1 Cover art of *Meon kil* (The Long Road)   73
2 Inner cover of *Seungrijadeul* (The Victors)   93
3 Illustration from *Seongjangui bom* (A Spring of Growth)   167
4 Illustration from *Yonghaegongdeul* (The Iron Workers)   173

Preface

More than 25 years have passed since I last visited North Korea. I traveled there in 1985 as a reporter working for a Tokyo-based, Korean-language daily newspaper published by Chongryun, the General Association for Korean Residents in Japan, which supported North Korea. It was June. Although Tokyo was entering the rainy season, Pyongyang was sunny and dry. My supervisor (in the guise of a tour guide) from the Workers' Party of Korea, North Korea's ruling party, kept teasing me that I was already 25 years old and yet had no marriage prospects. He called me *rocheonyeo,* an old spinster. I was intrigued: I had always thought that women who continued working long after college graduation were admired in North Korea, as they were seen as contributing to the revolution. At least this was what I could recall from the contents of *The Works of Kim Il Sung* that I had read as a student. As those readers familiar with my first book, *North Koreans in Japan: Language, Ideology, and Identity* (1997), may recall, I was born and raised in Japan among Koreans who regarded North Korea as their fatherland, this despite the fact that the absolute majority of them (including my parents and grandparents) originated from the southern provinces of the Korean peninsula.

When I returned to Japan in 1992, seven years after the visit to North Korea described above, as a doctoral student in Social Anthropology at the University of Cambridge, I recognized a

continuing sense of commitment to North Korea among the
people I had previously known as *dongpo,* or brethren. North
Korea was alive and well in the minds of these Koreans in
Japan, many of whose children and other family members had
relocated to North Korea after the introduction in 1959 of a
scheme allowing Koreans in Japan to be repatriated to North
Korea (see the Introduction to this volume). After a period as
an academic nomad, taking up a postdoctoral fellowship at
the Australian National University and more or less settling
in the United States as a professor and educator, I decided to
take another look at this strange country, a nation to which the
American media could not refer without resorting to terms
such as "rogue," "terrorist," "subversive," or "inhumane." As
far as I was concerned, this was the land to which dozens of
my former classmates had been repatriated from Japan.

Whenever I heard news of defections, nuclear weapon development, starvation, or any one of a series of calamities af-
fecting that country, I would think of these people, all appearing as they had when I had last seen them, their youthful faces
filled with hope and anticipation. Every year, from my first
year at elementary school right through until my graduation
from high school, I would send off classmates and their families
to North Korea, sometimes multiple times in one year. Some
chose this path because it was very difficult for them to survive
financially in Japan, others due to particular personal circumstances. It might be useful at this point to cite the case of one
of my classmates in sixth grade, whose father, a prominent scientist, decided to contribute to the betterment of our "socialist
fatherland" by attending an international conference in Europe
as a member of the North Korean delegation. Since the Japanese government did not allow Koreans to re-enter Japan in
those days, his father ended up stranded in Pyongyang after
the conference. My classmate, along with his mother and his
brothers, therefore, decided to be repatriated to North Korea
in order to join his father in 1972. A few letters reached us in
Japan after his repatriation, although these later became rarer
until, finally, around 1975, we heard a rumor that the family

had been relocated to a mountainous village. Since then, no one has had any word of the family's whereabouts or even whether or not its members are still alive. In other cases, individuals decided to be repatriated on their own, without their families, in order to fulfill dreams that would have been unattainable in Japan due to the ethnic discrimination suffered by Koreans living there. To my knowledge, only one or two of my classmates attained their dreams in North Korea. Others are not talked about.

It is still very strange for me to think (let alone understand) how it is that I now call the United States home, raising my children here and mired in the mundane aspects of everyday life, from faculty meetings to grocery shopping, while others with a very similar background to my own ended up in a place called North Korea, a place that in a strange way used to be familiar to me. I was educated in a school system that consistently fashioned itself in the North Korean–style revolutionary mold, seeking to cultivate loyalty for the Great Leader and the North Korean state. In this sense, I could well have ended up as one of those people who were repatriated to North Korea. Although my education was one of ideological indoctrination, it took place in Japan, a so-called free society. This meant that I was able to avoid, along with my classmates, total immersion within the institution known as North Korea. Instead, we were able to distinguish between what was required of us in the North Korea–influenced community of Koreans in Japan and what was deemed as normal and mainstream in Japanese society at large. For those who were repatriated from Japan, however, this duality was absent.

Today, North Korea no longer holds any political, let alone moral, sway, over those Koreans living in Japan, as its credentials as a national polity have plummeted on multiple fronts. In spite of globalization, North Korea continues to keep its doors tightly shut to the outside world, leaving our knowledge of it both fragmented and disjointed. I felt the keen need for intervention, which spurred me to write this book.

I also undertook this study in order to redeem our own grace vis-à-vis North Korea, a nation that tempts us to lose our humanity in the face of its incomprehensible behavior. I wrote this book in order to demonstrate that we can treat it just like any other human society. While no anthropologist has yet to set foot on North Korean soil in order to conduct ethnographic fieldwork, it is still possible to envision an ethnological study of this nation, as I shall argue in the Introduction of this book. Above all, anthropology does not simply provide us with the training for fieldwork; it teaches us to appreciate and try to critically understand human cultures, our own as well as those of others.

In writing this book, my position is an ambivalent one: I am an outsider, but I used to be located in a position that may be deemed as that of an insider. As has been stated earlier, throughout my school education, I was immersed in North Korea's official public discourse of loyalty toward the leadership, the North Korean version of nationalist commitment, and its own depiction of the ideal of Korean reunification. As I read through North Korean texts as I prepared to write this book, I was constantly reminded of how much I knew about how language was used in North Korea. Yet, at the same time, I found myself a stranger adrift in a sea of politically loaded and at times almost comedic usages of conventional social science concepts. As I continued to write, I tried to maintain that tension within myself, the tension that comes from being simultaneously insider and outsider. If the reader finds some of my prose untamed and raw, it may be attributed to this tension.

I dedicate this book to all of my former classmates who were repatriated to North Korea between 1966 and 1978. A couple of my teachers were also repatriated. A few of my Korean neighbors also took that route. I think about them occasionally and whenever I do, I find myself left with deep bewilderment. Writing this book is one small attempt at coming to terms with my helplessness when faced with this situation.

All translations of North Korean texts are my own. I have retained North Korean pronunciation—for example, Rakdong-gang rather than Nakdonggang—while following the recently standardized South Korean method of romanization, where applicable.

Reading
North Korea

An
Ethnological
Inquiry

INTRODUCTION

A Journey into the Abyss

This book may please neither human rights activists nor xenophobes. Anti-communists and diehard Stalinists may also dismiss it. But many readers may be intrigued by its take on North Korea—one derived from a look at state-society relations, drawing upon an ethnological approach that is based on a close reading of selected literary texts published in North Korea.

I neither advocate for North Korea nor directly accuse it of wrongdoing. Further, I avoid ridiculing it or questioning the legitimacy of its existence. The picture of North Korea that I present is neither a monstrosity nor, as North Korea's own nomenclature would have it, a paradise on earth. There has been enough demonization on the one hand and self-embellishment on the other. I therefore refrain from taking either side, and instead look at North Korea from an entirely new angle.

My intent is to conduct an ethnological study of North Korea, just as any anthropologist or ethnologist would vis-à-vis his or her field, but with an important qualification. My specific focus will be on the way in which the connection between the people and the Great Leader is secured, as this connection appears to be one of the most important and meaningful social relations among North Koreans. Here, as the reader will soon find out, I hold the Great Leader (Kim Il Sung, the father) and the Dear Leader (Kim Jong Il, the son) to be separate entities. It is the father, now deceased, and his position vis-à-vis the people, to which I specifically point when I refer to the Leader. The world regards Kim Jong Il as Kim Il Sung's successor; however, this a misunderstanding, or at least an incomplete understanding. Kim Jong Il did not succeed all of Kim Il Sung's powers. Father Kim was not only the Supreme Commander of the Korean People's Army, the title that Kim the son now holds, but also *suryeong*, the Leader, a title which the son does not and will never have, since there is only one possible *suryeong*, Kim Il Sung. Kim Jong Il is referred to as *chidoja* or *ryeongdoja*, both meaning leader, but never *suryeong*. *Suryeong* is also translated into English as the Leader, but this hides the fundamental semantic difference between *ryeongdoja* and *suryeong* in the North Korean context. I will discuss this distinction more extensively below.

North Korea is one of a very small number of nation-states in today's world into which no outside ethnographer has ventured with the specific purpose of conducting anthropological fieldwork. This is extraordinary, considering that the North Korean state has been in official existence for more than 60 years, having been established in 1948, and considering that anthropologists from western and other industrialized nations have ventured to most of the territories on earth during this period.

There are books written by former diplomats assigned to North Korea or by reporters who worked in North Korea covering it for certain periods. Some of these works include references to the everyday lives of so-called ordinary North Koreans (Bradley 2006; Lankov 2007, for example). There are books by photojournalists, novelists, academic researchers, and even tourists who have visited North Korea and then published reports of their discoveries. However, such works typically have been the product of short stays in the country, certainly when compared with anthropological ethnographic fieldwork, which usually lasts for one or two years (as suggested by Poivert, Fenby, and Chancel 2007; Harris 2007). Furthermore, the itineraries of such trips are usually strictly controlled by the state, with visitors taken to pre-arranged, pre-designated sites by official guides, under conditions that differ markedly from the spirit of anthropological fieldwork.

There are also memoirs and expositions (such as Kang 2005; Choe and Sin 1988) by former detainees, deserters, and defectors who lived in North Korea for extended periods. While these undeniably carry a wealth of information on North Korean society, such accounts must be considered with particular caution, due to the overly politicized circumstances surrounding the publication of this genre of literature. In sum, none of the existing studies of North Korea that claim legitimacy based on the argument that they are derived from first-hand experience withstands comparison with the conventional criteria of ethnography.

While being ethnographically informed, ethnological studies do not have to be premised upon ethnographic fieldwork. Yet, the ethnological study aims to lay bare the logical undercurrents of the culture that it examines. Whereas the term "ethnography" denotes a genre of writing, "ethnology" refers to a scholarly discipline, an attempt to understand, among other things, an ethnos, its ethos and values. For that purpose, ethnographic data is extremely useful. But other data, including historiography, art and literature, media reporting, and even state-crafted propaganda, are equally useful. Not all ethnographers are ethnologists, but by the same token, not all ethnologists have carried out fieldwork in the cultural environment about which they study and write.

In writing this book, I define myself as an ethnologist of North Korea who has yet to conduct ethnographic fieldwork there. My strategy is a hybrid one, relying on no linear or chronological scheme. I make frequent reference to existing ethnological studies that have informed my investigation of North Korea because of the commonalities and contrasts they help illuminate in relation to cultural logic, structure, and the operative mode of everyday life. In fact, I place more emphasis on these than on the various books on North Korea currently in existence, as the majority of the latter fall into one of the three categories discussed above: advocacy, accusation, or ridicule.

As such, this book seeks to make a break with overly politicized positions. Yet, I maintain that political institutions and political (not politicized) relations are of prime importance when trying to understand North Korea's cultural logic. In this regard, it is more appropriate to regard the political domain as the target of this study. In North Korea, everything — including life, death, love, body, and the person — is political. Further, the political and the social are indissolubly connected. It is this excess, or the oversaturation of North Korean society with the political, that is the object of my inquiry.

For this purpose, it would appear crucial to closely examine the connection between individuals and the Leader. In studying these ties, I shall focus on three separate, yet intricately connected realms of inquiry — love, war, and self — followed by a concluding note offering a comprehensive analysis of the political foundations of North Korean society. But how are we to proceed in an ethnological study that penetrates to the heart of these fundamental issues? To gain data, I analyze and interpret the rituals and language embodied in North Korean literature, concentrating mainly on works published during the 1970s and 1980s, with additional references to earlier literature. I complement these literary analyses with data drawn from my own visits to North Korea in the 1980s and conversations with Koreans and others who have visited North Korea during different phases of its history.

Most important, however, is the framing of this book as an ethnological study of an unknown land. For this reason, the remainder of this Introduction is dedicated to clarifying my methodology as well as briefly outlining its theoretical and historical background.

Anthropo-ization

There is a reason behind my use of the neologism that heads this section. During the nascent phase of ethnology in the nineteenth century, European scholars sat in their offices in Oxford, Cambridge, London, and Paris, imagining the rituals and customs of remote peoples and writing about them as constitutive elements of humanity, *anthrōpos*, past and present. Studies of "primitives" by these armchair anthropologists were, in other words, endeavors that presupposed a connection between them, the "uncivilized," and us, the "civilized." The primitives, with their bizarre practices and customs, were seen as bearers of remnants of our past. Even after functionalism moved to the core of British Social Anthropology, with use values conferred upon bizarre and unfamiliar institutions—thereby paving the way for cultural relativism—"primitives," now variously referred to as natives or locals, were never placed outside of the *anthrōpos*. They were humans, just like us, albeit inferior.

The dehumanization of the objects of ethnological study is a phenomenon that has been observed on a number of occasions in more recent years—but I am not referring exclusively here to colonialism and/or racism. When Bronisław Malinowski, an Austrian Pole studying anthropology at the London School of Economics, was stranded in Australia during World War I as an enemy national, he had a golden opportunity to study the Trobriand Islanders in their archipelago off New Guinea. All of their seemingly bizarre and arbitrary institutions—the *kula* ring, the avunculate uncle and matrilineal kinship, the eyelash-biting courtship ritual, and the bachelor hut (*bukuma-tula*) where boys and girls stayed overnight to develop premarital sexual relationships—were introduced as parts of a splendid system that humans had created. However different they might have been from us, the intention was not to introduce them as a nonhuman species: they were placed within the frame of humanity (Malinowski 1961, 1987, and 1992). When the British military high commission in Sudan needed E. E. Evans-Pritchard to work on the Nuer in the 1930s, it was not because they deemed the Nuer to be nonhuman (although maybe less human). Fascinated by the Nuer kinship system, their ghost marriages, female marriages, leopard skin chiefs, and their ambivalent relationship with the Dinka, Evans-

Pritchard rendered them human, if not on an equal footing with Western civilization (Evans-Pritchard 1969, 1971).

It was much later, when the Iron Curtain was drawn and humans in opposing camps ceased to attack, invade, inquire into, be curious about, and indeed, touch each other, only regarding others as competitors or as objects of propaganda, that we discern the start of a more explicit and systemic form of dehumanization of the other.

Before Vietnam, there was Korea. Between 1950 and 1953, combat zones had not yet been penetrated by the global media and images of war had not reached living rooms. Consequently, details of the Korean War—the number of human casualties and the extent of destruction, for example—remain open to dispute and in some ways unidentifiable to this day. Although radio, newspapers, photo journals, and magazines carried extensive coverage of the war, the absence of television meant that the Korean conflict left behind very different memories to those evoked by the later Vietnam War (see Cumings 1994). This war was the first example of a new kind of fight, the first of many in which the United States was the prime mover, yet where the institutional mechanism of the United Nations was utilized. It was also the first of many in a series of what later came to be viewed as proxy wars, battles fought between two parties that each represented the interests of one or the other of the dominant superpowers, the United States and the Soviet Union.

No notable synchronic sociocultural studies were produced in relation to Korea and the Koreans during the Korean War, in contrast with Japan during World War II. Whereas anthropologists—and notably Ruth Benedict, working for the wartime enemy studies effort—were able to humanize the Japanese by delineating the intermingled hyper-connections between the seemingly fanatic kamikaze bombers and other imperial ultra-nationalists and the sociohistorical background and presuppositions of the Japanese during World War II, no such effort was deemed necessary during the later Korean War (Benedict 1946; Ryang 2004, Chapter 1). Why was this case?

The answer, it seems, can be traced to the way Americans imagined Koreans, that is to say, in how they were not thought of as humans. There was no armchair anthropologist of Korea, as Ruth Benedict had been for Japan. The war was fought, not in order to understand, conquer, and eventually occupy Korea, but to eliminate it altogether. Here, I hasten to add that the object of elimination was confined to the northern half, viewed as the "invader" of the U.S.-occupied south. If classic anthropologists were later criticized for having been sentries in relation to imperial expansion and colonization, North Korea did not even warrant such status. The aim of the United States and the other nations that followed it in the name of the United Nations was to eliminate North Korea from the face of the earth, or perhaps not even that: they did not care. The study or understanding of its culture, therefore, had no place in war.

The dehumanization of North Korea goes back to the end of World War II and the beginning of the Cold War, just prior to the beginning of the Korean War. Already, Western POWs were complaining that their prison guards were Koreans, not Japanese, since, in their eyes, the Koreans were less human than the Japanese, the latter having had the guts to fight against the Allies, and the former having been powerlessly colonized by and subordinated to them.

Dehumanization of the other was carried out by North Koreans, too, perhaps even more ferociously, if less effectively, internationally speaking. Ever since the Korean War, North Korea has referred to the United States with the mandatory suffix *nom*. This is a derogatory term denoting worthlessness and baseness. But if the term *nom* borders on implying a marginal form of humanity, more explicit is the phrase "U.S. imperialist wolves" or *seungnyangi mije*, which literally banishes the American from the human race as a whole. Furthermore, the term consigns the United States to the level of carnivore animality. Accordingly, the following anti-U.S. slogan came to take on an intense ferocity: *mijeui kageul tteuja*. Direct and unambiguous, it calls for the mutilation (into millions of pieces) of U.S. imperialism. Since *mije*, U.S. imperialism, is *seung-nyangi*, a wolf, tearing its limbs apart and gutting its organs would not incur humanly moral wrath of any sort. The effects of such phraseology are unmistakable: by the time a North Korean is old enough to speak, these terms have been adopted as part of his/her everyday discourse, extinguishing any concept of Americans as possessing an even remotely human side. It is, in other words, very hard for North Koreans to come to terms with the idea that Americans are fellow humans. My point, in sum, is that systematic, deep-rooted dehumanization of the other is recognized equally in North Korea and in the United States.

The challenge at this historical juncture, therefore, for the anthropological and ethnological study of North Korea is to (re)anthropo-ize the faceless Koreans. The task is unclear, though, and even more uncomfortable than the one faced by Ruth Benedict vis-à-vis Japan during World War II. For, no meaningful military (let alone social, political, or cultural) contact between North Korea and the United States (or the West, broadly put, for that matter) has occurred since 1953. And rather than being registered as "insane," as were the Japanese involved in kamikaze bombing sorties, the Rape of Nanjing, and the Bataan Death March, North Koreans have come to be labeled as "unknown" and, hence, even less human. (Re)-anthropo-izing North Koreans should, thus, begin with the recognition that we are dealing with a people that are unknown, yet a people nevertheless.

The usual recourse of an anthropologist in this case would be to pack up and leave on a fieldwork expedition. This is not possible in this case, as stated earlier. Under the current conditions, under which no viable fieldwork is possible, how else do we attempt to get to know North Korea?

Culture at a Distance

The supposedly facile quest to conduct ethnographic fieldwork can become, of course, a naïve wish—not only in the case of North Korea, but also, historically, in other places, including the most famed field sites of classical anthropology, such as the land of the Nuer and the Trobriand Islands. First, to make an obvious point: without utilizing archival, literary, historical, or census data, and without recourse to other studies and forms of documentation, no ethnographic fieldwork can be successful. That is to say, producing a good ethnography is not simply the outcome of having gone there and seen it all (as discussed in Clifford and Marcus 1986; Clifford 1988; Marcus and Fischer 1994). Secondly, moving on to an obscure, yet more important point: anthropo-ization is not simply about interacting with the other as a fellow example of humanity, but also about deeming the other a dignified being deserving of respect.

Ethically speaking, it is important to remember that the term "respect" is derived from the Latin *re-specere*, or, to look back at, to look again. Ethicist Karen Lebacqz emphasizes this concept in her essay exploring the position to be taken vis-à-vis the human embryonic stem cell. According to her: "Respect is owed not simply to persons, but very precisely to those who are always in danger of being cast outside the system of protection that personhood brings" (2001, 152–53). Thus, respect can be a concept that not only makes interpersonal human relations viable, but also renders different societies and cultures as counterparts even to the most self-assuredly "superior" nation-states.

If looking at a person again holds the key to entering into a dignified human relationship with that person, to dignify a culture requires multiple acts of re-looking. At first, it might seem ironic to realize that strenuous attempts of this kind were made at the height of Cold War tensions. But, with the Iron Curtain precluding them from conducting viable fieldwork on the territory of the opposing ideological camp, scholars, and especially anthropologists, tried nevertheless to do so, since not doing so would be to succumb to the temptation of the simplistic yet popular language of the propaganda at that time.

It was Margaret Mead and her associates, students of Franz Boas at Columbia University, that strived to establish as a skill set this kind of attempt to "re-look" at distant others. Mid-twentieth-century Boasian anthropology is branded as the Culture and Personality School, which was grounded in the belief that if one had a full understanding of a given culture, one also had a comparable understanding of the typical personality that this given culture produced. The advantage of this approach became clear in the turmoil of World War II, as it became impossible for Western anthropologists to freely travel to remote corners of the world in order to conduct the fieldwork that had been a central element in the structural functionalist approach favored by British Social Anthropology. For this group of researchers, literature, film, public imagery, and other media materials were considered equally important (if not more so) to field data gathered on site (Beeman 2000). Furthermore, Mead and her associates (including Benedict) proposed that if anthropologists could not interview native peoples in their own lands due to war and other limiting circumstances, then interviewing overseas residents would be equally profitable for researchers in their attempts to understand that particular culture. Mead, the principal flag-carrier for this approach, called it the study of "culture at a distance" (Banner 2003, 412–14). (Incidentally, anthropologists and other researchers had already employed this method in relation to Japanese and Japanese-American internees incarcerated by the Roosevelt administration during World War II [Ryang 2004, Chapter 1].) Needless to say, "culture at a distance" was to flourish during the Cold War period, revamped and reinforced as national character studies.

Although Mead and Benedict worked closely with each other, the two women did not employ quite the same methods: Mead was more psychologically disposed, whereas Benedict, who was also a poet, enjoyed using literary sources (see Lapsley 2001; Ryang 2004, Chapter 1; Lummis 2007). Due to Benedict's untimely death in 1948, she did not have the chance to explore the approach that came to be known as "culture at a distance," as such. Nonetheless, this does not change the fact that she concurred with Mead, Gregory Bateson, Geoffrey

Gorer, and others in her belief that a culture (and the typical personality associated with it) could be studied without the need for on-site ethnographic fieldwork. I pay particularly close attention to Benedict, as her work on Japanese culture, *The Chrysanthemum and the Sword*, stands out as different from other works carried out by scholars in this group. For example, based on interviews with Japanese nationals in the United States and American citizens of Japanese descent (utilizing the "culture at a distance" method), Gorer (1942) concluded that the excessive atrocities committed by Japanese soldiers in occupied territories was due to the strict toilet training to which they had been subjected as infants. Benedict's work also came out of the wartime enemy studies sponsored by the Office of War Information, but it tried to do something other than label Japan and the Japanese: by utilizing literary and autobiographic sources from Japan's traditional warrior culture, Benedict (1946) attempted to explain how Japan's cultural logic allowed one to view a kamikaze bombing mission as the utmost demonstration of honor and dedication to the Emperor.

My aims in this book are not unrelated to those of Benedict in *The Chrysanthemum and the Sword* and, for that matter, to the study of "culture at a distance," in that I, an anthropologist, am studying the cultural logic of a society without conducting fieldwork. I am not, however, seeking to come up with some kind of empirical research manual using literature, broadly understood to include film, radio, novels, stories, textbooks and other media—as attempted by Margaret Mead. Nor am I trying to find out how North Koreans think and act and what kind of typical personality they might have; rather, I propose to abstract the cultural logic that runs through North Korean society as an undercurrent to its human relations. In order to do so, I maintain that the way the North Korean leader is represented to North Koreans provides a crucial key to understanding connections between people in that society. In this regard, literary sources published in North Korea provide us with abundant examples of how such connections are articulated and represented in idealized but also concrete terms.

aren't those all controlled by gov't

One particular point to note is that in a society like North Korea, literature is not always produced as a two-way outlet: both as a reflection of social reality and as a constitutive part of that reality. It is, rather, produced on the part of the state apparatus in order to ideologically unify the masses, with the specific intentions of political mobilization and ethos building. Writers are assigned to write certain stories, following designated storylines that are aligned with current policies of the government. As such, it would not be an exaggeration to claim that there are no free writers in North Korea, as their creations occur strictly within the parameters of state control. This is one of the main reasons why my sources are limited.

In this book, I choose to introduce the reader to a total of some fifteen texts that I deem to be of key importance in illuminating the cultural logic that runs through North Korean society. I have selected those out of close to 50 volumes that I surveyed, a number of them being collections of short stories. Although I allude to the existence of so-called key texts, it is difficult to define what makes a particular text key to a society's cultural logic. In some ways, all texts are key texts in North Korea, since each writer is given a specific task involving the promotion of state policy at a given time. The arena in which writers can compete to show off their literary styles and skills is, accordingly, extremely narrowly defined. Furthermore, in North Korea, those books regarded as politically more important are produced in a collective fashion and do not bear the individual names of their authors. These books are assigned as part of revolutionary education in schools and workplaces. This makes it difficult for researchers to assess their value. Whereas individually authored books allow us to make comparative interpretations, paying attention to the prose and storylines deployed in each example, a collectively produced book is nothing more than the official mouthpiece of the state. This does not mean that individually authored books are less important or less political. Finite and impoverished in quantity and quality as they may be, these too are produced by state-trained, state-approved writers who write from a position of authority and privilege vis-à-vis ordinary North Koreans. Readers in North Korea are inherently seen as the object of education. As such, we can assume that these books play an important trend-setting role in North Korea's otherwise rather monotonous and impoverished cultural environment.

Moreover, it is possible to claim that data exists even in the most arid of fields, if we look carefully: propaganda, slogans, official publications, clothing, gait, and even eye movements can be used as data allowing us to gain an understanding of a given society. Indeed, scholars have gone about their work in restricted environments using limited materials yet coming up with insightful research (for example, Whyte 1983 on China). Closely and critically examining North Korean literature—no matter how limited it may be—in this case will yield extra-textual information, approximating what anthropologists would usually call field data. As such, as I hope the reader will understand, this book is not about literature or textuality per se. I will not embark upon analyses of the literary establishment, the politics of literary creation, the publishing mechanism in North Korea, and so on. Rather, I treat literary texts as sources of data—just as Ruth Benedict did in *The Chrysanthemum and the Sword*. I rely on literature as a form of textual and archival material that can give us a window through which we may obtain a certain glimpse of North Korean society. My treatment of this body of data is, thus, of an interpretive manner, rather than an empirical or factual one.

A "Guerrilla State"

The ideological origins of North Korea, as have been argued by a number of reputable scholars, go back temporally to the period of colonial occupation and rule by the Japanese (1910–1945) and spatially to Manchuria, to what is today northeastern China (Park 2005; Armstrong 2004; Cumings 1981, 1990). Contiguous with the Korean peninsula, Manchuria was a pivotal locale for the Japanese colonial authorities from early on, playing a key role in Japanese economic, political, demographic, and territorial expansion toward the Asian continent. Japan's securing of infrastructural hegemony started early with the establishment of the South Manchurian Railway Company in 1906. Its assets increased from 160 million yen shortly after its incorporation to 1 billion yen by 1930. The company's expansion was accompanied by mass migration of Japanese settlers as well as the construction of military bases, as in the case of the Kwantung Army. These activities culminated in the founding of Manchukuo in 1932 and the restoration of Puyi, the last emperor of Qing-dynasty China, under the rubric of multiracial, multiethnic, and multilingual culture-building. Although such a slogan was firmly rooted in the absolutization of the Japanese emperor as the benefactor of all Asians, unlike in Korea, where colonial rule led to the annexation of the Korean royal family by the Imperial family of Japan through intermarriage, the Japanese project in Manchukuo had a different face from the outset. This was a new kind of endeavor, an adventure, and a speculative investment. Indeed, the Japanese were willing to invest heavily, and they did. Further, its objection to relinquishing this new territory led it to withdraw from the League of Nations in 1932 (Harada 2007; Katō 2007).

As it happened, 1932 was also the year when North Korean history books claim that the anti-Japanese Korean Revolutionary People's (guerilla) Army was founded in Manchuria by the then twenty-year-old Kim Il Sung. In North Korea's historiography, the modern era begins with Kim Il Sung's birth on April 15, 1912, two years after the beginning of Japan's colonial rule of the peninsula. Kim's paternal family had moved from southeastern Korea a couple of generations prior to his birth, their clan lineage being the Kims of Andong, a southern family. Kim's father, Kim Hyeong-Jik, attended a missionary high school, Sungsil School, in Pyongyang. While at Sungsil, sixteen-year-old Kim Hyeong-Jik married eighteen-year-old Kang Ban-Seok, daughter of a prominent local Christian family. The Kangs, Kim's maternal family, were devoutly Christian and ran a missionary school near Pyongyang. Due to Kim Hyeong-Jik's involvement in underground political activities of an anti-

Japanese nature, he was arrested and imprisoned in 1918. While in jail, Kim Hyeong-Jik taught himself Oriental herbal medicine and, after his release, embarked on a new career as an herbal doctor. Then, in the early 1920s, Kim Hyeong-Jik, Kang Ban-Seok, and their three young sons migrated to Manchuria.

Seen in this way, Kim Il Sung came from an immigrant family that had been uprooted and displaced on numerous occasions. At the same time, in terms of faith, his family was firmly Christian. The standard North Korean textbook outlining Kim Il Sung's revolutionary history would always describe an episode in which the twelve-year-old Kim made a solo journey from Manchuria back to the village of his birth in Korea in 1924 in order to "receive a Korean education" at his maternal grandfather's missionary school. Soon, however, his father's health deteriorated, and he crossed back over the border in 1926. Given that his maternal grandfather was one of the most prominent church elders in the area and ran a Christian school, how much of his formative education was "Korean" and how much "Christian" is an interesting question. It would suffice to say that from early on, Kim Il Sung's life was diasporic, nomadic, and in some ways "guerrilla-like"—namely, devoid of a secure base.

Soon after his return to Manchuria, his father died. After briefly attending a Chinese academy and then a large private high school in Jilin, one of the sociocultural centers of Manchuria, he gradually emerged as a notable anti-Japanese activist and then as a guerrilla fighter. Legend has it that when crossing the Yalu River again in 1926, Kim turned back to have one last look at his fatherland and swore never to return to Korea unless the country had achieved independence—another episode involving multiple displacements.

This, in large part, is exactly what happened. Kim's return to Korea was indeed in October 1945, about two months after the surrender of Japan and the liberation of Korea. During the intervening twenty years, he had lived in various parts of Manchuria, waging guerrilla warfare against the Japanese alongside like-minded men and women, both Chinese and Korean, before moving to the Soviet Union after 1941 or thereabouts. There, he married Kim Jong Suk, a guerrilla comrade, who gave birth to Kim Jong Il in 1942. Kim Il Sung led a guerrilla-like life struggling against Japanese rule during his entire adulthood prior to the liberation of Korea, and this story helps to explain why Haruki Wada (1992), a leading scholar of Kim Il Sung and of anti-Japanese guerrilla history, has styled North Korea as a "guerrilla state."

The term "guerrilla state" summarizes the logic upon which the North Korean state was founded and has come to be legitimized. According to North Korea's foundation myth, Kim Il Sung was the supreme commander of a Korean guerrilla unit that operated independently of the Chinese and the Soviets. The authenticity of Kim's claim to leadership is derived from his guerrilla warfare against the Japanese. This is not entirely untrue: Kim indeed fought courageously against the Japanese. Whether or not his unit was independent of other units, Chinese, Soviet, or Korean, for example, is a separate question. Furthermore, whether or not Kim Il Sung was so revered by the masses is even less clear. Nevertheless, it is true that Kim Il Sung was widely known in Korea proper: "Kim Il Sung had [. . .] a decisive asset. Compared to Choe Yong-Gon, Kim Chaek, and others, who were active in [guerrilla fighting in] northern Manchuria and therefore [. . .] hardly known inside Korea proper, Kim Il Sung was most widely known in Korea, because he was active in southern Manchuria and had a record of waging battles in northern Korea" (Wada 1992, 331; my translation). Indeed, in the words of Dae-Sook Suh: "Kim Il Sung was a Korean patriot who gallantly took up arms for his country against the Japanese militarists and can claim a place in the annals of modern Korea for what he accomplished" (1995, xiii).

According to Wada's research, between 1953 and 1967, individuals that had not been members of Kim Il Sung's Manchurian guerrilla group (referred to as the "Manchurian faction") were systematically eliminated from the North Korean political arena. By the time the Fifteenth Assembly of the Central Committee of the Workers' Party of Korea was held in May 1967, the key posts in the party were occupied by Kim's close battle comrades, all of them Manchurian veterans. This was openly confirmed at the Fifth Congress of the Party in 1970, where Kim Il Sung's ideas came to dominate North Korean life under the slogan *yuilsasang chegye*, translatable as the "sole ideological system" (Wada 1992, 377–80).

By the 1970s, however, the guerrilla state was beginning to lose the battle—not at the hands of the United States, but as a result of an altogether more banal and inevitable phenomenon: aging. Key leaders, including the top military commander and veteran anti-Japanese guerrilla fighter, Choe Yong-Gon, had died by the mid-1970s and Kim Il Sung himself, much younger than the others, turned 60 in 1972. It was during the 1970s and 1980s that what I call the notion of Kim Il Sung the sovereign and the sacred, no longer simply Kim Il Sung the great man, began to emerge. This was a topological shift of Kim's existence.

A Sovereign Being

During the two decades of the 1970s and 1980s, Kim Il Sung was enshrined as sovereign. While he was routinely referred to as the Leader (or more precisely, the Great Leader), during these decades he was beginning to be viewed no longer as a man or even as a human. This does not mean that he was therefore seen exclusively as a deity, since he was not conceived as someone who belonged only to a higher, normally unreachable, and immaterial realm. He was, rather, understood to be a form of existence that is untouchable, yet ubiquitous, an entity that exists for its own sake, its very nature filled with love and wisdom. It was also believed that because of this very nature, this entity, whether intended or not, would act as the foundation of society and that, in its name, people would commit themselves to extreme causes and acts.

During the 1970s and 1980s, through lifelong normative immersion in an environment filled with admiration and gratitude for Kim Il Sung, North Koreans acquired a form of self-identification that was in unison with ideas of/about Kim that, at the same time, always involved placing themselves in a lesser, subordinate capacity to that of Kim. Seen from the outside world, the way in which North Koreans relate to Kim Il Sung is one of the most—if not the most—enigmatic aspects of North Korean society. Defectors' tales are replete with recollections of how North Koreans are indoctrinated, from early childhood, into thinking of the Great Leader as a being that loves them unfailingly and also as an object of their deepest love (see Kang 2004). As the title of Barbara Demick's book on North Korea would have it, children grow up singing songs expressing deep gratitude to Kim Il Sung for his love and care and declaring that they have "nothing to envy" in the entire human world (Demick 2009). This over-the-top rhetoric incorporates a sober form of logic if we understand the mechanism connecting Kim Il Sung with North Korean individuals.

Here I am not alluding to a forceful, terror-inducing system of threats and punishments, despite the fact that references to such an environment are typically included in the tales of defectors—and indeed with good reason. Rather, I am trying to look at the ideological mechanism that enables North Koreans to be proud of being the recipients of Kim Il Sung's leadership. According to this way of thinking, individuals owe their lives to this entity, the leadership, not simply in a spiritual way, but in a comprehensive manner extending, for example, to the bodily, material, social, and familial aspects of their lives. As such, this entity presides over every dimension of society. Whether this entity is man, woman, or child no longer matters. For, it is around the position or locus of the leadership that the fabric of social relations between members of society has come to be woven.

Is this entity a symbol of North Korean society? The answer is only partially affirmative. The leadership is in some ways too awe-inspiring and sacred to be casually replicated, due to the fear of being considered an impostor, despite one's actual intentions. On the other hand, a metaphorical or metonymical piece of this entity is to be carried by everyone everywhere at all times, as it is imperative that people should be able to feel constant proximity or spiritual contact with this sacred being. It was no coincidence that during the late 1970s and early 1980s it became the rule for all North Koreans to wear Kim Il Sung badges (with different designs according to one's rank) on all public occasions, positioned on the left-hand side of the chest, close to the heart. His portrait penetrated every household, school classroom, workplace, office, public building, and square. Naturally, the intervention of a regulatory body is required in order for the measured distribution of such tokens to take place. Thus, in North Korea, the nation-state and its various apparatuses together play a pivotal role in disseminating Kim Il Sung's ideas and words, also producing officially-sanctioned portraits of the Great Leader (in all sizes, filling gigantic tapestries as well as miniature lapel pins).

Unlike in the case of God in the context of Protestantism, one cannot claim to have Kim Il Sung inside one's mind and thereby "privatize" him, so to speak. There is no such a thing as having one's own personal Kim Il Sung, as opposed to the Protestant proclivity for holding one's belief in God in the most personal and private part of one's heart. Kim Il Sung is a national sovereign and his existence is inseparable from the collectivity of the North Korean nation. But, unlike royal state figureheads (as in Britain or Japan, for example), whom everyone reveres but does not learn from or understand, Kim Il Sung is believed, emulated, and upheld as a virtuous role model. ← what evidence ?

As such, there is a certain religiosity in the relationship between North Koreans and the entity called Kim Il Sung. Yet, this religiosity differs from the situation in the United Kingdom, where Queen Elizabeth II is also head of the Church of England. Everyone in Britain understands that she holds the highest nominal position in the church, but no one worships her in lieu of God. In this sense, the Queen is a mere office-holder. Kim Il Sung, on the other hand, has no church or church-like assemblies or establishments, but his existence itself is the object of worship, while he is seen as the utmost form of existence that every North Korean is supposed to emulate (although everyone at the same time knows that it would not be possible to do so). He is a truly self-sufficient being, a sovereign being.

I proposed earlier that a topological shift occurred with respect to Kim Il Sung's position in North Korea during the 1970s and 1980s. Before, as can be seen in Wada's view, Kim Il Sung was a man, a great man, a military strategist, a leader, a political visionary, and a national hero. As such, if he were to die, he would be mourned, but it would be understood that when he was dead, he would be truly dead and gone. After the 1980s, however, Kim Il Sung came to be viewed somewhat differently, as a being that does not die and lives forever. This would be the case even after Kim Il Sung the mortal dies — as indeed happened in North Korea, but not simply because his body was embalmed and artificially preserved.

Before, Kim was not only revered, but also expected to possess and display certain attributes, gifts, and skills, such as theoretical rigor, linguistic ability, political farsightedness, and other examples of technical finesse, aside from showing his characteristic benevolence and warmth. As such, Kim had to perform certain duties in return for the respect accorded him by the people. But, after the topological shift that I am proposing to investigate, Kim became an entity of which almost nothing came to be expected. In other words, his existence itself represented meaning, purpose, and an end in itself. Thus, he simply had to exist — this is precisely the notion of the sovereign proposed by Georges Bataille (1993).

Bataille's exploration of the sovereign emphasizes his capacity to pursue consumption for the sake of consumption, pleasure for the sake of pleasure. He does not produce and does not consume as a reward for production. He does not love others — does not find worth in others — and loves only himself. He is not bound by necessity. He lives in excess. He lives for the sake of living, not for the sake of achieving a set of goals. His life itself is the end, not a means (1993, 178–79). And it is on this point of understanding Kim Il Sung as sovereign that I part from the currently pervasive understanding in South Korea and the United States of North Korea as a neo-Confucian state with Kim Il Sung as its ancestral founder — as I shall argue below. What I mean here will be more clearly understood by turning to Kim Il Sung after his death.

A Perpetual Ritual State

In July 1994, just a few days before his scheduled second meeting with former U.S. President Jimmy Carter, the news of Kim Il Sung's death took the world by surprise. At 82, he was well advanced in years. But, as he had not been known to the outside world as having been suffering from any serious conditions or illnesses of note, rumors inevitably followed. Whether Kim Il Sung was assassinated or not is neither my concern nor within the scope of this study. More interesting is what followed Kim's death, notably, the situation I call a "perpetual ritual state."

As mentioned, Kim Il Sung's body is preserved and exhibited for regulated public display. An expansive structure named Geumsusan Memorial Palace was built for the purpose of housing Kim Il Sung's relics as he used them while he was alive: the limousine in which he was chauffeured around, his desk with the desktop stationery arranged exactly as he left it, the train carriage that was reserved for his travel, his uniforms and other items of clothing, his books, his notebooks containing his handwritten notes, his eyeglasses, fountain pens, hats, shoes, gloves, and so on. North Koreans are given the "privilege" of visiting this palace as a reward for hard work and devotion. Every day, group tours visit the palace, forming long lines, proceeding in a slow, orderly, yet emotionally overwhelmed manner through rooms and halls filled with serene music. At a glance, this ritual of mourning appears to go on literally forever in the scheme of the North Korean concept of remembering Kim Il Sung.

But what separates North Korean practice from the usual mortuary rites is that these individuals would have approached their leader in a similar manner — solemn yet emo-

Souce b

tional, overwhelmed with awe—even while he was alive, and as such, rather than simply being remembered, Kim Il Sung is perceived as still being there with them. Indeed, in state discourse, the Great Leader or *suryeong* never dies, and neither does his preserved body. It concurs with the slogan adopted by the North Korean state shortly after Kim's death: *Widaehan suryeongnimeun yeongwonhi uriwa hamkke* or "The Great Leader lives eternally with us." Accordingly, the state has designated Kim as Eternal President. This event is worthy of note, as it follows that the tenure of the office of president was made permanent along with Kim's life itself—in other words, that his death has earned him eternal life.

With this inversion (the Great Leader's death being an eternal life), North Korea entered an ongoing ritual for celebration: rather than mourning Kim's finished life in what Heonik Kwon (2010) characterizes as "national bereavement," North Korea is celebrating Kim's eternal life, granted by way of death. No matter how many people are starving, the million-strong Arirang mass games go on. The capital Pyongyang is filled with lesser versions of Arirang, held indoors and outdoors, all year long. Men and women, old and young, participate in parades, dance nights, and festive evenings of song and music. People stay after hours at their places of work to practice repertoires and dance steps, choruses and rounds, in order to participate in such events. Enormous amounts of time, energy, funds, and human effort have continued to be expended on a wide spectrum of activities and large-scale mass celebrations following Kim Il Sung's death.

Diverse genres of performance art are unified by themes depicting the epic history of North Korea, beginning with the birth of the Great Leader and ending with his eternal life. In between, there are depictions of his early anti-Japanese activities, his guerrilla warfare and postcolonial leadership, the military and political victory in the Korean War, the period of post–Korean War economic and social reconstruction, the consolidation of his ideological corpus under the keyword *juche* ("self-reliance"; see below), and so on.

North Korea's perpetual ritual state today would be better understood in terms of the dual morphology portrayed by French ethnologist Marcel Mauss, whose interpretation of the circumpolar life cycle of the arctic Eskimo led him to conclude that Eskimo life was divided into two radically opposed seasonal forms. During summer, when game was plentiful, the collection and consumption of food was carried out with each family making up one unit. Families gathered and consumed food separately and there was no need to distribute game beyond immediate household boundaries. Scattered in their family tents, members of the village only rarely gathered in one place.

In wintertime, life took on the form of a collective, extended ritual. More precisely, life was saturated by ritual. Whereas summer rituals were reduced to a simple and cursory format, in winter, even small events were loftily celebrated, and the smallest transgression thoroughly cleansed. Longhouses accommodating multiple families (which Mauss suspected as sharing kinship relations) were built, with a cluster of such longhouses forming a settlement. Typically, each settlement would contain a large assembly house where villagers frequently gathered. Sheltered from severe weather and sub-zero temperatures, they spent their time engaged in fiestas, plays, and rituals. Often, couples exchanged partners during this period, although the exact details of the patterns and principles involved are not known. As such, winter life presupposed different kinship relations, reproductive arrangements, and (economic) units of consumption, to those found during summer. Mauss (1979) termed these two forms of Eskimo life a "dual morphology."

Turning to North Korea, we can see that the current continual staging of mass games and performances resembles the winter life of the Eskimo. Life involves engaging in mass ceremonies. In this space of ongoing ritual, non-ritual or ordinary social relations are suspended. Rather than remaining bound by this-worldly relations such as kinship and marriage, individuals, as participants in ritual, assume close and direct relations with gods or a sacred being. In North Korea in the aftermath of the death of Kim Il Sung, the supreme social relationship in society came to be unequivocally designated as that connecting the individual with the Great Leader. According to this schema, no other connection should interfere with this connection, and no form of social relationship should stand between the two parties.

As such, I am in fundamental disagreement with the proposition that North Korea is a neo-Confucian state, tending to explain its social relations in terms of kinship with Kim Il Sung as the national ancestor (Kwon 2010; Kang 2001). Certainly, Kim Il Sung was referred to as Father Marshal, *abeoji wonsunim*, until Kim Jong Il came to take the term father, as in Father General, *abeoji janggunnim*. Kim Il Sung is more often referred to as *eobeoi suryeong*, the leader that is both father and mother to people. These terms appear to pertain to the realm of kinship. But that does not warrant Kim's positioning as the national ancestor. For one thing, this characterization is overly logocentric. Moreover, if we look at the system of traditional Korean kinship relations, in what way could a father be the ancestor of the nation? According to Korean tradition, the (male) members of the entire lineage are collectively related to the ancestor. And, importantly, each lineage is independent and, therefore, unrelated. Thus, men (traditionally, women were disenfranchised) had to pledge dual loyalty toward the ancestor on one hand and the monarch on the other. It was only in the case of members of the royal family that the seat of loyalty coincided: in relation to both the father/ancestor and the king. Furthermore, as I will show in the following pages, ideas such as "family" or "collective" are not very helpful in understanding social relations in North Korea and the relationship that North Koreans have with Kim Il Sung, the sacred: North Koreans are each alone in their relationships with Kim (see Chapter 3 of this volume). Introducing the notion of Confucianism, in my view, not only muddies the waters here, but also shows a misunderstanding of the core nature of relations between the North Korean people and their leader (see the Conclusion of this volume).

Two Crucial Decades

How was a society such as today's North Korea formed? This state of affairs did not come into being overnight. In my view, a reasonable amount of preparation took place during the 1970s and 1980s, although there was a notable shift in emphasis between these two decades. It was during this period that Kim Il Sung was transformed from a theoretico-ideological leader into an ethico-spiritual one. It was also during these years that Kim Il Sung came to be viewed as the center of people's souls rather than as the focus of their ideological identification as North Koreans. Let me offer a few examples in order to substantiate this claim.

We have seen that it was at the Fifth Congress of the Workers' Party of Korea in 1970 that North Korea came to uphold *yuilsasang chegye*, Kim Il Sung's sole ideological system of ideas, otherwise known as *juche* (Cheung 2000). This concept insists that the destiny of the nation lies in the hands of its own people, and hence places the utmost emphasis on political independence, economic self-reliance, and military self-defense. During the early 1970s, North Koreans were made to memorize the works of Kim Il Sung (including public speeches, committee reports, and so on) by heart, word-for-word. This period also saw absolute logocentrism established in relation to Kim Il Sung's very existence itself. All public self-criticism sessions, the standard form of ideological training in North Korea, were required to be opened with correct and exact quotations from Kim Il Sung's published works. One was required to avoid even the slightest misquote, as this would be seen as evidence of insufficient or false loyalty towards the Great Leader. Men and women avidly studied Kim's teachings, memorizing hundreds of pages, including speeches, annual New Year's greetings, and entire party congress reports. Perfect memorization was rewarded with public recognition in addition to the awarding of prizes and medals.

From around the late 1970s through to the time of Kim Il Sung's 70th birthday in 1982, however, this national passion quietly faded away. No longer did North Koreans engage in exact reproductions of the utterances and writings of Kim Il Sung as if they were mantras, and the practice of quoting his teachings verbatim was dropped from self-criticism sessions. Instead, more artistic and iconoclastic methods of representing and disseminating Kim Il Sung's image became the norm. As I shall show in the chapters to follow, this can be seen in literary works produced in the 1970s and 1980s. Unlike in the 1960s, when mainstream literature in North Korea was dominated by autobiographies and memoirs of former anti-Japanese guerrilla fighters, with Kim Il Sung depicted as a fellow fighter or comrade, the 1970s and 1980s saw an increase in the number of novels being published, and this genre becoming the major object of leisure consumption as well as voluntary self-education. Similarly, the 1980s saw an increase in the number of feature films produced, together with the expanded use of performance art, such as musicals.

This trend can, in part, be ascribed to the aging of the leadership. Kim Il Sung delivered a massive quantity of reports and speeches right up until his 70s. After entering old age, however, there was a reduction in the number of speeches and written works he produced, and accordingly a fall in the number published. Similarly, as noted earlier, former participants in anti-Japanese guerrilla warfare were dying out by the end of the 1970s.

Simultaneously, and in some ways more importantly, it was during the late 1970s and early 1980s that Kim Jong Il began to display real power in the political arena. His artistic proclivity, particularly his visual and sensory-oriented approach (through dance and film, for example; see Kim Jong Il 1992), contrasting with the previous logocentric approach aimed at disseminating Kim Il Sung's teachings through an emphasis on reading and memorizing, appears to have played a key role in shift of Kim Il Sung's image in North Korea from sagacious to benevolent, theoretical to ethical, and ideological to spiritual.

Needless to say, both representations of Kim Il Sung existed in North Korea from the outset, long before the 1970s. Kim was referred to as warm, virtuous, and loving toward people,

while at the same time wise, knowledgeable, politically experienced, and so on. The shift, therefore, was rather subtle.
Nevertheless, it was an important transformation. In the 1980s,
unlike in the late 1960s and early 1970s, people no longer had
to intellectually understand Kim Il Sung, speaking his words
and reproducing his teachings in public. It became more important to sense or feel Kim Il Sung's potency. Accordingly,
his original theoretico-ideological formula, *juche,* came to assume a different form. Previously, everyone had been supposed to study *juche,* reading about it, memorizing its theory,
and becoming familiar with its standard vocabulary. In the
1980s, it became more important for people to be able to com-
petently perform songs from feature movies and reproduce
catchall phrases and slogans in public — in other words, North
Koreans became more performance oriented. Previously, citizens had spent hours reading and memorizing the works of
Kim Il Sung, but from the 1980s, they came to spend more
time practicing dance steps for public performances and goose
steps for parades.

The 1980s saw another important change in the environment,
this time explicitly concerning North Korea's relationship with
Koreans living in Japan. A substantial number of overseas Koreans in Japan had supported North Korea from the very early
days of the expatriate movement immediately following World
War II, when the peninsula came to be divided into two opposing camps. At the time of Japan's surrender to Allied forces
in August 1945, there were said to be about 2.4 million Koreans
living in Japan. Most of them had moved to Japan after the
outbreak of the Pacific War due to wartime economic demand
in Japan proper. Many among them were brought to Japan
against their will, while others semi-voluntarily opted to move
to Japan in order to gain a better livelihood. For the majority
of Koreans in both groups, however, once the war was over,
their sources of income vanished, precipitating them to be repatriated to the Korean peninsula. Although this took place in a
rushed and haphazard manner due to the insufficient provision
of repatriation facilities by the Allied forces then occupying

Japan as well as the Japanese authorities, by 1946, the number of Koreans living in Japan had fallen to approximately 600,000 (Ryang 1997, 80).

From early on, Koreans remaining in their former colonial metropolis were starkly divided into two camps, each respectively supporting North and South. For many decades following the partition of Korea, the former group benefited from a mass support base and effective ideological apparatuses. These included the organizational network known as Chongryun, the General Association of Korean Residents in Japan, and a network of Korean ethnic schools. Chongryun members proclaimed themselves to be overseas citizens of North Korea, despite the fact that the majority of its followers originated from southern provinces of Korean peninsula that were now incorporated into South Korea.

Reflecting the tensions of the Cold War era, the treatment afforded Chongryun-affiliated Koreans by the Japanese government consisted of civil and political deprivation. Not until the early 1980s did this population have any form of permanent residence in Japan. This was in contrast with those Koreans in Japan who pledged loyalty to South Korea by applying for South Korean nationality in the midst of Cold War tensions; the latter were able to obtain permanent residence in Japan from 1965.

Early in 1959, as a result of negotiations between the Japanese and North Korean Red Cross organizations, and with the active assistance of the International Committee of the Red Cross, Japan and North Korea opened up a one-way repatriation route to North Korea for Koreans in Japan (Morris-Suzuki 2007). Repatriation was on a strictly voluntary basis, but once an individual had left Japan, he or she was not allowed to reverse their decision. This was because Koreans in Japan had no such civil rights in Japan at the time and Japan and North Korea did not have formal diplomatic relations (a situation that continues to the present day). A pro-repatriation campaign run by Chongryun combined with the enthusiastic maneuverings of a Japanese government eager to rid the country of Koreans led to a total of about 90,000 Koreans choosing to be relocated to North Korea from the 1960s through to the mid 1970s, never to return to Japan (Ryang 1997, 113–15; Ryang 2000). This number included a diverse range of people—from families impoverished to wealthy and politically dedicated; from children abandoned and orphaned to well-provided and gifted—all sharing one common fate: they would never return to Japan. Families and friends left behind in Japan consequently had to give up any hope of ever seeing them again—until the day when Korea would be reunified through the initiative of North Korea, or so they believed.

The granting of permanent residence to Koreans in Japan in the early 1980s was one of many legal reforms implemented by the Japanese government due to its ratification of the International Covenants on Human Rights in 1979. With permanent resident status, most Koreans in Japan (and not just those who supported South Korea) were now eligible to apply for re-entry permits to Japan. This enabled the families of those who had earlier chosen to be repatriated to North Korea to visit their long-lost kin there. Ordinary citizens of Japan are prohibited from visiting North Korea, but in 1981 the Japanese government began permitting such visits (and re-entry to Japan) for the Korean families and relatives of repatriates based on humanitarian principles, the same argument deployed in 1959 when originally opening up the repatriation route (Ryang 2008, Chapter 3).

The post-1981 visits to North Korea by Koreans living in Japan were, in many senses, groundbreaking. Initially, they greeted the opportunity to make such journeys with great enthusiasm, believing that finally they would be able to actually see their political fatherland with their own eyes. Furthermore, for many, it offered the chance to be reunited with their repatriated family members and relatives for the first time in decades. On multiple levels, therefore, the initial visits were emotionally overwhelming. But soon, it became clear in the eyes of the visitors from Japan that North Korea was not exactly "a paradise on earth," as the propaganda would have it.

In the face of the dire needs of their repatriated family members, families in Japan began avidly sending Japanese-made goods and cash. On the other hand, with the involvement of Korean entrepreneurs in Japan, trade between Japan and North Korea expanded in a covert fashion, the so-called repatriation route now transformed into an active channel for the flow of goods, cash, and humans between the shores of Japan and North Korea. The pro–North Korea Chongryun also took advantage of this opening, building its own facilities on North Korean soil for the re-education of its cadres, in addition to hotels for Korean tourists from Japan.

It was via this channel that, from around the early 1980s, stores for the North Korean cadre began filling up with Japanese-made goods, including electrical appliances, entertainment systems, luxury items, and precious goods. While this marked a real beginning in the nation's opening up to the outside world, albeit in an unconventional and restricted way, it was also true that, for North Koreans at large, this window of contact with Japanese products engendered much envy, desire, and frustration, in some ways necessitating more effective population control by way of restriction on one hand, and on the other, enabling North Korean authorities to be able to materially reward model citizens by giving them limited access to the Japan-made products and advantageous service-sector positions dealing with visitors from Japan. Unlike most of Pyongyang citizens who were subjected to compulsory Friday labor or *keumyorodong* (weekly all-day field labor on Fridays), waitresses and cleaners in the newly-opened hotels for Chongryun visitors from Japan were exempt from this chore—they were selected on the basis of pedigree as well as good behavior and achievement. The massive flow of visitors and goods from Japan starting from the early 1980s was represented in North Korea as a reflection of the fervent loyalty of Koreans in Japan for the Great Leader. Indeed, upon Kim Il Sung's 60th birthday in 1972, it is said that Chongryun collected a total of 5 billion yen from Korean residents in Japan (Matsubara and Tokita 2007), which was turned into gifts for Kim, including Mercedes-Benz automobiles, color television sets, various kinds of industrial machinery, home electrical appliances, trucks, bulldozers, excavators, agricultural machinery, an assortment of Japanese and other foreign luxury goods, jewelry, silk, delicacies, and even foodstuffs such as abalone and the famed Koshihikari rice (from Niigata prefecture).

The Emergence of Kim Jong Il

The 1980s were also important in the advancement of Kim Jong Il as the nation's new leader. The differences between Kim Il Sung and Kim Jong Il are numerous — as in any comparison of father and son. Four points are perhaps most noteworthy: Kim Il Sung's diasporic and uprooted upbringing as opposed to Kim Jong Il's sheltered and protected one; the former's Christian-influenced formative years contrasted with the latter's secular, Soviet-influenced infancy; the former's military experience and the fact that he genuinely risked his life for his nation and the latter's lack of such a personal history of publicly displayed bravery; the former's intellectual rigor and his copious literary production and the latter's visual, artistic, and sensory orientation.

Kim Jong Il was born in 1942. There are contradicting theories regarding his birthplace — whether it was in the former Soviet Union or on Mount Baekdu in the northern border region, the locale now associated with the sacred imagery of the guerilla battles against the Japanese. According to today's North Korean political mythology, Kim Jong Il's childhood was filled with virtuous episodes and noble sagas. Basically, however, he had an extremely secluded, protected, and comfortable childhood, far out of touch with reality, to say the least. He was educated at a select boarding school in Switzerland, lavished with exquisite items from Europe, Japan, and the United States, and generally not given any kind of discipline. I do not, however, suggest that he was responsible for this upbringing — there are more than a few world leaders who are completely out of touch with the day-to-day realities of their own peoples. My point is simply that he did not earn his current position of leadership by his own efforts or as a result of his elevation to such a position by his comrades, as was the case with his father, but was accorded his position entirely due to the fact that he was the first-born son of Kim Il Sung.

After graduating from Kim Il Sung University in 1964, Kim Jong Il emerged as a key player during the 1970s, especially in the field of artistic production. Politically speaking, however, it was during the 1980s that Kim Jong Il was given positions of national importance: during this decade he was appointed to the Politburo, the military commission, and the secretariat of the Workers' Party of Korea. In 1982, he was made a member of the Seventh People's Assembly, and in 1991 made supreme commander of the North Korean military. It was during these years that Kim Jong Il began putting his name on what were seen as important oeuvres on the principles of *juche* (Kim Jong Il 1982, 1984, 1985). The period from 1980 to 1991 saw the steady emergence of Kim Jong Il, firstly as heir apparent, then as heir designate, and finally the only living heir of the now deceased Great Leader. (As stated earlier, however, since Kim Il Sung was declared Eternal President after his death in 1994, Kim Jong Il is not the North Korean president.)

In the 1980s Kim Jong Il was involved in the production of innovative new movies, as well as the development of new musical genres and performing arts in North Korea, and it is no coincidence that the aforementioned shift in emphasis from a logocentric to a sensory-oriented relationship with the leadership took place. As feelings replaced logic in North Korea's public discourse, the arts, and especially the performing arts, took on a distinctly different meaning for North Koreans.

At the same time, this was also the period when North Korea came to be associated with or suspected of involvement in a series of high-profile abductions and terrorist attacks. In 1978, influential South Korean director Sin Sang-ok and his wife, leading actress Choe Eun-Hui, were captured and taken to the North, where they were held until 1986. In 2002, it was confirmed that North Korea had kidnapped a large number of citizens of Japan from its shores during the late 1970s and early 1980s. North Korea was later implicated in the 1983 Rangoon bombing, in which many South Korean dignitaries were killed, as well as the bombing of Korean Air Lines Flight 858 in 1987. The first case noted above is of particular interest in the context of this discussion, as it was said that the abduction of Sin and Choe was carried out upon a directive from Kim Jong Il himself. Indeed, it is said that he planned to set up a world-class film industry in North Korea, and that he had decided that bringing in Sin and Choe would boost such efforts. Regardless of the authenticity of this story, it is true that the 1980s were boom days for North Korean films — with diverse storylines, sophisticated character construction, substantial budgets, and popular success (Choe and Sin 1988).

The world professes to know little about this reclusive and unconventional leader. It has been said that he is "amazingly well-informed and extremely well-read" and "can talk about almost any subject" (Cumings 2004, 47), is ignorant and awkward with people, has a bad temper, loves shooting and hunting, and is overweight while his nation is gripped by famine (Oh and Hassig 2000, 92–93). He is also said to be a debauched womanizer with multiple mistresses, one of whom lives in Japan with his secret daughter and visits him with the daughter every year ("Kim Jong Il's Mistress" 2009). Further, he is said to possess a "shining ability to look toward the future" and a "sense of mission that enables him to be thoroughly responsible for the fatherland and the revolution" (*"Widaehan"* 2009), in addition to having "outstanding political ability," "extraordinarily ideological and theoretical brilliance," and the "highest human virtue" (*"Keullodanchedeureseo"* 2009).

Who Kim Jong Il truly is and what he is really like, in my view, are not as important as where he stands in the overall cosmological scheme of North Korean society. My concern is not about his position in the government, the party, or the military; rather, my focus lies in the symbolic topography of leadership in North Korea. How Kim Jong Il is related, in terms of his position or placement, to the Eternal President, his father Kim Il Sung, is therefore of primary interest to me in the context of this work. If Kim Il Sung's death "froze" the office of presidency, does it then follow that North Korea is to be eternally ruled by a dead man? And, if so, what is the positional value of Kim Jong Il? While I do not claim to have answer to these questions, I believe looking at 1980s literature in North Korea might give us an interesting clue.

Kim Il Sung, the Eternal President

Kim Il Sung is the fourth and most recent world leader to have his body embalmed for preservation and public exhibition—following Lenin, Ho Chi Minh, and Mao Zedong. The embalming and eternalizing of a leader's body is, in my view, of great significance, as it fundamentally alters the corporeality of the sovereign. In thinking about this issue, it might be helpful to consider a debate that raged among lawyers in Tudor England. According to the Tudor English judges, the king had two bodies—the body natural and the body politic. The latter, often also referred to using the term "mystical body" (Kantorowicz 1957, 15), is seen as knowing no infancy, old age, imbecility, or disability, and it never dies (Kantorowicz 1957, 7–14). Thus, even though the king's natural body is dead, his politico-mystical body does not die—it lives forever. This parallels to some degree Tibetan thinking as it relates to the Dalai Lama: after the body in which the Dalai Lama's soul has been residing ceases to breathe, his soul travels in order to reincarnate in another person's body. Thus, the holiness represented by the Dalai Lama never dies.

On the other hand, the embalmed body of the king (the king's body natural) does not die either. Its organs and cells may cease to function, but the body (if not the life) continues to exist. Embalming resembles mummification, in that in both cases, the eternity of life is encapsulated in the body—a physical, material, corporeal entity—as opposed to an immaterial entity, such as the soul. Since ancient times, humans have viewed body and soul in separation, particularly at the time of death. In ancient Japan, when someone died, the bereaved sponsored a ritual called *tamagoi*, meaning "begging for the soul." This ritual reflected the idea that death meant the departure of the soul from the body and that, therefore, by beckoning the soul back to the body, the dead would come back to life (Ryang 2006, Chapter 1). Mummification has been a source of human fascination since ancient times. Death took a person's soul away, but as long as the body was preserved, it was believed, the dead would be brought back to life some day. As such, even though the body's functions might have ceased, preserving it carried significance, as no dead person could be revived without a body to which to return. The body natural of the dead, thus, did not die at all times in history, just as the body politic or mystic body of the Tudor monarchs never died either.

It was the ancient Egyptians who nearly perfected mummification techniques (Pettigrew 1834), in the belief that life went on after death, albeit in a different form. As such, death was a transition from one form of life to another. In China, historically, a dead parent's body was kept in a coffin and placed in a quiet and cool part of the family dwelling for years, this being deemed the utmost form of completion of the duty of filial piety (Pettigrew 1834, 19–20). While this may not strictly imply eternity of life, its end was not clearly marked, either. Indeed, even today, many cultures do not view death clearly as the end of life. Even in our secular, late-capitalistic contemplations, death more often than not presupposes continuity rather than discontinuity.

In North Korea, Kim Il Sung is revered as an exceptionally supreme and sacrosanct being. It is also true, however, that every individual aspires not only to be loyal and dedicated, but also to be close to him, in the belief that such an effort will earn that person eternal life, or more precisely, eternal political life. Death that occurs while dedicating oneself to the Great Leader or *suryeong* is, in other words, equivalent to eternal life. In this sense, Kim Il Sung's embalmed body, as it were, is a reminder of this mechanism: since Kim Il Sung never dies—not only in terms of body politic but also body natural—dedication and loyalty toward him need also to remain eternal. As such, his embalmed body is not a mere symbol, but an actual and material reminder of the necessity for eternal and endless loyalty. Thus, Kim Il Sung alone is eternally the president and not even his biological first-born son can replace him. Let me reiterate: Kim Jong Il the *ryeongdoja* (the Leader) can be replaced, but Kim Il Sung the *suryeong* (the Great Leader) is irreplaceable.

This brings us to the question of the positionality of Kim Jong Il. His father is not replaceable, but he is, and his successor may or may not be his own son or kin. Despite his current position of authority, he can be replaced, as the distinction between Kim Jong Il's body politic and body natural is more easily discerned when compared with Kim Il Sung. In other words, his body natural (unlike that of Kim Il Sung) will die when he dies, while the exact whereabouts of his body politic is not clear as long as his father presides over North Korea as the one and only Eternal President.

On December 18, 2011, Kim Jong Il was announced dead. In the ensuing national funeral ceremonies, Kim Jong Un, the youngest son, was referred to as the leader who has embodied Kim Jong Il's ideas and guts. Born in 1984 to Kim Jong Il and his now deceased mistress Ko Yeong-Hui, who was repatriated from Japan to North Korea during the 1960s and became a top dancer, he is only in his late 20s. The youngest Kim did not deliver a speech at the state funeral, following his father's precedent; Kim Jong Il did not speak at Kim Il Sung's funeral in 1994. What was striking in Kim Jong Un's public appearance was that a deliberate effort was made to approximate Kim Jong Un with Kim Il Sung, rather than Kim Jong Il, as far as his presentation was concerned. Jong Un wore a dark *inminbok*, a Mao-inspired suit jacket, which his grandfather favored, rather than his father's signature zip-up jacket. His hairdo was modeled after the young Kim Il Sung's photo taken at the welcome rally for him in Pyongyang in October 1945, when Kim Il Sung was 32 years old. It will be interesting to observe how this young man with virtually zero credentials will hold up during these times of stress in North Korea and in the future. One thing is clear: like his father, Kim Jong Un will never be *suryeong,* the Great Leader, as this title is reserved solely for the Eternal President Kim Il Sung.

Chapters

As mentioned, the main body of this book consists of three chapters, each exploring one aspect of North Korean society and each based on a particular theme: love, war, and self. Across these chapters, I introduce, analyze, and interpret about fifteen North Korean novels published during the 1970s and 1980s. While each chapter pursues different sets of inquiries, their three themes are closely interconnected. Chapter 1, "Love," looks at how the concept and discourse of love became a pivotal element in the ethos of North Korea during the 1970s and 1980s. Sensory reactions, such as tears, trembling, excitement, heightened voices, and other non- or extra-linguistic forms of bodily behavior often depicted in 1980s literature in situations where individuals were receiving the overwhelming love of the Great Leader are, in fact, reflections as well as constitutive parts of a highly disciplinary regimentation of "love education" implemented from a very early age. The language of love, as clustered around Kim Il Sung, is interpreted and analyzed by using a selection of literary products that circulated in North Korea during the 1970s and 1980s. Inspired by Simone Weil's notion of love, I will inquire as to how love can be so useful, yet so burdened by semantic complexity. Consequently, I will also look at the need to adjust or simplify this complexity in a society like North Korea with respect to the way individuals are connected to the leader.

Chapter 2, "War," looks at the consistency and constancy of the discourse of war at the core of North Korea's national and political identity. Ever since the outbreak of the Korean War in June 1950, North Korea has maintained that it has never ceased to be at war—with the United States. A state of emergency declared during the Korean War has thus become a normal condition of existence in North Korea (Armstrong 2009). As I shall also argue, a peculiar ethos has emerged as a result of North Korea's ongoing self-identification as a nation at war.

Drawing on the works of Giorgio Agamben, I will explore how the state of emergency becomes a core element in North Korea, acting as an important adhesive between the people and their leader. This state of affairs did not, however, arise overnight. By comparing selected short stories published from the early 1950s (during the Korean War) through to the 1970s, we can see that the emergence of this emergency consciousness (so to speak) in North Korea actually postdates the ceasefire of 1953, becoming consolidated in the 1970s and 1980s.

Chapter 3, "Self," addresses a question that can be applied to all of the chapters of this book, since the notion of self — its transition and transformation — encapsulates the development of North Korea itself before, during, and after the 1970s and 1980s. In this chapter, I focus on the way in which the self, or more precisely, the language of the self, paradoxically exists outside of the self. It belongs with the sacred being — in the case of North Korea, the Great Leader. This does not mean that the self does not exist or is irrelevant in North Korea. In contrast with the commonly held assumption that the self is subsumed in totalitarian societies, erased in the name of the collectivity, the self in North Korea has become an extremely important element in securing the continuity of this society. Using Michel Foucault's notion of care for the self as a starting point, I shall discuss how the self came to play such an important role in North Korea, as it is care for the self that enables North Koreans to be positively connected to their leader.

In the Conclusion, "On the Social and the Political," I will look at the way in which the social and the political overlap in North Korea, and inquire as to whether this is an important aspect of what we understand to be totalitarianism. In today's world, characterized as it is by diverse forms of state intervention, whether it be in relation to disaster recovery, home loans, the "war on terror," or border controls, hitherto clear-cut differences between totalitarian and liberal-democratic states have become far more difficult to establish. Unlike during the era when Hannah Arendt (1974) wrote on totalitarianism with Nazi Germany and the Soviet Union in mind, we no longer have a clear understanding of an uncontrollable desire to enter into fusion with a particular political movement as evil. Here and there in the world today (including in the so-called free world and democratic societies), we can find individuals and groups committed to radical movements and causes — whether they be South American guerrillas, Islamic extremists, or American religious fundamentalists. In the face of what appears to be an excess of the political, an intellectual reconfiguration becomes necessary in order to understand, or at least achieve a satisfactory interpretation of, the very notion of the political. A political commitment to the radical requires a destruction of the ordinary, which resembles abjection and/or transgression. In North Korea, transgression occurs in the form of an excess of the political as embodied in what I earlier called the perpetual ritual state. Here, ritual is not primarily religious, but it bears a distinctly political nature. I hope to present a discussion on the political, or more precisely, the excess of the political, and the way in which this aspect of human life dominates other aspects of life for North Koreans.

By entitling this Introduction "A Journey into the Abyss," I refer to the Greek term denoting a bottomless sea. North Korea has appeared to be entering such a place since the death of Kim Il Sung. The world community bears moral responsibility for facing this society squarely, not from a sense of philanthropy or altruism, but because, ultimately, the rest of the world is not free from North Korea, what happens there, or how people live and die there. I am not, however, alluding to the possibility that North Korea's crude nuclear arms program can destroy the rest of the world. Rather, it is the uncertainty that the world feels in attempting to grasp North Korea that should prompt us to show deeper interest in, and concern for, this nation. I chose the term "abyss" in order to allude to the uncertain journey, in intellectual terms, on which we are about to embark in the pages that follow. Whether North Korea will yield to our conventional wisdom and repertoire of understanding and comprehension will become clearer as we work toward the completion of our journey.

ONE

Love

Attempting to envision her native France in the period following the years of Nazi occupation, Simone Weil veers toward
a notion of spirituality in which religiosity does not play such
a central role. Instead, she places greater emphasis on the idea
of the soul, seeing this as one of the most important concepts
upon which to rely when reconstructing and reconfiguring the
postwar world. For Weil, the soul is an imperative element in
making us human. Roots, in turn, provide the structure that
surrounds and nurtures the soul. Using more contemporary
terminology, this might be called "home," although her notion
of roots is less materialistic and more oriented toward ideas
or ethos. She does not forget the importance of the collectivity,
going so far as to state: "The degree of respect owing to human collectivities is a very high one," viewing each one as
unique, irreplaceable, and embodying continuity with respect
to the future while at the same time having its roots in the
shared past (Weil 1952a, 8).

   Among the many elements that constitute food for the soul
listed by Weil, I find liberty and obedience most relevant to
our understanding of love in North Korea. According to Weil,
one of the preconditions for liberty is a society's goodwill:
"Those who are lacking in goodwill or who remain adolescent
are never free under any form of society" (Weil 1952a, 13).
Here, goodwill is not simply an act of blind charity or one-sided

giving: it has to be accompanied by restrictions, limitations, and self-constraints based on knowledge of and concern for others as well as for the self. Thus, society's goodwill is closely intertwined with the personal goodwill of individuals; neither can exist without the other. Obedience, on the other hand, concerns love between the leader and the masses. Weil writes: "Those who keep masses of men in subjection by exercising force and cruelty deprive them at once of two vital foods [for the soul], liberty and obedience; for it is no longer within the power of such masses to accord their inner consent to the authority to which they are subjected" (Weil 1952a, 14). For, in Weil's vision, obedience must not be imposed on others; instead, people need to obey by generating inner consent, which is a dignified choice and must not be confused with submission or servility.

Weil's contended notion of love is also somewhat self-effacing, or rather, self-eliminating, the ideal being ultimately moving closer to god. God, for her, is an ultimate sovereign (as in Bataille 1993, 197–211; see Introduction above), in that he does not have to, or cannot, love humans: God loves only himself. Humans, on the other hand, must continue to love God forever in order to attain virtue and status akin to that accorded sacred beings. This love is one-sided. However, at the same time, as with consent and in contrast with submission or servility, this love is based on the will to love, not on a structure or mechanism forcing one to love. Such love does not know sacrifice, as sacrifice in itself denotes victimhood. Whatever this love requires of humans, it is not sacrifice—it is honor, joy, and happiness.

Love is a sign of our wretchedness. God can only love himself. We can only love something else.

God's love for us is not the reason for which we should love him. God's love for us is the reason for us to love ourselves. How could we love ourselves without this motive? It is impossible for man to love himself except in this roundabout way. (1986, 270)

In this understanding of love, people are at liberty to obey — they choose to obey this sovereign being—God for Weil and the Great Leader for North Koreans. And people love each other, because of their love for God or for the Great Leader. The reader will see that the North Korean literary works that I introduce in this chapter are dominated by abundant references to the Great Leader's endless love and protagonists' aspirations to move closer to him. They also contain clear references to other concepts that Weil argues as being critical to the construction of a new society in post-Nazi France, including roots, societal goodwill, consent, liberty, and the soul. This is as if to highlight the fact that, as in the case of Weil imagining post-Nazi France, the writers of these North Korean literary works of the 1970s and 1980s were helping to build a brave new world.

Great Love

In the following passage from the story *Uri hakkyo* (Our School) by Choe Sang-Sun, Kim Il Sung pays a surprise visit to a village school in the mountains during the Korean War:

"Marshal Kim Il Sung!" "Here comes the Marshal!" Children ran toward [him]. He embraced each and every child in his bosom. Miss Jeong-I, the art teacher, also ran toward him. Her skirt danced in the breeze. Her legs, however, froze the moment she saw the benevolent figure of the Leader smiling gloriously amongst the children [*aideulsoge seosiyeo hwanhi useusineun jaaerousin suryeongnimui moseubeul poeomneun sungan*][. . .] everyday, in happiness or in difficulty, she looked toward his image deep inside her heart, that Leader, whom she longed for and longed for. Two streams of tears rolled down her cheeks. . . .

The Supreme Commander [Kim Il Sung] laughed out loud, as if to lovingly admonish Miss Jeong-I, who was crying like a child.

. . . .

He carefully examined the pencil. Its tip was worn out. He stood there, without a word, as if in deep contemplation. Miss Jeong-I and his aides were worried, because obviously he was pained by the shortage of pencil supplies for the children. U-Seong [a child] quickly understood what he should say: "Dear Marshal! We have many, many good pencils at home. I'm just being thrifty and careful. . . ." He looked at U-Seong with the most gentle and loving gaze. Smiling, he stroked U-Seong's back many times gently and warmly. (Choe 1974, 10–14)

The discrepancy between Kim Il Sung's war image (as commander or military leader) and the image that is depicted here (as benevolent, laid back, full of warmth and love) should be clear to the reader. The depicted image does not reflect the actual Kim Il Sung during the war. Even as a fiction, this image is anachronistic and exhibits a time gap between the 38-year-old Kim Il Sung in 1950 and the 62-year-old Kim Il Sung at the time of the story's publication in 1974. While the above story depicts an image of a warm-hearted elderly leader, filled with love for his people, this image is set against the background of the Korean War that happened when Kim had not even reached his 40s. This is an example of a typical pattern of reconstructing or reconfiguring Kim Il Sung as a loving and benevolent leader during the 1970s and 1980s, retrospectively applying such an image to stories of his younger years. Reminiscent of Tudor English notions of the king's body politic, which knows neither old age nor imbecility, here applied in inversion, Kim Il Sung is portrayed as someone who is always old and mature, yet beautiful and brilliant. This implies that he did not accrue his virtues as he grew older, but that he was born with such innate natural gifts.

As I shall more fully explore in the following chapter, Korean War motifs abound in literary works produced in North Korea during the 1970s and 1980s. Unlike stories written during the war in which, to the best of my knowledge, Kim Il Sung never appears in person, stories written later and set against the background of the war often include him as one of the (major) protagonists. There is a set pattern, mostly, in the way he is treated in these stories, presumably a result of party policies and the detailed directives handed down to state-employed writers; as stated previously, all writers in North Korea are state employees. But, there are also subtle differences between writers in the way in which delicate expressions of love both for and of the Leader are depicted. Let us compare two stories.

The first example is, just like *Uri hakkyo* above, set against the background of the Korean War:

How can Comrade Kim Il Sung envision an enormous range of things [regarding the nation] amidst the raging flames of war, finding huge meaning in miscellaneous, almost invisible things! The aide [Kim's aide] realized that although he was raised close to the Leader during the anti-Japanese guerrilla struggle, he still was not able to grasp the true greatness of the Leader. At the same time, the aide was over-whelmed by endless joy, as if fresh strength were pouring into his chest. (Ko 1970, 23)

This story by Ko Byeong-Sam, entitled *Malgeun achim* (Pure Morning), is one of the short stories contained in a collection entitled *Binnaneun jauk* (Brilliant Footsteps), published in 1970. This is one of the earliest efforts on the part of the North Korean state to reconstruct and refashion Kim Il Sung during the Korean War as a far-sighted, sagacious, benevolent, and remarkable leader capable of planning long-term national goals. The above-quoted story revolves around Kim's idea of building an underground theater in Pyongyang, eventually reaching the point where he orders engineers and architects to gather in Pyongyang in order to start designing the capital city ahead of the Korean War ceasefire. Judging from the storyline, which shows the war progressing in a slow and stagnated fashion, the story is set around 1952. After the rapid occupation of all but the southern tip of the peninsula by the North Korean People's Army following the outbreak of hostilities on June 25, 1950, the amphibious landing by U.S. troops on the peninsula's west-central coast of Incheon on September 15 tipped the scale, with the Americans soon crossing the 38th parallel and entering territory previously controlled by Kim Il Sung's government. On October 16, Pyongyang fell. However, North Korean defenses were soon strengthened through the participation of the Chinese People's Volunteer Army. By the end of 1950, the war was heading toward a stalemate, and in June 1951, the Soviet delegate to the United Nations, Yakov Malik, proposed a truce. Following negotiations that lasted for a little over two years, a truce was signed on July 27, 1953.

In the above story, Kim Il Sung is supposed to be already starting to envision the reconstruction of the North while the truce negotiations are ongoing. The aide, who is a major protagonist alongside the Leader, is depicted as a child of one of Kim's close comrades, since, as can be seen in the above quoted passage, he was raised near Kim, suggesting that his parents fought against the Japanese alongside the future leader. The novella ends with a scene in which People's Army soldiers become excited and overcome by emotion as a result of the encouragement and warmth shown them by Kim Il Sung as he outlines his brilliant vision for the rebuilding of Pyongyang, believing that North Korean victory in the war is assured.

It is interesting to note that Kim Il Sung's intelligence and far-sightedness (in starting ahead of time to design and envision the reconstruction of North Korea's capital) is only of secondary emphasis in this story. It is the emotional responses to his sagaciousness on the part of the People's Army soldiers and his aide that are highlighted—their feelings of gratitude and joy, deeply moved as they are by his warmth. Thus, rather than emphasizing how wise and smart Kim Il Sung is, the story ends up stressing his personal warmth and his ability to touch people emotionally.

The next story, *Keun simjang* (A Big Heart) by Choe Hak-Su (1970), is set during the period of post–Korean War reconstruction between 1953 and 1958. During these years, decisive moves were made toward the Sovietization of the North Korean economy. A collective form of agriculture was introduced that combined locally autonomous cooperative farms and state-operated farms. Key industries such as iron and steel production and mining were completely nationalized. It was also during this period that Kim Il Sung launched his now-famous "on-the-spot" guidance, known in Korean as *hyeonji-jido*. These were spontaneous town hall–style events, though always held at worksites rather than in assembly halls, in which people gathered around the leader in order to learn from his words of encouragement and advice. Their magical effects were usually enhanced by their surprise nature. Stories of such encounters cannot be considered entire fabrications; indeed, Kim visited many factories, offices, schools, and farms and, as many examples of documentary footage from this period can confirm, North Koreans welcomed him passionately wherever he went. But the extent and frequency of such guidance visits, including how warmly Kim engaged with people, remembering every worker and his or her personal circumstances, the makeup of their families and so on, has been grossly exaggerated in North Korea's official discourse. Literature has played an important role in enhancing this type of image, and I quote from *Keun simjang* here as an example. The quoted section relates to a scene where the Great Leader is paying a surprise visit to a factory:

"Thank you for your hard work." The Great Leader smiled at the workers, whose faces were filled with joy. He approached the closest machine operator. He was a good-looking young man. His hair was cut so short that it was almost spiked. Overwhelmed, he kept squeezing a student cap in his hand. "Let me look at your work." The young man could not move, since he was incredulous at having the Great Leader stand in front of him and talk to him. [. . .] Finally, the young man started to operate the machine. "Well, you should wear your cap when working." The Great Leader took the young man's cap from his hand and put it on his head in person. The young man was enthralled and stood immobile for a while. [Once he started to work,] it was obvious he was not a skilled worker. [. . .] "Isn't this machine too high for you? Let's see . . . why don't we raise your stand, here." [. . .] Upon this encouragement, the young man smiled, his face reddening. [. . .] "I see that you are a high school graduate. I can tell from your school cap. Why did you come to the factory [to work]?" "[. . .] Since everyone's contributing to socialist construction, I could not be happy spending my time at college. I can always go take evening classes." [. . .] "You can of course contribute enormously to our socialist construction by going to college. And, if you want to, you can always come back to the factory after graduation," [said the Great Leader]. "But," the young man hesitated. "Feel free to tell me anything," the Great Leader said gently. The young man responded: "If I were to study in the evening [. . .] and work in the factory during the day, I'd be contributing double the amount. My father also told me that it would be a good idea to first participate in work in this way and go to college later if I wanted to." The Great Leader smiled satisfactorily. "Right. Very good. Where does your father work?" "He works in the metal department." "What is his name?" "Pak In-Seop, Sir." "Is that right?" The Great Leader looked at the young man very lovingly and nodded many times. Clearly he was remembering his visit to the metal department two years earlier. "I can see your eyes look like your father's," said the Great Leader. [. . .] The Great Leader looked around and gently remarked: "This young man's father is a veteran member of our working class who has worked in this factory since the colonial period [under the Japanese]. He came back to the factory one day after the [Korean War] ceasefire and gathered all sorts of pieces of steel to produce the first metal product. He is the cornerstone of this factory." [. . .] "I'm certain you will be a great member of the working class. [. . .] You have a great father. Learn from him. [. . .]," said the Great Leader to the young man. The young man's eyes, which had been shining with joy so far, became clouded with swelling teardrops. He was so moved and so deeply touched that he could not even utter the words to bid the Great Leader farewell. (Choe 1970, 34–38)

In the above-quoted excerpt, one striking element is how well the Great Leader remembers the details of individual family circumstances and, more importantly, that he recognizes and praises every little contribution individuals have made toward national reconstruction. He remembers the personal history of the young man's father simply by recalling having met him two years earlier. He even recalls how the father's face looked and recognizes that the father and son share similar-looking eyes. He is also seen to pay detailed and concerned attention to the well-being and comfort of the worker by adjusting the height of his stand, and is extremely personable, offering to put the cap on the worker's head. He is then portrayed as being very observant: a quick glimpse at the cap makes him realize that the worker is a high school graduate. And he is eager to learn why the young man is foregoing the opportunity to attend college, which is, in North Korea, a special privilege. The Great Leader is satisfied and appears to be very proud of this young man, who states that he is willing to make a contribution to the national economy by both working and learning—namely, doing the work of two people.

In the above conversation scene, however, the Great Leader's attentiveness, observational ability, and accurate memory are not presented as mere skills, but are depicted as surface expressions of a core character that is consistently underpinned by his endless love for the people. Here again, he appears ageless, or always and already mature (in mortal terms), leading us to recall the notion of the two bodies and the seemingly universal age of the Tudor kings discussed earlier. Assuming that the visit depicted in the above story took place right after the ceasefire in 1953, we may assume Kim Il Sung to be around 42 or 43 years old. But his behavior and demeanor as he interacts with the young man—referring to the man's father and offering encouragement to everyone present—are more in line with those of a benevolent, old, and wise man, a man much older than one in his early 40s.

Novels of the 1970s and 1980s thus portray Kim Il Sung as an almighty, all-seeing, and all-perceiving wise man who is deeply affectionate and loving toward his people. But as can be seen from the above excerpts, the Great Leader in this period is still portrayed as a human being. He takes humanly care of people. During the 1970s and 1980s, it was still possible for North Korean writers to depict the Great Leader as human, exploring his inner feelings and making him one of the protagonists of a given story. This practice became rare in literary works produced from the 1990s on, as these were written under even stricter party supervision and published with more official and auspicious-looking covers. In other words, in literature published since the 1990s, Kim Il Sung leaves the human world and appears as a bundle of virtues. No longer are authors allowed to fully describe what we would call Kim's personal feelings. This was still possible during the 1970s and 1980s, although, as I shall argue below, there is a subtle shift from the 1970s to the 1980s in terms of Kim's positionality.

Let me cite one more example by Ko Byeong-Sam, "Pyongyangeun noraehanda" (Pyongyang Is Singing). Written in 1976, and almost resembling a sequel to the 1970 *Malgeum achim* (Pure Morning) by the same author quoted earlier, this short story shows how a writer's words put emotion into the heart of the Great Leader. Like the earlier work, it is also set against the backdrop of the Korean War, and depicts the completed construction of the underground theater in Pyongyang conceived by the Great Leader:

The Supreme Commander [Kim Il Sung] was thinking about the soldiers who had crafted such beautiful musical instruments out of burnt wood and broken parts of the murderous weapons of American imperialism. He recalled their faces and imagined that he was standing side by side with these men and women. [. . .] [Listening to a musical broadcast from the Moranbong underground theater,] The Supreme Commander smiled coolly, longing to hear the tune played by a young soldier on a *jeottae* [Korean traditional flute], and recalled the memory of that old soldier who had conjured up such a delicious meal for him out of almost nothing in the field. His deeply penetrating thoughts were with the everyday lives of soldiers on the front line. [. . .]

The Supreme Commander, who is the personification of love for the people and our people's history and strength, approached the strategic map and drew lines on it while listening to the music broadcast. His hand, holding a red pencil, stopped moving momentarily as he imagined the soldiers' futures, the day that every one of them would return to their homes. At that moment, his eyes gleamed with endless love for the people. [. . .]

"Long Live the Iron Fighter, Our Supreme Commander Comrade Kim Il Sung!!" "Long Live Our Great Leader, Comrade Kim Il Sung!!" "Long Live! Long Live!" The radio continued with the soldiers' chants. Their tears, their overwhelming emotion, and their determination were transmitted as if they were breathing right [there] in the same room. The Great Leader approached the radio and turned the volume down a little, as if to suppress his burning desire to embrace each and every soldier closely to his bosom. (Ko 1976, 31–33)

North Korean literary production today does not allow this kind of intrusion (albeit fictional) into Kim Il Sung's emotional world. The author, Ko Byeong-Sam, is a well-known writer who was active in the 1970s and frequently assigned to produce stories with Kim Il Sung as one of the protagonists, the ultimate honor and privilege among North Korean writers.

What interests me in the above excerpts is the depiction of the deep love that Kim Il Sung feels toward his people, and the fact that, yet again, this love is still humanly love. Kim Il Sung is human here precisely because he expresses love just like any human would — through smiles, shining eyes, musing about and longing for the beloved, showing a desire to embrace them — in this case, the people or soldiers that he cares about. His love is reciprocated by loyalty, dedication, and faith on the part of the soldiers, whose on-air chanting of "Long Live" is almost explosive. A loving leader and his loyal people, a loving commander and his dedicated soldiers — these are the images of love that the 1970s stories depict. Here, the love between the leader and his people is mutually strong and assumed to be limitless.

Greater Love

The Great Leader's all-pervasive presence is perhaps matched only by George Orwell's Big Brother, an entity who watches all people all the time, no matter where they are (Orwell 1949). Whereas Orwell's Big Brother in *Nineteen Eighty-Four* is the personification of a sinister control-freak, Kim Il Sung in the 1980s is the sender of a loving gaze that enwraps the entire nation, shining even into the darkest shadowy nooks of the country and brightening up the minds of even the most depressed men and sorrowful women. This section explores two short stories, *Haeppicheun kkeudeopsi* (Sunshine Forever) by Kim Dong-Ho and *Mirubeol jeonseol* (The Legend of Miru Plain) by Kim Sam-Bok. Both are published in *Inminui hanmaeum* (One Heart of the People), a collection of short stories published in 1983 in which all twelve pieces feature the Great Leader as the main protagonist. Each story presents Kim Il Sung in a subtle yet interesting variety of ways as a being with feelings. Yet, we will see below that he is, in fact, quite suprahuman in terms of his capacity and virtue, thus subtly shifting him toward the realm of deity. Just like the gods of Greek mythology, Kim

Il Sung can be playful, angry, whimsical, and very, very intelligent, endowed with suprahuman capacities. Whereas the Greek gods can enjoy a division of labor, each retaining his or her own unique personality, Kim Il Sung loses his personality due to his all-pervasiveness and extreme versatility. In fact, he loses his gender and age along with his personality—he is gender-free and does not age.

Set a little after the Korean War, *Haeppicheun kkeudeopsi* is devoted to Kim Il Sung's *hyeonjijido* or on-the-spot guidance. The story takes place when the Great Leader is on the road back to Pyongyang at the end of a long and busy guidance trip. His aide is breathing a sigh of relief because after tonight's drive, the Great Leader will reach Pyongyang and be able to catch up on some much-needed rest. When their car passes by a town, the sight of a snowman catches the Great Leader's eye. It is a snowman in the image of an American soldier, in North Korea usually referred to as *migungnom* or the American bastard. The *migungnom*'s head is dislocated and his "helmet," made from a bucket, has been thrown to the ground. Children have shot many fatal snow bullets at it, and so this American bastard's chest is torn open. It is in the front yard of a kindergarten. "Let us see what is happening," says the Great Leader, and instructs the chauffeur to park the car. Children are playing *kunsanori* (translatable as "the military game"), but as soon as they see the Great Leader, they gather around him, screaming joyfully. "Marshal!! Our Father Marshal!," the children shout. They grab the Great Leader with no reservation, while he happily smiles and embraces them in his bosom. He straightens the scarf of one child and warms up the hands of another. "Tell me, what game are you playing?" "We're playing the military game to catch the *migungnom*." "Who did best?" "I did, I did," a little boy screams. "I caught ten *migungnom*!" "That's great!" Then another boy thrusts himself forward, claiming that he has caught a hundred of them.

The Great Leader goes inside the kindergarten building with the children and asks them to show him a toy gun that they have used to catch Americans. A little boy brings a rifle-like toy. The Great Leader recognizes that the toy has been produced at the local Saenal toy factory. The children, knowing no modesty, demand that their Father Marshal make the factory produce a toy gun that has "real bullets" in it. "You want those . . . ," the Great Leader gently murmurs. The aide is getting irritated by the children and their demands, since he is worried sick about the Great Leader's much needed rest and wants to get out of the kindergarten so they can be on their way to Pyongyang. Once they are back in his car after saying farewell to the children, the Great Leader asks the chauffeur: "How far is B district from here?" "About twenty miles, Sir." "That is not bad," the Great Leader says and, turning to the aide, suggests: "Comrade Assistant, let us visit B district." The aide is momentarily assaulted by a sense of deep disappointment, and recalls that their car has already gone past the turn-off for the road to B district. "That's fine. Let's still go. Let's go back, Comrade Chauffeur," says the Great Leader. The car thus performs a U-turn and heads to B district, where the Saenal toy factory is located.

Once they arrive, the Great Leader meets the director of the factory, who is overwhelmed at this surprise visit. The Great Leader requests that all new products be shown to him. The director takes him to a display room, where the Great Leader takes a particular interest in the face of a doll. "Let us look at the art department," he suggests. When they enter the art department, they find a young woman working on her own, drawing faces on dolls. Caught by surprise, she is unable to collect herself. "Please sit down! Don't be like that. There, let's sit," says the Great Leader and brings a chair for the woman. "Here. Now, let me see how you will finish drawing the other eyebrow." The woman's face beams with joy and excitement, but she calms herself down and focuses on finishing the face. "Ah, this is very good," says the Great Leader and asks her whether she needs any materials or art supplies. She says there is nothing she needs, since the party and the government have given her everything she needs. The Great Leader tells her:

"You must let me know whether you need anything. . . . I have some suggestions. Your doll's face needs to be a little prettier. And the choice of colors for the doll's dress is rather poor: rather than using black and red, use various colors." [. . .]

"You said you were only twenty years old? But, you should think of yourself as even younger, as young as four or five, when you draw dolls' faces for children. [. . .] It is particularly important to give children a clear recognition of colors. So, pay special attention to your choice of colors, OK? We Koreans traditionally made children's clothes in a variety of colors and called them *saektong jeogori* [multi-colored dress]. This is not simply because this would make children look pretty, but we Koreans always used this method to teach children how important it is to recognize all sorts of difference in colors. Do you understand?" (Kim Dong-Ho 1983, 192)

Already, the woman's eyes are filled with pure, transparent tears. The Great Leader kindly looks into her eyes, strokes her back, and leaves the art department, having given her great encouragement.

After visiting the art department, the Great Leader asks the director which product is most popular. Hearing that it is the toy gun, he requests to be taken into the gun department. After examining a few products, he comments:

"These are very well made." "Great Leader, we have about twenty skilled workers with Level 8 certification." "Twenty? . . . that is wonderful. But, I wonder . . . since you have that many skilled workers, maybe your products should be a bit better than these?" The Great Leader affectionately looked at the director, whose face had been filled with joy and pride. But then, momentarily, the director felt tension, without being able to figure out why. The Great Leader gave a very friendly laugh. "No big deal. What I mean is that we could come up with a device by which the toy gun could have genuine toy bullets, so children could actually shoot at objects, rather than imagining it." The director was caught by surprise, and then his tension returned. [. . .] "Comrade Director! Although these are only toys, we still have to make it possible for children to shoot at objects in reality. That will be the only way to let the children enjoy their military games and let them have the joy of catching and shooting *migungnom*. [. . .]" The director was so overwhelmed by this wise advice that he stood there with his mouth half-open. (Kim Dong-Ho 1983, 193–94) [. . .]

"I'm leaving you with an important assignment for children's emotional development." "Great Leader!!" The director's heart was filled by the Great Leader's love and trust, and that was all he could say as his throat choked with warm tears. [. . .] The Great Leader's car headed to Pyongyang at last. The aide was unable to suppress his excitement. He was so deeply moved by the Great Leader's extraordinary sagacity and love. This road, the road that stretched almost endlessly in front of the car, was the road of love, benevolence, and the endless virtue of the Great Leader. That is right! Any road that the Great Leader traveled would be filled with a sea of flowers of love and our people, on the flower waves of this great love, are progressing vigorously toward communism. (Kim Dong-Ho 1983, 202)

Even when the Great Leader is actually (somewhat sarcastically) criticizing the director, the director is taking it as love; even when the Great Leader is making a few complaints about the doll painting, the woman artist is overwhelmed with a sense of honor and gratitude. What does this tell us? The love of the Great Leader is everywhere; his entire existence consists of love. Therefore, even comments that appear to be critical and negative to outsiders are understood to be loving and affectionate by the North Korean recipients. This unconditional pre-understanding that whatever the Great Leader does consists of love or delivers love is consistently and constantly shown in the North Korean literature of this period. This is a subtle but clear departure from the 1970s novels introduced in the earlier section, in which Kim Il Sung was emotional— almost vulnerable in his own love for the people. As I stated, love then was still humanly love, mutual love between the human leader and his people, as can be seen in the depiction of Kim's own desire to embrace soldiers, for example (see above). The love depicted in the novels from the 1980s departs from this, by showing no vulnerability or humanly emotional movement in the Great Leader's love, which is constant, never changing or diminishing, and only ever growing. Here, Kim does not show desire; rather, his love is an absolute attribute that does not bear humanly weakness.

Another point to consider is the way in which an instantaneous supposition is established whenever Kim Il Sung comments on something: the factory director is caught by surprise and awe-struck by Kim Il Sung's suggestion about making a toy gun that shoots toy bullets — as if this were not something that a toy producer could have thought of in the past; the female artist gratefully listens to the Great Leader as he gives her his version of color theory. In both cases, sagacity and wisdom belong to him, and no experts can match this great being that knows everything about everything. But the underlying message is that his superior sagacity is the result of his all-encompassing love for the people.

Mirubeol jeonseol starts against the backdrop of the very early stages of the Korean War, in the late summer of 1950. Despite his busy schedule as Supreme Commander, the Great Leader pays a surprise visit to a farming village in the mountains called Miru Plain. This place is named after the Korean verb *miruda,* meaning to postpone or put off, as its climate and geographic features make it unsuitable for farming. Due to the high altitude and dry conditions, it has been impossible to secure irrigation for the fields in this village, and the farmers there have struggled against hostile environmental conditions for generations. The story begins with the heroine, Ok-Sil, a young mother and farmer, encountering the Great Leader quite unexpectedly on one dark night. Ok-Sil is pulling a cow cart in the dark. Since there are only a few metal pails in the village, everyone takes turns fetching water from low-lying areas and bringing it back to the village. Ok-Sil is carrying her baby on her back and wearing her husband's worn-out slippers, since her shoes are already torn and she wants to save them for daytime farm work. She is pushing the cow to move faster so that she can make as many rounds as possible that night when she is caught from behind in the long, bright rays of car headlights. Ok-Sil moves her cart to allow the cars to pass by. However, instead of passing by, the cars stop beside her.

The Great Leader emerges from the first black car. Ok-Sil stands back, awestruck and completely speechless. "You are

Love

working hard! Where are you headed on such a dark night as this?" the Great Leader asks. "Well . . . I need to bring water from . . . ," but Ok-Sil cannot continue, her heart so overwhelmed and still incredulous about what is happening—meeting the Great Leader on this narrow mountain pass. "Is this for your field?" "Yes." "Where do you have to fetch this much water from?" "The place called Seoktalri." "From that far? And where is your village?" "Myeoneurikol, Sir." "I believe there is a well there." "That is correct, Sir, but that well has dried up completely." The General gazes affectionately at Ok-Sil's sweaty face and begins to tell his companions and aides the following story:

"Last year, I met an exemplary farmer from Hwanghae Province. He was from Myeoneurikol in Miru Plain. He told me a legendary story about a young wife. As a young bride, she worked very hard to serve her in-laws by fetching water day and night. One day, she was too exhausted to carry on any further and had a breakdown. Then, right at that spot, a well burst forth. Miru Plain was known to be a hard place for young daughters-in-law because of its droughts and tough farming conditions. And many farmers had to postpone [*miruda*] getting brides and that is how it came to be called Miru Plain. I remember the name of the farmer. I'm sure you know him—it is Kang Yun-Chil." Listening to the General's story, Ok-Sil had been feeling uncomfortable, because Kang Yun-Chil was her husband. She said, "Well, actually, that farmer is this baby's father [Ok-Sil's husband, a traditional form used in Korean female speech when referring to one's own husband]." "Ah, very well. I'm glad we are meeting in this way!" [. . .] The General was very pleased with this encounter. "How is Comrade Kang Yun-Chil?" "He joined the People's Army." Ok-Sil told the General that upon joining the People's Army, her husband had left her with the important task of farming. [. . .] The General [...] reminisced about that farmer Kang, who had told him that now that the General had given back to Korean farmers the farmland that they had lost to the Japanese [during the colonial era], the farmers of this nation would do their best to improve the food situation. He walked slowly, as he thought about him. [. . .] "What is your name?" asked the General. "Pang Ok-Sil, Sir." "The baby is so young. Is it a boy?" "No, it's a baby girl," Ok-Sil answered, embarrassed [because sons were favored in Korea over daughters]. The General smiled and fondly said, "That's wonderful! Daughters are treasure." He continued, "I gather there is no one at home that can take care of your baby and that's why you are playing a double, triple role, working all day and even after dark like this. [. . .] I feel awful. You farmers should not have to live with difficulties like this. . . ." Ok-Sil felt despondent at the thought that her appearance was giving the General great anguish and worry. "General! Our life is so, so much better compared to the pre-liberation days. We are the owners of the land to be cultivated and, unlike before, we live like humans now." Ok-Sil's answer was sincere. The General looked carefully at Ok-Sil's clothing and work tools. Ok-Sil was embarrassed about her husband's slippers, and she hid them by pulling her long skirt lower. The General pretended that he did not notice, and looked away toward the prairie under the moonlight. [. . .] "Comrade Ok-Sil, please write to Comrade Yun-Chil and tell him that once the war is over, you will together cultivate the fields of Miru Plain and make them into the nation's best land." "General, I will do so without fail." "I am very, very happy to meet you today. This meeting has made me feel confident about our victory over the Americans. Let us meet again after our victory at war." The General held Ok-Sil's hands warmly for a long time, and then, finally got into his car. Ok-Sil could not stop crying and stood on the mountain pass, as if she had forgotten about having to deliver water. After a couple of days, a military officer came back to Miru Plain. He brought Ok-Sil a brand new pair of women's shoes and told her that they were a gift from the General. After identifying that the pair was the right size for Ok-Sil's feet, the officer said, "Wonderful. Now our Supreme Commander has one fewer issue to pain him." (Kim Sam-Bok 1983, 256–63)

In the next scene, a couple of years after the end of the Korean War, presumably around 1955 or 1956, the Great Leader is receiving a report from the official of the Agricultural Ministry who excluded Miru Plain from future irrigation plans. The Great Leader asks the official whether he has talked to the farmers of Miru Plain in person. Relieved, the official responds, "Yes." The Great Leader prods further, asking what his thoughts are about this proposal. The official responds by referring to his meeting with a "young female labor team leader" (Ok-Sil) who was upset in the beginning but later accepted the plan. The story notes that the Great Leader's face showed dissatisfaction and he turned away from the official. The official was very worried, since he thought an inadvertent error, of which he himself was not aware, may have caused grave pain in the Great Leader's heart. He tried to justify himself, saying: "After we had talked carefully, the female team leader understood us very well and asked me to let you know that they would do their best to lessen the Great Leader's burden." The Great Leader quietly asked, "Is she Ms. Pang Ok-Sil?" "Yes," answered the official, surprised at the Great Leader's knowledge of this woman's name. "I know her very well. She is very close to me." The Great Leader could not calm himself down easily and began pacing the room. Ok-Sil! That Ok-Sil who prioritized the [needs of the] nation over her village's water situation and her own pain at having to fetch water from miles away every day and every night! That genuine daughter of Miru Plain! "These are our people! We won the victory at war precisely because of these people, and precisely because we have them, we are rebuilding our new life here on our soil." [. . .] "We must feel rewarded when we are able to deliver greater happiness and joy to our people. Let us travel together to Miru Plain tomorrow." The official was too embarrassed and so full of regret that he could not raise his face. [. . .]

In the car, the Respected and Beloved Leader asked the local party committee chairman, "What happened to Comrade Kang Yun-Chil?" The chairman could not raise his head and said with regret, "He was sacrificed with dignity in a battle while crossing the Rakdong River [in southeastern Korea]." "That is a terrible loss. He had big dreams. . . ." The Great Leader turned his sad face toward the window and painfully recalled his memory of the heroic soldier. "Comrade Ok-Sil must have suffered a lot." [. . .] The party chairman reported to the Great Leader that despite her sorrow and bereavement Ok-Sil had worked heroically during and after the war and had been playing a key role in motivating members of the agricultural co-op toward greater productivity and better crop quality. [. . .] The car reached Myeoneurikol. [. . .] The Great Leader suggested that he and the party chairman walk to Ok-Sil's house [as everyone was working in the fields] and wait for her return there. [. . .] Under the eaves, a little girl was tending her own flower garden. [. . .] "Are you alone?" asked the Great Leader. She ran toward him and politely bowed. "What a very good girl you are. Have you been to school already?" "I have, Sir." "What grade are you in?" "I'm a first-grader, Sir." The Great Leader squatted down to look into the girl's face more attentively. She had large, bright, beautiful eyes. "So, you must be that little one whom your mother carried on her back during the war." The girl simply smiled. [. . .] The Great Leader came out to the yard. At that moment, Ok-Sil, along with her co-op members, arrived home. "Mommy!" Her daughter ran toward her. "Comrade Ok-Sil, how have you been?" The Great Leader's countenance brightened up with joy at seeing her again. "Oh, our Great Leader, how have *you* been?" But Ok-Sil could not say any more because of the endless tears that covered her face. She lowered her head. The Great Leader looked at her as if she was his long-lost daughter. Just like many years before, Ok-Sil looked attractive; her tall stature, sharp eyes, and straight lips all showed her strong will and determination. "You've changed quite a bit since the war. You must have had a hard time." [. . .] "Great Leader, we are just fine." "I heard about your situation. I heard how strong and brave you have been. I know how brave your husband was as well. I'm sorry he did not return, but we have you here, don't we?" Ok-Sil began sobbing. "Mommy, why don't you put your white shoes on?" Ok-Sil brushed her away. "Well. . ." "Mommy, you said you'd only wear them if you could meet Father Marshal one more time, right?" Ok-Sil did not know what to do. She was so elated yet embarrassed at the same time. Her daughter went inside the house and brought out the unworn pair of white shoes. "Come on, Mommy, put these on!" Ok-Sil's fingers trembled. Our Beloved and Respected Leader took the shoes from the girl and said to Ok-Sil, "I sent this pair to you back then because I saw you were wearing your husband's worn-out slippers when you had to walk so many arduous miles along the mountain pass. Why have you not worn them even once to this day?" When the Great Leader said this, the aides and officials accompanying him all broke into tears. [. . .] "If we had not had that war, we would have included Miru Plain in our irrigation map. [. . .] We must try now. I feel strongly about it now that I've seen this place again. [. . .] This girl's father asked us to raise her in this happy future fatherland of ours. We must [fulfill that wish]." [. . .] [Ok-Sil's daughter] tried not to cry. For, even at her tender age, she understood that although her father would never return home, she had found out that there was a bosom even bigger and warmer than that of her own father. (Kim Sam-Bok 1983, 267–73)

In the end, Miru Plain receives water through the newly constructed irrigation system. The story ends with a scene where farmers are sending off the Great Leader with tears running down their cheeks, passionately repeating their cries of "Long Live!" The novel concludes with the following passage:

That wish, that wish that Ok-Sil and her husband had made together after Liberation came true today. That wilderness of Miru Plain is now beautifully tamed, and endless horizons of fertile fields spread in front of everyone's eyes. The ears of crops dance with joy. Rich water runs through ditches, passing on the legend of the irrigation of Miru Plain. That is right. This is a new legend of Miru Plain born in the age of the Workers' Party of Korea. (Kim Sam-Bok 1983, 278)

The Great Leader here (again) is depicted as someone who can remember every detail of each individual's circumstances, but above all as someone whose love is boundless and endless in nature. His bosom is deeper and warmer than that of an individual's own father; he is as loving toward Ok-Sil as her own husband was, if not more so. Ok-Sil's physical reactions to the Great Leader—tears, trembling, losing her voice, embarrassment, elation, and so on—are those easily recognizable among infatuated teenagers in the presence of their beloved. But, the author uses the father-daughter metaphor when capturing the Great Leader's love for Ok-Sil, despite the fact that Ok-Sil, a young mother, might only be ten years or so younger than the Great Leader, their age difference being insufficient for a father and daughter. Further, it is difficult to imagine a daughter exhibiting this type of bodily reaction to her father. This jumbled, many-faceted, complex, all-consuming and all-compatible love is the love that is embodied by the Great Leader, and derived from the very inner core of this great being.

Love's Eternal Triangle

How does a North Korean find worth in another human being? To find another individual worth noticing, worth helping and caring for, worthy of protection or education, or worthy of a minimal level of respect: such acts are necessary for any society to be viable. Without such investments, society would collapse. Collectively, I would call these acts examples of "love." As Simone Weil writes, "Among human beings, only the existence of those we love is fully recognized. Belief in the existence of other human beings as such is love" (Weil 1952b, 64).

In any society, love thus defined creates engagement, inter-action, and relationships between humans. Here, we assume that love flows around the population in diverse, uncircum-scribed, and (mostly) unprescribed directions, while these di-rections would follow discriminatory contours, reflecting par-ticular prejudices and predilections. Although this does not cancel out the hierarchy or selectiveness of love, I assume here that we tend to be both recipients and givers of love, mostly at the same time. It would be interesting, therefore, to recall that at the beginning of this chapter, we identified Weil's view of God's love as being of a sovereign kind, in that God does not have to love us mortals, only loving himself. We, on the other hand, must love each other, and by so doing attain our love for God: we love each other because each of us loves God. Putting this in a North Korean context, we will see in this chap-ter the intriguing yet wholly understandable—if only via the conundrum of interpretation—way by which North Koreans love themselves, their humanly comrades, and of course, their Great Leader.

In the following pages, I explore love's whereabouts in North Korea using the novel *Meon kil* (The Long Road) by Jeong Chang-Yun, published in 1983. I conducted a similar exercise (see Ryang 2009) using another North Korean novel, published in 1974 under the title *Yonggwangroneun sumswinda* (The Steel Furnace Is Breathing) by Yun Se-Jung. In that piece, I tried to substantiate that love's primary location in North Korea could be found in the connection between the Great Leader and each individual and that North Korean men and women love each other precisely because the other loves the Great Leader. According to this proposition, love in North Ko-rea is always born from within a triangle involving a man, a woman, and the Great Leader. I called this love "sovereign love" following the notion of the sovereign as a form of ex-istence that is only the object of love and does not love anyone other than himself, as proposed by Bataille (1993, 178–79, 198) and as suggested in the Introduction to this book. In this form of love, I stressed, love for the Great Leader constitutes an all-consuming form of dedication, while the Great Leader does not have to reciprocate. Paradoxically, however, the Great Leader is perceived as an all-loving, most benevolent figure, and this has led to the precondition where the population is expected to show him unconditional love in return. We will see that in this novel, *Meon kil*, the plot for this revolutionary love conundrum thickens even further.

Meon kil is set in the field of mining and metallurgical research, and its protagonists include scientists, miners, technicians, medical doctors, factory workers, and their families. The entire story revolves around a research project that aims to develop a new iron alloy, Teu-13, to enhance the quality of iron production. Professor Pak Si-Bong, one of North Korean's leading senior metallurgists, has proven that it is theoretically possible to produce this material, but none has yet been produced. This task has been given to the hero of the story, Choe Jung-Yeol, and Professor Pak's other disciples.

The novel opens with two long-winded letters. One is from Jung-Yeol to Seon-Hui, his high school sweetheart and includes lengthy quotes from Seon-Hui's previous letter to him, and the other is from Jung-Yeol to his mother. Seon-Hui's letter had declared that their relationship was over, but she demanded that Jung-Yeol respond to this announcement. The reader quickly learns that this is a prologue for Jung-Yeol's new life, and that what Seon-Hui deems as love is something that Jung-Yeol will reject throughout the remainder of the novel.

After completing her college medical training, Seon-Hui had returned to her hometown, a mining town where she and Jung-Yeol had been high school sweethearts. Before enrolling in an engineering college, Jung-Yeol had also worked as a miner there. Their close ties were not affected by the long-distance relationship that they had to maintain while Seon-Hui studied at medical college and Jung-Yeol worked as a miner. However, as soon as Seon-Heui returned to the town, Jung-Yeol left for college, where he would major in metallurgy. Seon-Hui was hurt by his departure, but even more so by Jung-Yeol's lack of communication once he started his studies. After a few years of separation and lack of communication, Seon-Hui declares the end of their relationship in a letter, which is quoted in Jung-Yeol's reply to her:

I have a feeling that we would live apart forever, because even if we were to be married for a hundred years, you would not spare a moment for your personal life [because of your dedication to research]. I'm no longer able to endure your indifference toward me. You have never written to me [during all these years], not even one line to make me happy. Don't you understand that, in order to nurture your love, you have to spend time and energy on it? You must know that there is nothing in this world (including love) that would not change in time. [. . .] I believed for a long time that there was no gap between you and me. I was happy. But these years [of separation] have made me realize that our lives are far apart and that a vast emptiness lies between us. Our young, innocent days are over. It makes me cry when I think about it, but no longer does the thought of you arouse the flames that used to burn in my heart. (Jeong 1983, 1–2)

Seon-Hui decides not to continue their romance based on her realization that marriage and family are not important to Jung-Yeol, and her further realization that she cannot do without happiness in her personal life. She continues, according to the quote in Jung-Yeol's letter:

Had I not known that there was a vast distance between ideal and reality, I would have still been happily intoxicated [with the idea that I would be married to a famous, dedicated scientist]. But [. . .] I now know that if you were to continue dedicating yourself to your research at this pace, there would be no room for the two of us. [. . .] I know it would be great if you were to live as a world-famous metallurgist, contributing to the scientific advancement of humanity. But, I'm not sure if that day will ever come. And if your research did not succeed after all these years, not only your [life], but [also] my own life would have been sacrificed for nothing. I'd rather go on as an ordinary person, without having to pay such a high price for life. I plead to you one last time: will you come with me to live the life of an ordinary person? Going to work and coming home, everyday, all year long, for many, many years and, in the evening, we would close the window blinds and enjoy "the world where only you and I exist." I want to live like that. I want to enjoy life and our youth. I want to cherish the small, mundane things in life, such as dinner parties and interesting conversations. [. . .] Our dreams seem to have drifted far away from each other. (Jeong 1983, 6–8)

The key to this letter, the logic of Seon-Hui's justification for ending the relationship, is her desire for them to have their own world, a world in which only the two of them exist. The first thing the reader registers is this idea of a private world of two lovers as the antithesis to the entire novel. In response, Jung-Yeol writes as follows:

I will tell you clearly where I stand. Even though your pleading must be very sincere, I will have to continue on my path. You say that you realize that there is a distance between ideal and reality. You don't seem to realize, however, that our nation is full of passion and longing for creativity and production. You don't understand the passionate heart of creative people and you say you'd rather live ordinarily, with stability and mundane happiness. Such a life may appear like a rainbow-colored dream to you now, but the day will come when you realize that that dream is totally meaningless. But, I will not criticize you. There is nothing wrong with your desire for mundane happiness. That is not a crime. Many, many people live that way and I, too, sometimes understand that the pursuit of ordinary happiness is important. But, I'm unable to accept your position as my own. My future without you will be lonely, but I have no choice but to go on my own path, and I know I will not regret it. Maybe, some time later, one night, I might be walking past the windows of your happy home. Even though [. . .] it might be freezing outside, I will not knock on your door begging for momentary warmth. (Jeong 1983, 8–9)

Jung-Yeol's stern declaration in his letter to Seon-Hui is that his relationship with her — and the love that it represents — is over: this is the beginning of the novel. We can register here at the outset a dyadic pair of contrasting concepts and lifestyles: a warm, mundane family life and a well-regarded, stable occupation (medicine) on one hand and on the other a lonely, uncertain, and ever-arduous life of research driven by a passion to creatively contribute to the nation. As we continue reading this novel, we will realize that this is not a simple contrast between private and public—what are contrasted here are different forms of love. And, although Jung-Yeol refrains from criticizing Seon-Hui, we will see in this novel that the pursuit of ordinary happiness in a world reserved only for two lovers constitutes a form of blasphemy in North Korea.

The second letter, from Jung-Yeol to his mother, is filled with his efforts to console his mother after the break-up of his relationship with Seon-Hui. Again, Jung-Yeol lengthily quotes from his mother's earlier letter, to which he is now responding:

That girl [Seon-Hui] got married yesterday to someone else. It caught me by surprise. I knew that you and that girl were close, closer than usual friends. Are you not capable of attracting and retaining one girl? Or is there another reason? This mother is quite saddened by this. I always thought she would be my future daughter-in-law. Her good reputation as a medical doctor in town secretly made me happy and proud. I feel lost. . . . (Jeong 1983, 10)

In response to this, Jung-Yeol tries hard to explain:

Mother, your words sadden me, not because of Comrade Seon-Hui's marriage, but because of the way I made you feel. All this son wants is your happiness and your peace of mind. I don't know how I can explain to you what happened. As you know, Comrade Seon-Hui is a beautiful girl—beautiful inside and outside. But, Mother, one never knows in this world. Someone who is even better than Comrade Seon-Hui could be your future daughter-in-law. I know I ought to let you know why we parted, but I also feel that I should not tell you very private matters that relate to our female comrade [Seon-Hui]. You worry about me not being able to attract a woman. [. . .] Please do not worry. I'm not that bad. And if I were to lose a girl, that's because I did not want her. One day, a girl will appear in front of me whom my heart tells me to grab by all means. When that day comes, I will do anything to take her and bring her home to show you. I have such strength, heart, and passion. In this sense, I'm just like my deceased father, as you know. [. . . It] looks like I'll be able to take about one week off. I'll make a point of going home to spend time with you and [my sister] Jung-Ok. (Jeong 1983, 10–11)

This letter is full of affectionate exchanges between mother and son. Also, it gives the reader some background regarding the makeup of Jung-Yeol's family. His father was a mining technician and died at a young age. He has one younger sister and a deeply loving mother. The letter shows that Jung-Yeol has a dignified personality, not slandering his lost love, but maintaining how beautiful Seon-Hui is both inside and outside. It also shows his maturity; rather than telling his mother what happened and, therefore, making her feel even more regretful, he provides her with relief by suggesting that he will get an even better girl. Note that he refers to getting a girl here somewhat as if it were a gift to his mother or a means of demonstrating his filial piety rather than a matter of his own personal taste and choosing. The letter also tells the reader that Jung-Yeol is 30 years old, in good health, has begun learning his fourth foreign language and, above all, that he is truly a kind and loving son.

Meon kil is unusually vivid, well written, and animated for a North Korean novel of this period. Its author, Jeong Chang-Yun, is capable of depicting individual characters as unique and idiosyncratic, including personalities that are stubborn, thin-skinned, neurotic, standoffish, alcohol-dependent, indulgent, solemn, or grim, for example. Unlike other North Korean novels of this period, which tend to depict short spans of time during the Korean War or the postwar reconstruction period, this novel spans the colonial, post-liberation, and contemporary periods, and is interspersed with citations from old Korean folklore as well as foreign authors and poets, such as Byron. Clashes between individuals, and their experiences of agony, betrayal, trust, rivalry, jealousy, failure, success, and love are also brought into the story in a more intricate and sophisticatedly complex manner than in other North Korean novels from this time. As with any historically expansive novels of this period, *Meon kil* also contains a chapter in which Kim Il Sung appears in person. Also, as in all other such cases, his appearance comes toward the end, decisively pushing and encouraging the protagonists to overcome any obstacles that lie in the way in their heroic struggles. In this regard, this novel does not deviate from others in its portrayal of Kim Il Sung. However, when compared to the stories of the 1970s, this 1983 novel shows that North Korean society is becoming more complex, reflecting class stratification if not according to economic status or income level than by socio-political rank and affiliation. At the same time, the standardized way in which Kim Il Sung appears in novels starting in the 1980s reflects his elevation in status from man to sacred being. In the novels of the 1970s, he is portrayed as a human protagonist. By the 1980s, however, he had become a fixed element in stories, increasingly devoid of human sentiment and described only on a surface level. Let us see in *Meon kil* how this process plays out as the hero Jung-Yeol strives to achieve his metallurgical innovation.

Jung-Yeol arrives in a town that is home to a metal factory, the August Factory, which has a research facility attached to it. Professor Pak Si-Bong of Kim Il Sung University in Pyong-yang has sent his disciple, Yang Bin, here to conduct research and ultimately produce Teu-13. Upon Jung-Yeol's arrival, the reader learns that Yang Bin has deserted his post as field researcher without completing his research task and disappeared with his wife, leaving the facility empty. Jung-Yeol and his friends have come to know this, but have not informed Professor Pak, as Yang Bin was the professor's favorite and most trusted disciple. Since the professor is advanced in age and in fragile health, his disciples are worried that if he gets to know about what Yang Bin has done, he will suffer severe distress and his condition will decline.

Jung-Yeol unpacks his bags in the small house that has been vacant since Yang Bin's departure. The first boarders to have stayed at the house were Professor Pak and his team ten years or so earlier. After Professor Pak, several interesting residents had occupied the house. One of them was a state-commissioned novelist who was known among locals for his white shirts and wide grey neckties. The novelist completed a long story on the working class struggle while living among the workers. During his stay, he gave the house the nickname *meon kil* or "long road," referring to the long road leading to completion, be it in relation to literary work or scientific research. The reader learns that the novel's title *Meon kil* derives from this episode and is tempted to imagine that Jeong Chang-Yun, the author of *Meon kil,* might have been the novelist with the white shirt and wide grey tie referred to in the story.

Jung-Yeol knew Yang Bin as his cell leader from his college dormitory. At Kim Il Sung University, dormitories were not privately operated; they fell under the strict supervision of the branches and committees of the Korean Socialist Working Youth League. Yang Bin was well known for his outstanding intellect, but he was always arrogant and unapproachable. Jung-Yeol, a couple of years junior to Yang Bin, recalls one incident in which he accidentally dropped his foreign language study notebook. Yang Bin picked it up and looked through it before telling Jung-Yeol to his face how deplorably poor the latter's foreign language skills were. Jung-Yeol was ashamed, but could not deny this, as Yang Bin was not only known to be a genius in his own field of metallurgy, but also fluent in a number of foreign languages. Yang Bin would regularly stay up all night, reading and studying. He knew nothing but research. Yang Bin completed his graduate studies two years ahead of Jung-Yeol and was assigned to the August Factory to take up the exciting task of researching and producing Teu-13. Five years later, Professor Pak received a delightful letter from Yang Bin, letting him know that the latter had been successful in producing Teu-9.8. This made the old master very proud, reconfirming the trust he had placed in his disciple. Now there would be only 3.2 points left to complete for the Teu material to reach the targeted value of 13.

Upon his arrival at the August Factory, Jung-Yeol learns that Yang Bin's research notes are missing. This is very bad news, since Jung-Yeol could have used them as a point of departure in his own efforts to achieve production of the remaining 3.2 points of the Teu material. Desperately searching for Yang Bin's notes, Jung-Yeol stumbles upon a personal journal written by a woman by the name of Ryu Po-Eun, a journalist for the local newspaper. Po-Eun was a close friend of Yang

Bin's wife, Ri-Sun. If Yang Bin were to have left his records with anyone locally, it would surely have been this woman, Jung-Yeol infers. Upon discovering the journal, he is unable to resist the temptation, and while knowing full well how undignified and unethical it is, he nevertheless reads through the pages of Po-Eun's personal reflections and daily records. From her notes, there is nothing particularly helpful in indicating where Yang Bin's records might be found.

Po-Eun happens to enter the room at this point and discover that a newly assigned researcher is reading her journal without permission. After retrieving her journal, Po-Eun flatly denies Jung-Yeol access to herself for the next few weeks, forcing Jung-Yeol to follow her around — from this coincidental encounter between the two, the reader knows immediately that a romance between the two will later develop. One day, forcing entry to her media car, Jung-Yeol finally succeeds in having a conversation with her:

Po-Eun said, "Comrade Yang Bin started from zero and reached 9.8, but you are trying to obtain 9.8 with no effort. And, in order to do so, you used a dishonorable method [by reading my journal]. Furthermore, you are stalking an unknown woman [Po-Eun herself] like some kind of coward. If this was the behavior of someone else, how would you see it?" [. . .] "You are mistaken," Jung-Yeol replied, "Of course, I admit that my desire for Comrade Yang Bin's records is the result of laziness to some extent, but more importantly, I need to save time. I need to bypass the first five years, so that we can obtain [Teu-13] as soon as possible for the nation's economic construction. Because of this, I threw away my pride and am behaving in this despicable manner. [. . .]" "Thank you," Po-Eun said, "for answering me honestly. But you must surely know how hard Yang Bin worked in order to reach the 9.8 point." [. . .] "Yes, I do. Reaching the 9.8 point is and will always be the accomplishment of Comrade Yang Bin. I just need to start from the 9.9 point." [. . .] For the first time since he had begun following her, she showed a smile that disappeared in a flash, however. That moment, Jung-Yeol felt an indescribable [sense of] hope being born in his heart. That hope was not simply about the possibility of being eventually able to obtain Yang Bin's research notes: it went beyond that, reaching the somewhat differently hued territory of the heart. (Jeong 1983, 83–84)

Some months later, Jung-Yeol eventually tracks down Yang Bin and his wife while Po-Eun happens to be staying with them. The three of them—Jung-Yeol, Yang Bin, and Yang Bin's wife—have quite a fierce exchange, while Po-Eun looks on. Here, Yang Bin and Ri-Sun are portrayed as cowardly quitters, while Jung-Yeol is still trying to restore Yang Bin's honor, proposing that he return to complete his research. Yang Bin painfully refuses. The reader is impressed by Jung-Yeol's big heart and by the fact that he is prioritizing the success of the research (for the benefit of the nation) over any feelings of personal vendetta. The reader is also informed through this exchange that deserting one's mission halfway through—be it research (Yang Bin) or a romantic pursuit (Seon-Hui)—is seen as undignified in North Korea. On their way home, Jung-Yeol and Po-Eun have a conversation on the train. By then, Jung-Yeol is fully aware how much he is attracted to Po-Eun. They are still awkward toward each other, though Po-Eun more so, since she still cannot forgive Jung-Yeol completely for having violated her privacy by reading her journal. Jung-Yeol confesses:

So far, I have always lived honestly, in the eyes of our fatherland, our Party, our revolution, my deceased father, my mother, and my little sister. I've always been completely honest with my professors, my college mates, and even my past lover. Yet, I read one woman's journal without permission. That was the one shameful crime I committed in my life. But, I still maintain: I was only trying to find clues about Teu-13, not [pry into] a woman's personal life. [. . .] My one-track mind, my stubbornness about the success of the research led me to commit such a shameful deed. [. . .] I have paid a high personal price for my research. I did not even try to retain the one beautiful woman who loved me deeply. I had believed that she would stay with me till the end of our arduous journey together, but I was mistaken. She was precious to me, but my ideal was even more precious. [. . .] I've looked for a comrade, a companion in life. I've been looking; sometimes in the darkness, sometimes on the riverbank, sometimes lost in a crowd, and sometimes absorbed in my own reflection. [. . .] I've longed to meet someone, someone genuine, and I believe I have found one, the genuine one. I happened to find this person during my search for Teu-13. (Jeong 1983, 186–88)

Po-Eun, in the face of this confession, remains poised and does not show her emotions easily. In fact, she does not show much emotion at all, saying rather coldly: "You shall have a [female] companion who will support you, care for you, and encourage you, but that woman will have to remain at a distance for a little while, or perhaps for a long time. . . ." (Jeong 1983, 188). Despite these cold words, the reader is told that Jung-Yeol has found reason for hope.

Back on the research front, it turns out that past experiments used half domestic and half imported materials, making the results unreliable. Jung-Yeol comes to learn that Professor Pak (who by then has passed away) was searching for a fungus that he had named "black fungus" or *keomeun peoseot,* known to contain a lethal poison. Black fungus was not easily found and, because of its porous surface, was prone to leaking the poison and was regarded as impossible to transport. Jung-Yeol begins his search for this material, but during his expedition, accidentally falls down a rocky cliff. He suffers horrific injuries, ending up with multiple facial stitches and a broken leg. Before he has completely recovered, he finds out that the black fungus is native to a little mountain village called Hoseongkol and he heads off in that direction. During his trip, he and Po-Eun cross paths, since Po-Eun also happens to be visiting this village while researching an article for her newspaper. After an arduous search, Jung-Yeol eventually discovers black fungi deep in the mountains. He packs them securely, but his backpack is not allowed onto the train. A female public transportation officer is outraged by Jung-Yeol's ignorance of the rules against the transportation of hazardous materials and severely criticizes him for potentially endangering public health. Embarrassed, Jung-Yeol decides to walk dozens of miles with the poisonous fungi on his back. When he finally reaches home, Po-Eun is awestruck: despite the fact that he has not yet fully recovered from his recent injuries, he has walked a long distance, burdening himself with the task of hand-delivering poisonous fungi in order to help the research project succeed, thus providing a path-breaking improvement to the national economy. Po-Eun finally realizes that Jung-Yeol is the one she has been looking for: "Po-Eun was overcome by a burning flame that enwrapped her entire existence. This flame was telling her that one season of her life had ended and a new one was about to begin. 'A true person . . . I will walk with him along his *meon kil* [long road],' Po-Eun could not stay inside the house. The beginning of this new season of her life was too all consuming to be contained indoors. She got out of the house and walked up and down the street. She was too uplifted and restless to sleep" (Jeong 1983, 358). Shortly after this, Jung-Yeol uses the black fungi to successfully raise the level of the metal up to 13 and thereby obtain Teu-13. This brings tears to the eyes of many veteran workers. Jung-Yeol is exhausted, yet overcome with a sense of fulfillment.

Love for the Great Being

Right after this, the Great Leader pays a visit to the August Factory, and Jung-Yeol receives the honor of a private meeting with him:

"So, you walked all the way from Hoseongkol, did you?" asked the Great Leader. [. . .] "You are brave. A courageous young man, indeed!" said the Great Leader to Jung-Yeol. He looked at Jung-Yeol with warm and trusting eyes and then turned toward the Cabinet members [who had accompanied the Great Leader for this visit], saying: "When I heard that one young man walked all the way from Hoseongkol to his factory, carrying the poisonous fungi on his back, I was very worried [about his safety]. But I was also enormously pleased to think that our young scientists are so incredibly reliable and admirable. [. . .] You must remember how difficult it was when we had just begun building our fatherland because of the shortage of intellectuals. So, we decided to produce one hundred million intellectuals, even if we had to go hungry. And look! Today we have such brilliant young intellectuals as this comrade." [. . .] The Great Leader turned to Jung-Yeol with a loving gaze and asked: "I understand you will be working on black fungi in order to dramatically increase our domestic metal yield. Now, is there anything the government can do for you?" "Great Leader, there is nothing I want from our govern-

장편소설

정 창 윤

Fig. 1   Cover art of *Meon kil* (The Long Road). Jung-Yeol walks dozens of
miles with the poisonous black fungi in his backpack. Illustration by Nam
Min-U.

ment. Nothing. . . ." The Great Leader looked at his Cabinet members
again and continued: "How amazing our young scientists are! But, I
demand that this comrade's experiment be suspended for the time
being, that is, until we can secure his safety in handling such a poisonous substance. Once we secure such conditions, he can come back
to a safe work environment." That moment, everyone could hear
Jung-Yeol's low sobbing. The Cabinet members also sobbed quietly.
[. . .] The Great Leader's eyes [. . .] also appeared wet. "Whenever I
think about the late Professor Pak Si-Bong, my chest is heavy with
regret that I was unable to give him better research facilities. Those
days were very hard for our nation. . . ." The Great Leader was unable to complete his sentence because of his sorrow. Jung-Yeol could
not recognize anything in front of him because of the endless tears
welling up in his eyes. (Jeong 1983, 369–72)

It turns out that the Great Leader and Professor Pak had known
each other ever since the beginning of the North Korean nation-

building project in the late 1940s. Professor Pak had a long, winding, and somewhat unorthodox personal history. As with all other technical and scientific personnel that became pillars of North Korea's national construction following the end of World War II, Professor Pak had studied under the Japanese colonial establishment. Following the partition of Korea, Pak decided at one point to cross the 38th parallel and head south to Seoul so that he could continue his research. He had had interactions with the Communist Party, the forerunner of the Workers' Party of Korea, and found its members pedantic and unimaginative. As a result, he had become convinced that the Party was not interested in scientific research.

Despondent about the future of his metallurgical research, he expressed his intention to leave the North. During the years immediately following partition (1945) and prior to the establishment of two separate regimes in the North and the South (1948), it was still possible, though cumbersome, for people to cross the 38th parallel in both directions. People did so for diverse reasons: for family reunions, in pursuit of careers, or because they liked or disliked the Soviet occupation forces in the North or the American military government in the South. It was after the Korean War ceasefire in 1953 that the two Koreas came to confront each other definitively and unequivocally as mutually hostile polities. Professor Pak was one of many intellectuals who had become pessimistic about the Communist Party's hard line against the intelligentsia.

As he pondered crossing over, one day he was taken to a hotel room by some uniformed men. In that room, he found himself facing the Cabinet members and military leaders. Once everyone was seated, General Kim Il Sung walked into the room and introduced himself: "I am Kim Il Sung. Let's walk over there." The two walked toward a window. Kim continued: "I sat here at the same table with a novelist who crossed over from the South to the North the other day, but today, I'm sitting with a professor who wants to leave Pyongyang for Seoul. [. . .] I was very happy here in this room the other day, but today, I'm saddened. When I was fighting as a guerrilla in the mountains, I used to become so happy when comrades came to join us, but when anyone left us, I was saddened, just like I am now." Professor Pak could not quite figure out why this meeting was taking place. The General continued: "It was yesterday. I heard the news that one scientist was arrested because he was trying to smuggle scientific results with him to the South. It pained me to see that our future scientific leaders had to leave us in this way, with invaluable data that would be so useful in building our nation. We all suffered under the Japanese, and yet we cannot fight together for our new nation, forcing our scientists to wander about." Kim continued: "I am a politician of this land [. . .] you are a scientist of this land. I gather we can frankly talk about this. [. . .] What is making you want to leave us?" Pak Si-Bong spoke honestly: "Pyongyang has declared a death sentence for scientists like myself. I have decided to part with Pyongyang in order to pursue my ideals and uphold my dignity as a scientist." Kim Il Sung gently responded: "It must be a portion of Pyongyang, rather than Pyongyang as a whole, that is vexing you." Kim Il Sung then looked at Pak and warmly yet firmly remarked: "I, too, have an ideal and I believe we can understand each other very well in the sense that we both are idealistic."

The moment he heard these words, Pak Si-Bong felt as if he were sitting next to his old teacher. The General's voice continued: "Our ideal is to build a communistic society on the soil of our fatherland. Just as you felt despondent because we don't have the foundations for scientific research, we did not have our own fatherland [until the liberation of Korea]. The reason why we fought against the Japanese is precisely because we wanted to recover our fatherland. [. . .] We are trying to found a research university in Pyongyang. [. . .] I'd like to propose that you work together with us. You trust me, and I trust you . . . Let us build our ideal, future Korea together." [. . .] "Dear General!!" Tears rolled down Si-Bong's cheeks. Until that day, Si-Bong had not heard Korean spoken in such a way. The General's words made him realize that words could grab his heart and conquer all of the organs and cells that constituted his body. [. . .] He did not realize that he could cry this much. His pure tears cleansed his eyes and showed him a new world that he had never seen, a world that he had always wanted to see, but thought was not available to him. But, now, he saw the hues that made up that world, hues that eternally colored his destiny. (Jeong 1983, 144–45)

There are a few interesting connections that one can see in the way Kim Il Sung is portrayed in this story. First, let us consider the use of the term "hues" in the above quotation, and one other use of this term: "That moment, Jung-Yeol sensed an indescribable [sense of] hope being born in his heart. That hope was not simply about the possibility of being eventually able to obtain Yang Bin's research notes: it went beyond that, reaching the somewhat differently hued territory of the heart (Jeong 1983, 83–84)." This latter passage indicates that Jung-Yeol is beginning to fall in love with Po-Eun. The former passage is the description of the brave new world that Professor Pak has come to recognize in the words of Kim Il Sung, words that grabbed his heart and conquered his body. It is interesting to see that heterosexual romance and a young scientist's reverence toward an equally young head-of-state (Kim Il Sung could not have been older than his mid-30s) take on an identical cosmology of new colors that have created a world hitherto unknown to the protagonist. Uncertainty, excitement, and extreme joy, accompanied by bodily reactions such as tears, trembling, a sense of being grabbed, a rise in body temperature, and so on, are classic symptoms of infatuation or of the rapid, almost violent, and uncontrollable manner in which one falls in love (see Fisher 1993). This type of response is reciprocated by Po-Eun: as we saw earlier, once she had identified Jung-Yeol to be her true love, she "was overcome by a burning flame that enwrapped her entire existence." (Jeong 1983, 358). On the other hand, Jung-Yeol's reaction to the Great Leader's love was "sobbing" and a "welling of tears," identical to Professor Pak's reaction to the General's kindness. All of the protagonists involved — Jung-Yeol, Po-Eun, and Professor Pak — show an overwhelming physical manifestation of love, the dividing line between romance on one hand and reverence and admiration for a superior, charismatic being on the other becoming difficult to distinguish. The only protagonist that does not show a bodily reaction or apparent upheaval of emotion is Kim Il Sung himself, except for the brief and modest show of emotion when "The Great Leader was unable to complete his sentence because of his sorrow" (Jeong 1983, 372) upon recalling how difficult things had been when Professor Pak initially started his research in post-liberation North Korea.

Pace Bataille and his exploration of the sovereign, the North Korean sovereign is a loving entity. The Great Leader is regarded as pre-equipped with endless love, *kkeudeomneun sarang*, toward the people. In this sense, the Great Leader is similar to Weil's God. And it is the people that are therefore expected to forever strive to repay this pre-accorded love from their Leader. The notion I briefly introduced earlier, that of sovereign love, is closely connected to this one-sided flow of love (from people to leader), which is nevertheless equipped with the pretension of two-way love (between people and the leader).

Unlike Weil's God, Kim Il Sung does not, however, love just himself. He loves the people. And, unlike Bataille's sovereign, he is supposedly capable of concerning himself with others' wellbeing too. Nevertheless, the way he loves people is indifferent to the question of reciprocity: Kim Il Sung never questions whether people love him back or not. It is always the people themselves that self-critically reflect upon and critically assess their love for Kim. As such, while adopting a two-way format, in reality, North Korean love flows only in one direction: from the people to Kim, from a people who constantly strive to elevate their love for Kim to an increasingly higher and purer level, where Kim's a priori love for the people is taken for granted. Furthermore, the people's love for Kim Il Sung is to be identified through their ties with each other in their common journey of dedication and devotion toward him. Along the long journey taken to demonstrate their loyalty toward Kim, men and women find companions in each other. This is how North Korean love forms an eternal triangle.

But here, we should stress the conspicuous function of gender in this novel. The most noble and sacred bond is reached between reverent male protagonists on the one hand and the revered Great Leader on the other. It is these male protagonists who are depicted as having personal interactions with the leader, while female protagonists receive the benefit of the leader's almighty benevolence in a second-hand manner through their relationships with the male protagonists. As such, male-female romance is only secondary to the leader-male connection. Following this, the male-male connection is of importance at the next level. In this novel, Professor Pak's disciple Jung-Yeol inherits the former's loyalty toward the leader and he is identified as a genuine intellectual and moral heir to the professor. As such, Jung-Yeol is the pillar of a story that conveys the proper channel of love for the leader. But there is also a hierarchy incorporated within these homoerotic (or should I shay homo-heroic) connections. Yang Bin is an imposter whose betrayal in the end endangers the professor's health and the professor ends his life shortly after learning of Yang Bin's cowardly act, as we learn in the story. The confrontation between Yang Bin the imposter and Jung-Yeol the genuine apostle is an important motif of the novel, in that it is an admonition against fake loyalty toward the Highest Being, the Great Leader. When the imposter is a man (rather than a woman), this is seen as being more deeply sinful, and in this case results in the death of the teacher.

Then there is the romance between Jung-Yeol and Po-Eun. Although this is an important element in Jung-Yeol's personal development, it is also crucial to note how the positioning of Po-Eun eloquently manifests her secondary role. For example, for a long time, Po-Eun is unable to see through to the true value of Jung-Yeol's humanity. Her ignorance is only saved by Jung-Yeol's incredible sincerity and moral principles. Similarly, the way Seon-Hui leaves Jung-Yeol right at the beginning of the story is seen as a symbol of backwardness, selfishness, the pursuit of petty bourgeois values and a meaningless, banal way of life. It is telling that such attributes and desires are embodied and carried by female protagonists. While Seon-Hui represents the worst of such values and Po-Eun an altogether more virtuous example, the two nevertheless share certain similarities in that they both have to work at catching up to the degree of commitment to noble causes displayed by Jung-Yeol: Po-Eun has to wait for almost the entire novel for this to happen, while Seon-Hui fails completely, even before trying. The last scene of *Meon kil* is indicative of this framework:

It is snowing. Some large, some small, flake after flake, snow falls endlessly. It is the last night of the year, a year full of struggles and progress. [. . .] Jung-Yeol stands on the banks of the Daedong River [in Pyongyang]. The young scientist Choe Jung-Yeol has climbed over many mountains of difficulties and trials this year. He has succeeded in producing six new metallurgical materials at the research facility provided for him by the Great Leader. This thankful year — Jung-Yeol's mind is filled with gratitude toward the Great Being. [. . .] Quietly, tears roll down his cheeks as he thinks about Professor Pak Si-Bong. [. . .] The young disciple is thinking about his master's final message: "Remember! Your research consists of only one area, the area that the Great Leader is concerned with." Jung-Yeol is re-digesting this message in his heart. He is etching these words in his heart one by one in order never to forget even one word. Ryu Po-Eun stands closely alongside him. Her coat, too, is getting covered in snowflakes. The sound of the New Year bell is heard. The bell is ringing, planting an invincible will in the minds of the people. The two are holding hands, hands that are warm with the determination to [journey an] even longer distance in the New Year. (Jeong 1983, 375)

In this final page of the entire novel, Po-Eun appears in the last couple of sentences. Until her name is mentioned toward the end, the reader is made to think that only Jung-Yeol is to appear in this last scene, along with his late professor, whose final words reconfirm that Jung-Yeol should follow his professor in his dedication to the Great Leader. In order for this Trinity to be delivered, the author began by eliminating Jung-Yeol's father as a renowned mining technician who had died long ago. In light of Korean traditional patrilineage, it is extremely useful to remember that the existence of a father or of a male ancestral lineage is a hindrance for North Korean individuals in the context of achieving a direct connection with the Great Leader free of any moral obstacle. Thus, in most of the well-read North Korean novels, of which *Meon kil* is one example, the protagonists' father is already dead. There are more novels with male lead characters than with female characters (although films and musicals do not follow this pattern), with such male protagonists usually raised by single mothers. The elimination of the father is necessary in order to both simplify and purify the connection between the hero and the Great Leader. While the story frequently includes romantic interactions between Jung-Yeol and Po-Eun, the essential goodness of their romance stands on the premise that these two are united in one identical purpose, to display loyalty to the Great Leader until the end of their lives. Good love and good romance in North Korea presuppose a perpetual triangle, where a man and a woman enter into a loving relationship via their dedication for the Great Leader. Such a relationship becomes wholly logical, if we are to understand the Great Leader not so much as a great man, but as a great being or "greatness," indeed, His Greatness.

The Leader Who Is Both Mother and Father

As can be seen in the above, in North Korean literature during the 1970s and 1980s, Kim Il Sung knows no age (or more precisely, no aging in any form) or defects, just as the body politic of the Tudor Kings knew no age, disability, or imbecility. Furthermore, he is all-loving and loves all. Whatever he touches feels love, turns into a loving being, and is determined to return this great love through dedication and loyalty. He is a hermaphrodite of love, whose love is not constrained by one gender—his love is gender-free. This is best captured in the North Korean adoption of the neologism, *eobeoi*, a compound word consisting of father (*abeoji*) and mother (*eomeoni*). *Eobeoi* is both: both mother and father at the same time. The fixed nomenclature *eobeoi suryeongnim*, or Father/Mother Leader, became standard in North Korea from around the early 1980s. It is interesting to note that when he is referred to by his military rank, the term *abeoji janggunnim* or Father General is used, as if to suggest that a military post is masculine. In such cases, Kim Il Sung is either portrayed as being young or depicted in a strictly military context, a pattern that became rare in the 1990s. Instead, Father/Mother Leader was the most frequently utilized epithet prior to his death in 1994.

In this understanding, Kim Il Sung's love is not heterosexual or homosexual, but devoid of, and beyond, sexuality. Neither is it defined by parental love or brotherly love or any of the categories of love that might be familiar to readers outside of North Korea. It is all-pervasive, chameleon-colored, age-less, sex-less, gender-less, and change-less. Yet, it is not religious in the sense that the Christian god's love is perceived. For, as can be seen in the stories I have dealt with in this chapter, Kim Il Sung's love is versatile, multi-directional, yet concrete: he is a parent to an orphan, he is a husband to a widow, he is a muse to a poet, he is an inspiration to an artist, he is a friend to the lonely and lost, and he is a son to a mother who has lost her own son in the Korean War.

There is, however, a subtle shift from the way that Kim Il Sung is depicted in the 1970s novels and how he is portrayed in novels written during the 1980s, as I stated earlier. While equally ageless and benevolent, perfect and awe-inspiring, Kim in the 1970s is a this-worldly and detail-oriented being. He remembers the details of an individual's family makeup, as in the case of a machine operator in *Keun simjang*. We can infer that North Korean authors were allowed (or ordered) to depict Kim's personal, humanly feelings. In the 1983 *Meon kil*, by way of distinction, Kim Il Sung is less concrete in his actions, more abstract and aloof. In *Meon kil*, members of his Cabinet or of a larger entourage surround Kim, placing him at a distance that is a few bodies removed from the protagonists. In the 1976 story, "Pyongyangeun noraehanda" (Pyongyang Is Singing; Ko 1976), Kim Il Sung cannot contain his urge to embrace soldiers of the Korean People's Army one by one. In *Meon kil*, he basically talks, though with warmth and wisdom. In the 1974 story, *Uri hakkyo*, Kim Il Sung strokes a boy's back many times when the latter tries to hide his hardship by using a shortened pencil. In *Meon kil,* he does not really touch anyone. As subtle as this shift may be, one can register in the 1980s that Kim Il Sung is becoming untouchable and moving toward the other-worldly realm, while the effects of his love remain constant and consistent—elating people, grabbing their hearts, and giving them enormous strength, pride, and joy—in short, transforming human beings.

Let us return to Weil. As we saw at the beginning of this chapter, she emphasizes liberty and obedience in her discussion of love. Love without these, quite predictably, parallels what Kim Il Sung and other so-called totalitarian leaders are perceived to be in the Western world: oppressive dictators who never grew up—self-centered, self-obsessed, always exploding in tantrums, and demanding the services that they require at any time and in any form.

Yet, North Korean literature has it quite otherwise: Kim Il Sung is the opposite—he is an ageless and benevolent being, whose mercy and love touch everyone, regardless of who they may be, and far from having never grown up, he is mature or more grown up than anyone else, as his age is rendered irrelevant. The uncanny point is that these two images—the adolescent dictator and the benevolent almighty one—are not that far apart. They share many commonalities. They demand, either via tantrums or charm, that everyone dedicate themselves to them; they absorb, either via force or benevolence, people's energies and passion; they change and mobilize people, either via coercion or encouragement. At the core of Weil's thinking, a person has free will, in that it is obedience and not servility or submission that makes that person follow a charismatic being. This love, however, is not a virtue that totally liberates—at least in our conventional thinking. According to Weil, liberty is attained, not achieved or won. The soul has to be able to know the Good, and it is love that leads the soul to know this state (and not the other way around). Thus: "It is only necessary to know that love is a direction and not a state of the soul. If one is unaware of this, one falls into despair at the first onslaught of affliction" (Weil 1951, 81).

The depiction of Kim Il Sung's love shown in this chapter has clear parallels with Weil's notion of God's love: "God can only love himself. . . . God's love for us is not the reason for which we should love him. God's love for us is the reason for us to love ourselves" (1986, 270). The Great Leader's endless love is not the reason why North Koreans love him, but his love is the reason for them to love themselves. And, on the basis of this self-love, which is attained in this roundabout way, North Koreans choose to obey, sacrifice themselves for, and dedicate their lives to Kim Il Sung. As such, their choice is a sovereign choice or a choice to obey according to free will. The only being not making any choice nor moving his soul in any direction is Kim Il Sung himself, as he is seen as being pre-endowed with endless love, while the North Korean people (or the protagonists in the examples shown in this chapter) are constantly *at liberty* to lead their souls toward obedience. This directional movement of the soul is manifested as love for the Leader, as we have seen. Here, Kim Il Sung does not change: he is, has been, and always will be loving, sagacious, mature, and perfect. Also, we can see that the people (the protagonists) display fierce and constant self-doubt, striving to improve themselves and agonizing over how much more they can and should love Kim.

The reader would realize that this notion of obedience based on free will, proposed by Weil during World War II, was to be taken up by Isaiah Berlin (1958) when publishing his view on the two concepts of liberty in the late 1950s. Written during heightening Cold War tensions in Europe, Berlin contemplated that there may be two contrasting yet mutually intertwining concepts of liberty. In what he calls negative freedom, one is free from the constraints of externally imposed controls, while in positive freedom, one takes control of one's own liberty in order to free oneself from obstacles, including one's own lack of knowledge and backwardness. In the latter — which Berlin posits closely resembles the situation under so-called totalitarian regimes — one is free to follow a charismatic leader that personifies one's higher, superior self. According to this concept, freedom does not stop where individual property begins, but is realized as a collective achievement. Needless to say, the free choice to love a leader, as portrayed in the North Korean novels introduced above, falls into this category of liberty.

It would be useful, then, to connect this concept of freedom with Charles Lindholm's (1993) exploration of the relationship between romantic love and charisma. Lindholm argues that for persons deeply involved in romantic love and those devotedly following a charismatic leader, self-elevation is perceived as the primary goal. In other words, it is believed that the self is improved through love for the person one adores or through love for the higher being one follows. If this is so, then, human worth in North Korea is found in love—a form of love that elevates you, me, indeed everybody, that is, love for the Great Leader.

As Weil states: "Among human beings, only the existence of those we love is fully recognized. Belief in the existence of other human beings as such is love" (Weil 1952b, 64). Especially in *Meon kil*, love for the Great Leader is seen as a force for good, and to recognize and cherish this goodness in a person is to love him or her, albeit in a roundabout way. Love among humans in North Korea, far from contradicting love for the Great Leader, only complements it. More precisely, a person's demonstration of love for the Great Leader is a most important condition for another to love that person.

TWO

War

In the aftermath of two of the most shocking disasters in the recent history of the United States—the 9/11 terrorist attacks in 2001 and Hurricane Katrina in 2005—the American people have lived, in varying degrees and durations, under conditions of heightened vigilance and caution, in which the complex lives of citizens are redirected and rearranged into a single framework: the state of emergency. Events such as these result in the disruption of ordinary routines, the destruction of infrastructure, the disabling of the diverse functions of a city's civic organizations, in addition to thousands of deaths and injuries—in a word, chaos and confusion beyond ordinary human social control. A state of emergency will be declared in order to put into immediate practice measures that are not available or able to be implemented during ordinary times. It allows authorities to take away an individual's personal freedom, private property, family connections, the normal elements of his or her existence, and other items cherished by so-called modern Western democracies. This leads us to the question: what if one never knew such things in the first place? Then, how would a state of emergency affect one's life? If one's life had always been subjected to a state of emergency from the outset—in other words, if one were to experience a state of emergency as a normal state of existence—how should such a thing as a war impact on one's ontological self-understanding in relation to life and the world?

This type of society is what Giorgio Agamben calls a camp society, where life always teeters on the edge of emergency—it exists only in such a state (Agamben 2000, 37). North Korea professes to be waging an ongoing war against the United States, a conflict that has continued ever since the outbreak of the Korean War on June 25, 1950. For North Korea, the armistice agreement of July 27, 1953 indicates only a temporary break from daily shootings, bombings, and killings (which, incidentally, is technically not wrong). War, in other words, continues to this day, not peripheral to but at the heart of the daily lives of North Koreans.

What does it mean to experience war as the foundation of one's daily life? Unlike many parts of the world scarred by civil war or foreign invasion, North Korea has not seen actual battles for more than half a century. This war, therefore, bears distinctly ideological characteristics as well as discursive effects. For this reason, it becomes necessary to explore how the conceptual reality of war figures in both the rhetorical and ontological horizons of North Koreans. This chapter will pursue the North Korean concept of war by reading closely some of the novels and stories published in this context.

Pre-1970s War Stories

While insisting on nationalism, loyalty toward the leadership, and patriotic commitment, stories written during the Korean War and the early 1960s differ in terms of theme and technique to those produced in the 1970s and 1980s: the former depict the inner feelings and delicate nuances of individual emotions. Further, the trivial personality characteristics of individuals other than Kim Il Sung receive more weight than in later novels. In other words, in these early novels written during the war, the connection between Kim and the people is not a direct one—yet. The absolute and direct connection between leader and people, at least in the world of literature, emerges after the ceasefire. In this sense, it is tempting to say that the state of emergency that requires national unity around Kim Il Sung vis-à-vis American imperialism emerged years after the ceasefire. As we shall see, literary production during the 1950s and 1960s displays clear evidence of what Western literary taxonomy would deem humanistic tendencies and is positioned surprisingly away from any sense of emergency. The irony, therefore, is that the sentiments and human interactions that writers tried to capture during the war were not as influenced by conditions generated by the emergency as were post-1970s works. Does this suggest that the direct connection between the Great Leader and the people is closely related to the emergence and sustenance of conditions pertaining to a particular kind of state of emergency and not so much about war itself or national crisis in general?

This inquiry begins with a short story produced in 1961. Entitled "Bultaneun bam" (Burning Night), this work is set in a small village called Solkol. The protagonist is work team leader Yeong-Ok, a young mother with an infant. Her husband is absent, having joined the North Korean People's Army, and he later becomes a war casualty. Not only is Kim Il Sung absent in person, but also is not given a central role in the story. Below, I allocate much space to this story because of its rather different take on war compared to *Mirupeol jeonseol*, discussed in the preceding chapter. In that story, the main protagonist, Ok-Sil, is also a young mother with an infant. Again, her husband is killed at war, just like Yeong-Ok's husband in "Bultaneun bam." Further, both women are work team leaders. In the preceding chapter, Ok-Sil received the benevolent encouragement and love of the Great Leader, even a warm gift of a pair of white shoes. Although her husband had been sacrificed for the sake of national victory at war, the Great Leader loftily rewarded Ok-Sil, her daughter, and her entire village with a modified irrigation plan that now included Miru Plain and therefore rescued the village from centuries of hardship due to a lack of water. We will see, however, that the story of Yeong-Ok differs greatly from that of Ok-Sil, despite their similar settings.

The story is set in a small village in Kangwon Province, which was divided down the middle along the 38th parallel during the Korean War. All of the young men—husbands and sons—are serving in the North Korean People's Army. The women are organized into a work unit and engaged not only in production but also in the war effort, clearing explosives and debris left over from American air raids and securing roads for transportation. Yeong-Ok is the team leader. All of the women, both wives and mothers, including Yeong-Ok, are regularly receiving letters from their loved ones at the battlefront, except for Hye-Ran, who got married a few days before the outbreak of war and has been living with her mother-in-law since her husband's departure for the front. Hye-Ran's mother-in-law, Mrs. Kang, is worried sick about her son and feeling very sorry for Hye-Ran, her new daughter-in-law, who had to send her husband off to war before getting to know him well. Yeong-Ok is painfully aware of this situation, and whenever she writes to her husband, asks him to tell all of his comrades to write to their families back home.

One evening, arriving home after dark, she realizes that her toddler son is still awake. Seeing his mother, he tells her that there is a letter waiting for her, adding, "It must be from Daddy!" Yeong-Ok has a strange feeling, because she only recently received his previous one. She opens the letter and reads: "Our respected Mrs. Hyeon, We are the fellow soldiers of Comrade Kim Hak-Cheol. Comrade Kim was injured in the eyes, yet refused to leave the trenches, and was hit by lethal enemy fire" (Li Jong-Ryeol 1961 [1976], 263).

Yeong-Ok feels the blood in her entire body draining away, and begins to sob sorrowfully. Cheol-Ho, her toddler son, is scared, asking whether his Daddy is mad at Mommy in the letter for some reason. Yeong-Ok is unable to say anything. Saddened and overwhelmed by the shock, Yeong-Ok wanders out of the house, leaving Cheol-Ho alone. She is in extreme despair. Why, she screams in her heart, has she not realized that something like this could happen to her? No one has received a death notice of a loved one in her village, yet she has to be the first one to receive such news. Why should such a thing as this happen to her and her family? She reminisces about the morning of her husband's departure. She wanted to prepare breakfast, but it was still very dark and the moon was shining. He told her, "When we win this war, I'll eat all I want," and left without breakfast. Those were the last words she heard him utter. Her chest aches with pain and she is not able to breathe. But, momentarily, the thought of Cheol-Ho brings her back to reality and she hurries back into the house—a makeshift structure, since her original home, as with many other houses in the village, had been destroyed in the air raids. Cheol-Ho has cried himself to sleep. She realizes that she has not finished reading the rest of the letter, and so picks it up and continues reading: "Mrs. Hyeon, please be strong. Comrade Kim [her husband]'s final words were as follows: 'Please write to my wife. Tell her not to be so sad and even on the home front, fight courageously as befitting the fighters of our Supreme Commander General Kim Il Sung'" (Li Jong-Ryeol 1961 [1976], 266). Having read it, despite her excruciating sorrow, Yeong-Ok decides not to reveal this news to others, and pledges to herself that she will fight more courageously in support of the war effort.

The next day, the villagers face an unusual challenge—after the air raid, they discover timers on two unexploded bombs lying in the fields. It is critical to get rid of them before they destroy the crops. Yeong-Ok approaches them and tries to move them to a wasteland area. Everyone is watching in dread as Yeong-Ok frantically tries to drag them out of the field. She tries to remember her husband's face, and momentarily feels like she can hear his voice: "Why so scared? We are at war!" Eventually, Yeong-Ok successfully removes them, but she is one second too late and the second one explodes near her. She gets violently thrown in the air and lands with a heavy thump. People are screaming for help, while trying to see what they can do to rescue her. Hye-Ran tries to see if Yeong-Ok's heart is beating, and then discovers a letter in Yeong-Ok's breast pocket—the letter informing her that her husband has been killed. At this news, the women surrounding Yeong-Ok are overwhelmed by pain and sorrow for Yeong-Ok. They understand that Yeong-Ok has kept the news from them in order not to diminish their spirits. They transport Yeong-Ok to the nearby town hospital. Upon returning to the village, they find Cheol-Ho, Yeong-Ok's toddler son, who is bewildered at not being able to find his mother. Women are sobbing, but a village elder tells them not to show their sad faces to the child. He turns to Cheol-Ho and tells him that his mother had to be at a meeting in town and that tonight he will treat him to potatoes and beans, a rare delicacy in such a time of hardship. The story ends with an image of the villagers continuing to work on clearing roads for the People's Army while feeling that "enormous strength is filling them and pushing them forward" (Li Jong-Ryeol 1961 [1976], 276).

Throughout this work, the only time that Kim Il Sung is mentioned is in the final words of Yeong-Ok's dying husband. There is no other mention of the Great Leader. In fact, the term "Great Leader," *widaehan suryeongnim,* is not used at all. Nowhere in the novel does the American enemy appear, and even in reference to air raids, burning village houses, and other acts of war, the United States is not mentioned as the party responsible for causing this much pain and destruction. More importantly, Yeong-Ok does not receive the news of her husband's death with dignity or honor, but in sorrow and pain: she breaks down. This is in contrast with Ok-Sil in *Mirupeol jeonseol,* whose husband's death is simply noted, her loss rewarded by the warm love of the Great Leader. Yeong-Ok has no such recourse. She loses her husband and he does not return. She is injured and hospitalized. The scene in which she loses control after receiving the news of her husband's death is one of a woman who has lost a loved one. In fact, she momentarily even forgets the existence of her toddler son, buried in her recollection of the affectionate days she has spent with her husband. Nothing substitutes for this loss, even her son, let alone the Great Leader.

There is no special reward for this courageous woman, no new pair of shoes, no kind visit by the Great Leader to the village, no embrace by His Greatness of the son that the hero has left behind. In fact, there is nothing Yeong-Ok gains by losing her husband in the story; there is no Kim Il Sung to resolve all problems and fill everyone's lives with love and happiness. Instead, the lives of Yeong-Ok and the rest of the villagers continue to be tough. Yeong-Ok has lost her husband, is left with a toddler son in a destroyed village, and faces an unknowable future in a war that shows no sign of ending. Furthermore, she is injured and hospitalized and the reader is not given any concrete sign that she would live. The final sentence captures this uncertainty and insecurity by simply suggesting that some kind of unknown yet powerful force is sustaining them. The ending of this 1961 novel is, in other words, a very abstract ending, when compared with that of the 1983 *Mirupeol jeonseol*, where Kim Il Sung gives love that is warmer than that of the real father of Ok-Sil's fatherless daughter and Miru Plain is filled with the water that will massively enhance its crop yield, thanks to the generosity of the Great Leader and the Workers' Party of Korea. Yeong-Ok and her fellow villagers, by contrast, are still searching for answers to the future amidst the uncertainty and difficulties of war. There are none of the usual references to glorious victory, revolutionary conviction, or other clichés found in post-1970s stories of the Korean War. Instead, the villagers' hard work and the difficulties they are suffering are portrayed in a dark and somber way, far removed from the optimistic pitch found in later novels. Even the extent of Yeong-Ok's injuries is uncertain—other than the fact that her heart is still beating, we are left with no consolation, unsure whether she will eventually recover or whether her son is to end up an orphan.

"Bultaneun bam" is included in an anthology of short stories of the Korean War entitled *Seungrijadeul* (The Victors). Published in 1976, this collection contains novels with war themes written as early as 1952, including "Pyongyangeun noraehanda" by Ko Byeong-Sam (discussed in the previous chapter). Ko Byeong-Sam's story is the only one showing Kim Il Sung as protagonist. Written in 1976, the year of the book's publication, it opens this anthology. It is most likely that the writer was assigned to write a 1970s version of Kim Il Sung

during the Korean War in order to publish the anthology, and
except for Ko's work, the rest of the stories were produced
between 1952 and 1966. Only Ko's work features Kim Il Sung
as the protagonist. Predictably, whereas Ko's "Pyongyangeun
noraehanda" revolves around the bravery and victorious progress of the North Korean People's Army under the wise guidance of Supreme Commander Kim Il Sung, the rest of the stories in this collection are much slower in pace, depicting in
detail the subtlety of human emotions and interactions, none
claiming victory in the Korean War in the exaggerated manner
of "Pyongyangeun noraehanda." We may recognize here an
evolving shift in the way the Korean War is remembered from
the 1960s to the 1970s.

Two more noteworthy stories are included in the above anthology. The first is entitled "Byeoldeuri heureunda" (The Stars
Are Flowing) by Paek Hyeon-U (1966 [1976]). This is a story of
a woman whom a North Korean People's Army (NKPA) unit
happened to include in its retreat operations following the
amphibious landing by U.S. troops at Incheon on the west-
central coast off Seoul. After North Korean troops invaded
South Korea on June 25, 1950, rapidly penetrating the South
and occupying all but the far southeastern corner of the peninsula, American troops staged the Incheon landing in September 1950, forcing the North Koreans to retreat northwards
while fighting difficult battles against the South Koreans and
Americans that were blocking their path. This was the most difficult period for the NKPA in terms of casualties and damage
during the Korean War. North Korean depictions of this period
are usually condensed into the story of a battle waged on
Wolmi Island off the coast of Incheon. These do not, however,
fit easily with the North Korean state's official take on the Korean War. While the state claims to have won the war, stories
of this difficult period of northbound retreat tend to accentuate
the superior force of the enemy in contrast to the strategic errors committed by the NKPA. Thus, while the story of Wolmi
Island hints strongly at the cowardice and callousness of an

단편소설집

승리자들

문예출판사 1976

Fig. 2 Inner cover of *Seungrijadeul* (The Victors). Artist unknown.

enemy that has adopted the deceptive and dishonest strategy (as seen from North Korea) of a surprise landing, the focus is placed on the heroic sacrifice of the NKPA soldiers who held firm, blocking the enemy from landing on the island and gaining time for more of their comrades to make their way to the North. Compared to this account of the Wolmi battle as the archetypal story of retreat with which we are familiar today, "Byeoldeuri heureunda" offers a slightly different take on this period of the war, as represented in the 1960s.

The other story introduced below is by Yun Se-Jung, a veteran novelist whose literary activities predate the liberation. His story, entitled "Kudaewongwa sindaewon" (An Old Soldier and A Young Soldier), is his first important work as an enlightened, reeducated writer under socialism (Yun 1952 [1976]). He later published the much longer *Yonggwangroneun sumswinda* (Yun 1974), which I have discussed more extensively elsewhere (Ryang 2009). As opposed to *Yonggwangro,* for which he was given the honor of being allowed to use an incidence of on-the-spot guidance by Kim Il Sung as the high point of the novel, "Kudaewongwa sindaewon" is a short piece that includes no real personal appearance by Kim Il Sung. Significantly, this novella was written during the war. The state selected certain novelists and commissioned them with writing assignments in order to encourage the North Korean soldiers and uplift their spirits; "Kudaewongwa sindaewon" was produced as part of this effort. But, as I shall argue more extensively below, the novel shows subtle yet significant differences with later literary productions such as Yun's own *Yonggwangro*.

"Byeoldeuri heureunda" opens with twenty people that are taking an arduous trek across the mountains toward the northern side of the 38th parallel, retreating from the south. Not only do they have to cope with sporadic enemy attacks, but they also must secure food as they proceed. On top of this, they have been forced to accept one woman to their group. When they were leaving Seoul, this woman, Song-Ryeon, insisted that she had to go to the North and that they take her along. She looks odd, and no one seems able to guess her age. She is wearing a thick, quilted winter coat that she never takes off, even under the midday sun of an Indian summer. Cheol-Ung, a young soldier, is perplexed by this woman, especially because she seems to be frank only with him. When they have to go through bushes and along difficult trails, she hesitates to accept anyone's support other than his, and it has come to be assumed that Cheol-Ung will take care of her. Cheol-Ung is very annoyed with this, thinking that he joined the army in order to fight the enemy, not to help a woman.

One day, the unit discovers that an older soldier, whom the younger soldiers call Uncle Tal-Su, is missing. After a while, Uncle Tal-Su reemerges and delivers some food that he has fetched from a nearby village. The unit holds a meeting to criticize his behavior, but he is happy to have been able to feed his comrades. In the meantime, the unit skirmishes with the enemy. The captain orders everyone to climb up a rocky hill immediately. Once up on the hill, Cheol-Ung discovers that

Song-Ryeon is missing. She was with them just before, he thinks, so why is she missing now? Then Cheol-Ung remembers that Song-Ryeon was worrying about her small bag being missing when they were climbing the hill. He gathers that she has gone back to retrieve it, and gets angry at her petty obsession with her meager possessions. A little later, Song-Ryeon is found climbing up the hill with her bag. Although angry, Cheol-Ung is worried sick, as enemy bullets are flying around her. When she is close to reaching the hilltop, her bag opens a little and a can falls out. Sadly, she watches it rolling down the hill. Cheol-Ung, however, finds it despicable that this woman has been hiding food in her bag while Uncle Tal-Su has been putting his life on the line in order to feed his brothers in arms. Following this incident, Cheol-Ung has been disheartened by Song-Ryeon, regarding her simply as a burden to the unit.

On one of the unit's many days of hard trekking, Cheol-Ung hears a painful scream. He turns around and sees Song-Ryeon collapse to the ground. She tells Cheol-Ung that she is about to give birth. In bewilderment and shock, Cheol-Ung finds a small nook and begins collecting leaves to make a fire. "Look here, everything will be all right." Cheol-Ung's voice sounds confident. Cheol-Ung is now guessing that Song-Ryeon must have left on her northbound trek with a grave sense of determination in spite of her condition. He asks her why she decided to join the unit. She tells him her story.

Song-Ryeon and her husband helped celebrate the "6.28 Liberation," referring to the liberation of Seoul by the NKPA on June 28, 1950, three days after the outbreak of the Korean War. Immediately afterwards, her husband joined the liberating forces as a volunteer. Working as a school teacher, Song-Ryeon was expecting a baby. One day, out of the blue, she received a visit from a childhood friend. This friend had gone over to the North after 1945, and was studying at Kim Il Sung University. She had come back to Seoul on a political mission. Handing Song-Ryeon a sealed letter, she asked her to open it only after the baby was born. She then left again for the North with the rest of the NKPA soldiers. Song-Ryeon could not resist opening the letter, and when the envelope became wet and began to peel after water had been spilt on it, she opened it. It was a letter written by her husband.

My dear Song-Ryeon, I hope you and the baby are doing well. I'm sorry I could not love you more. I'm sorry I have to leave you alone in this world. But, I want you to know that I fought courageously for you and our baby, for the future of all of us. Without being embraced in the bosom of our Great Leader, we have no life or happiness. [. . .] My precious Song-Ryeon, [. . .] I'm asking you to carry on the journey that I could not finish, that is, to give a free fatherland to our child. I love you, Song-Ryeon. I really want to see our baby's face. Be happy and well. Please raise our child as a fighter who is loyal to General Kim Il Sung. September 13, 1950. Written on Wolmi Island. (Li Jong-Ryeol 1961 [1976], 150–51)

Song-Ryeon then learned that her husband, injured in the battle of Wolmi Island, had been transported to a hospital, where he later died. He had written this letter as his death note, and his comrades had entrusted Song-Ryeon's childhood friend to deliver it to her in person. Having read the letter, and after a period of agonizing, Song-Ryeon decided to leave for the North, following the retreating NKPA soldiers. She was living with her mother, who had been widowed long ago. The idea of leaving her mother alone pained her greatly, but in light of her own pregnancy, she knew she would not be able to take her mother with her. One night, she wrote a short note letting her mother know that she was going to join the NKPA on their return to the North and left while her mother was sleeping.

Upon hearing Song-Ryeon's story, Cheol-Ung is unable to hide his tears. At that point, the captain and Uncle Tal-Su come to find them. The captain is surprised at the sight of the fire they have made and harshly questions Cheol-Ung about it. Cheol-Ung explains Song-Ryeon's condition to him. Uncle Tal-Su is happy, telling everyone that he has been collecting seaweed, a traditional postpartum food in Korea. Cheol-Ung then realizes that Uncle Tal-Su has been aware of Song-Ryeon's pregnancy all along. The captain alters his plans, ordering the unit to do its very best to secure a safe environment in which

Song-Ryeon can give birth. Half of the unit is now assigned to distracting the enemy, while the rest concerns itself with protecting Song-Ryeon. Uncle Tal-Su is taking good care of her when, a little later, a baby's cries are heard, to the elation of all. Song-Ryeon asks Cheol-Ung to fetch her bag. He then realizes that the can of food he saw was baby formula. She was keeping this bag close to herself because it contained the minimum supply of food she would need for her baby. Cheol-Ung is overwhelmed by emotion and admiration for Song-Ryeon. After the delivery, Song-Ryeon insists that the unit leave her at this spot. The unit crossed the 38th parallel a few days earlier and therefore, Song-Ryeon insists, she has fulfilled her husband's last wish by giving birth to her baby in the North. But the captain, Cheol-Ung, Uncle Tal-Su, and the rest of the soldiers refuse to leave her and her newborn at this place. They all depart together, supporting Song-Ryeon and her baby. Cheol-Ung mumbles, "What would the name of the baby be?" The captain suggests: "How about Puk-Seong ["northern star"]? Don't we look up at the North Star every night, longing for the day we are embraced by General Kim Il Sung?" "Fantastic!" Everyone agrees. Song-Ryeon, too, is very happy with this name.

"So, mother of the baby, do you like this name?" the captain asks. "Yes, I like it." Song-Ryeon answers, walking side by side with Cheol-Ung. Her voice is quiet, but filled with the pride of a new mother. "What's the baby's family name?," someone in the front line asks. "It is Kim," answers Song-Ryeon. She mumbles the baby's full name, "Kim Puk-Seong, Kim Puk-Seong." [. . .] Her eyes shine, reflecting the stars of the night sky. "Older sister [as Cheol-Ung is calling her now], how are you doing?," [. . .] as Song-Ryeon trips over a small branch. "I'm all right," answers Song-Ryeon, as she leans her left cheek on Cheol-Ung's right shoulder. Her cheek is warm. Cheol-Ung strengthens his secure grip on his gun. Above their heads, silent stars are flowing past. [. . .] Tonight, the North Star shines unusually brightly. [. . .] The unit, now consisting of 21 people, is steadily marching toward the North. (Li Jong-Ryeol 1961 [1976], 161–62)

There are a number of points in this story that draw our attention when considered in light of the conventions found in North Korean literature after the 1970s and 1980s. Firstly, the term *sarang* (love) is not used primarily in reference to the connection directly formed between the Great Leader and the people. In this case, Song-Ryeon's husband liberally applies this term in relation to his wife. His final note, though short and staccato in expression, reveals the deep personal affection and attachment he feels toward his wife, his regret at having left her behind, and his regret at not being able to fulfill his desire to see their soon-to-be-born baby and raise it with her. References to the Great Leader have him as a supporting factor in relation to the triadic family of husband, wife, and baby. The existence or position of General Kim Il Sung is an important anchoring point for their familial love, but he does not intrude into the family, as in post-1970s novels.

Secondly, the way the soldiers treat Song-Ryeon is complex and ambivalent. Author Li Jong-Ryeol repeatedly uses the term *injeong* (human emotion) as something that the presence of Song-Ryeon invokes among the soldiers. Although it is not a good idea to take a woman with them, this emotional aspect of human relations means that they are unable to leave her behind. In other words, despite her obviously being a great burden to the unit, Song-Ryeon is included in its northward retreat out of a basic concern for her welfare, not as a result of any burning sense of loyalty she may feel toward Kim Il Sung or any determination she may have to dedicate herself to the North Korean revolution. In fact, according to the story, the unit takes her in without inquiring into or verifying her loyalty to Kim Il Sung. The story suggests that she ends up following the soldiers into the North as a product of chance or circumstance. It would be unlikely, perhaps in reality, for a pregnant woman to follow retreating soldiers. But, precisely because of this unlikelihood, it would be more readily expected that a North Korean novel of the 1970s would emphatically depict Song-Ryeon as already possessing a firm sense of loyalty toward Kim Il Sung and a determination to serve North Korea. By contrast, Song-Ryeon (as depicted in 1961) is described as someone who simply wants to go to the North with rather obscure and unclear motives (from the soldiers' point of view). Later, it turns out that she is the widow of a South Korean volunteer soldier who joined the NKPA in its famed battle on Wolmi Island and was sacrificed, but Song-Ryeon herself is consistently portrayed as someone who is not quite politically aware. Only her deep love for her husband motivates her to fulfill her husband's wishes. The soldiers do not try to politically educate her or enhance her revolutionary consciousness. They simply help her give birth to a baby deep in the mountains, this again portrayed as a basic act of humanity and humanly feelings (*injeong*) by the soldiers. There is no big speech by the captain, Cheol-Ung, or Uncle Tal-Su characterizing this act as part of the revolution or the struggle against the American enemy. The story captures the unit's action as something that its soldiers feel they are obligated to do—as humans, not as revolutionaries. In this connection, it is interesting to note that the term *injeong* is seldom used in the currently available North Korean lexicon; instead, the term that depicts humanly bonds in North Korea today would be first and foremost *dongjiae*, revolutionary camaraderie.

Thirdly, the relationship between Cheol-Ung and Song-Ryeon is portrayed, albeit subtly, as a quasi-romance. From the outset, Cheol-Ung, who is younger than Song-Ryeon, is singled out as Song-Ryeon's partner, since she is unable to feel comfortable with other, older men. Cheol-Ung first appears as someone who knows next to nothing about women or girls. He is displeased that she has chosen him, obviously because he is not intimidating and does not pose an extra burden as a member of the opposite sex (Li Jong-Ryeol 1961 [1976], 137). In the course of the unit's retreat, Cheol-Ung ponders about this unknown woman, wondering whether she is married or a virgin, *cheonyeo* in Korean (Li Jong-Ryeol 1961 [1976], 136–37). After assuming that she has selfishly kept a can of food away from the soldiers, he develops a strong dislike for her, his attitude becoming that of someone who has been saddled with an extra burden—it is only because she has been with them this far that he now feels obliged to take care of her: "As is often said, there can be nothing beautiful in a person you hate, and from then on, Cheol-Ung simply regarded Song-Ryeon as a burden [*miunsaram kounde eoptago ihubuteo Cheol-Ungeun saenggak halsurok Song-Ryeoniga jimeurobakke yeogyeojiji anatta*]" (Li Jong-Ryeol 1961 [1976], 142).

But when Song-Ryeon reveals to him that she is about to give birth to a baby whose father is the husband she has lost at war, Cheol-Ung realizes how much he cares about her and her safety. He feels that he has become solely responsible for her well-being and the safe delivery of her baby. At this point, Cheol-Ung calls her *ajumeoni* (madam), the form of address for a married woman. He learns that she is the widow of a revolutionary soldier, and this leads him to view her with increased respect. In the last scene, Song-Ryeon makes physical contact with Cheol-Ung by leaning her cheek against his shoulder, Cheol-Ung responding to this move by tightening his grip on his gun. Symbolically, this can be seen as Song-Ryeon proposing that he protect her and her newborn in place of her deceased husband and Cheol-Ung responding in the affirmative. In this scene, Cheol-Ung addresses her as *nunim*, older sister. Affectionate kinship terms are used, rather than the more formal, non-kinship term *ajumeoni* (madam) that he has used up to that point. Also in this scene, the North Star shines on the couple and their baby, as if to allude to their presumed future together as one family unit or at least threesome that have a very special bond. Again, no mention of Kim Il Sung is made in the last scene—he is only represented metaphorically by the North Star shining in the sky; that is to say, he does not interfere in romantic relationships, unlike in the later novels explored in the previous chapter.

"Kudaewongwa sindaewon," by contrast, is a story about friendship and camaraderie between two male soldiers. The plot itself is rather simple. A small unit receives a group of new enlistees during the Korean War. Su-Cheol, sub-captain of the unit, immediately notices one bright-eyed young man by the name of Seong-Gu. At the welcoming party, Su-Cheol cannot take his eyes off Seong-Gu, enjoying Seong-Gu's shy and youthful smiles. Later, Su-Cheol makes a request to the unit captain that he be entrusted with Seong-Gu's education and training. Thus, the pairing of the two men is officially arranged. Every day, in and out of battle, Su-Cheol tries to show Seong-Gu how to use his weapons, as well as teaching him what kind of mental state a soldier should maintain when faced by the enemy. In one of these scenes, Su-Cheol asks Seong-Gu about his family. Seong-Gu tells him that his father was murdered by enemy forces during the occupation because his father was a card-carrying member of the Workers' Party of Korea. He left his mother and younger siblings back home and joined the army in order to avenge his father's death. Seong-Gu then eggs on Su-Cheol, asking him to talk about his past military prowess. Su-Cheol is a decorated officer with many heroic tales to tell. But he chooses to tell Seong-Gu one story from a time when he was still immature and inexperienced, nearly risking his life but eventually succeeding in singlehandedly capturing a total of fourteen American soldiers. Seong-Gu is very excited to hear this story, and views Su-Cheol with renewed admiration.

During one battle, under intense enemy fire, Su-Cheol notices Seong-Gu outside the trench. Later, after the fighting has subsided, Su-Cheol questions Seong-Gu as to why he was standing outside the trench, giving the enemy a good target. Seong-Gu shyly smiles and replies, "Well, I wanted to see what it's like to be in the middle of firing bullets." Su-Cheol is speechless, since it shows how naïve and unprepared Seong-Gu is. At the same time, however, Seong-Gu is so adorable in the eyes of Su-Cheol in his innocence and youth that the latter cannot find angry words. During this battle, one North Korean soldier was killed. After burying him on a good spot on a hill, Su-Cheol turns to Seong-Gu and asks, "You saw that, right?"

"Saw what?" Seong-Gu could not quite understand the intention of Su-Cheol's question. "That comrade whom we just buried . . . he was fine and well this morning." Seong-Gu looked at Su-Cheol in silence. "Comrade Seong-Gu, you told me earlier that you wanted to see what it was like to be in a battle. But war is not fun. What if you were to be shot? [. . .] I was worried sick about you." [Seong-Gu apologized, but Su-Cheol continued his criticism.] "I don't understand how you could think about war in that manner. Are you not afraid of anything?" [. . .] "Have you never thought about life? The lives of our youth?" "I, I have actually thought about it," replied Seong-Gu rather determinedly. Su-Cheol was interested to know more about this and said, "Alright. Tell me about it." "Only a life that is lived in dedication to our Great Leader is a most honorable and beautiful life.[. . .]" Su-Cheol was glad and followed up Seong-Gu's words by saying, "And a death achieved in dedication for our Great Leader. That death is fundamentally different from any other human death. A death that kills even one more of our enemy." [. . .] "I want to tell you one thing, sub-captain." "What is that?" "Earlier, I was not playing." [. . .] Seong-Gu's voice trembled a little. "Let me hear this," Su-Cheol responded, lighting his cigarette. "I'd like to tell you everything. At the time of our retreat [after the American landing at Incheon in September 1950], we suffered severe air raids and since then, I was not able to overcome my phobia about bullets and bombs. I struggled with my cowardice and, with great determination, enlisted. I made up my mind about two things upon enlisting: that, in exchange for my life, I would safeguard our revolutionary achievement as brought about by the Great Leader, and that I would avenge my father's death. [. . .] I've listened to your words very carefully, but I still wanted to [. . .] try [and see] whether I could really withstand the sound of bullets and bombs in the battlefield, because I had been so scared. That was why I dared to stand outside the trench in such a way earlier in the battle." Su-Cheol stood up, "Is that true?" "Yes. I'd like to be as brave as you and I also want to [achieve] revenge for my father and others that have been killed by the enemy. I really do." "Thank you, Seong-Gu, for telling me this. I have just heard a great story. You really are my comrade." Su-Cheol hugged Seong-Gu's shoulders tightly. "Comrade Seong-Gu, let's fight together. I, too, lost my family, in fact my entire family, [killed when] U.S. soldiers occupied my native village. I would never ever again let my home village be occupied by the enemy, even if I were to die one thousand times." (Yun 1952 [1976], 93–97)

After this confession, which reinforces the bond between the two men, Su-Cheol and Seong-Gu are selected for sentry duty. While they are monitoring an enemy unit, gunfire breaks out, and Su-Cheol sends Seong-Gu back to the unit. When Seong-

Gu comes back, Su-Cheol is not to be found in his original spot. After a little while, Seong-Gu discovers Su-Cheol lying on the ground. Shocked, Seong-Gu quickly presses the side of his face to Su-Cheol's chest and identifies that he is alive. Seong-Gu successfully evacuates Su-Cheol from the battlefield. After the gunfire has subsided, it is declared that Se-Cheol is badly wounded and is to be transported to hospital. On his stretcher, Su-Cheol says, "I can go since, instead of myself, my comrade Seong-Gu is here." Seong-Gu plays these words over and over in his mind (Yun 1952 [1976], 103–8).

Although written by the same author, Yun Se-Jung, the 1974 work *Yonggwangroneun sumswinda* (discussed in the previous chapter) differs significantly from "Kudaeweongwa sindae-weon" in its treatment of human relationships. The camaraderie between Su-Cheol and Seong-Gu is portrayed as the result of a very close male bond, which is not so much a machismo-oriented relationship as one based on top-down caring and bottom-up respect. In their capacity of young learner and old mentor, both admire each other's respective qualities. In the beginning, Seong-Gu's charm is of a physical kind—Su-Cheol is irresistibly attracted to the latter's innocent smile, young physique, and youthful demeanor. By contrast, Seong-Gu's admiration for Su-Cheol does not depend on the latter's physical appearance—in fact the novella has almost nothing to say about Su-Cheol's build or facial characteristics—instead it is based on Su-Cheol's courage and bravery at having captured fourteen enemy soldiers singlehandedly. Furthermore, as we would note from the excerpt above, both men have aspects of fear and vulnerability, albeit in different forms. Su-Cheol, despite his prowess and proven courage, still reminds Seong-Gu about the vulnerability of human beings, when burying their deceased comrade. Seong-Gu, on the other hand, is keenly aware how much he is scared of war, and, by extension, death. While the story sketches the development of Seong-Gu, showing how brave he has become, it is nevertheless atypical or contrasting with the Korean War novels in the post-1970s period, in that the fragility of NKPA soldiers is depicted; in the post-

1970s novels, a NKPA soldier is typically not afraid of anything, including death in this world.

The relationship cultivated between Su-Cheol and Seong-
Gu evokes C. S. Lewis's notion of friendship, which places it
higher than romantic love and affection, though below *agape*,
God's love or love that is as good as God. In friendship,
friends are able to accept each other for who they are (Lewis
1960). They are not petty or narrowly demanding the other's
attention, because the basis of their bond is often placed in a
common goal or interest and is open to the outside world. As
such, the circle of friends can expand exponentially. This is
precisely why the strong friendship between Seong-Gu and
Su-Cheol is not a hindrance to the battle actions of the unit
since the soldiers share a common goal.

While this homoerotic connection ultimately rests on loyalty
toward the Great Leader, there is room for other emotions and
orientations as well, including a desire on the part of both
characters to achieve revenge for the families they had lost
during the American occupation of North Korea. Seong-Gu's
fear of battle, his honest admission to having such fears, and his
youthful straightforwardness and beautiful physical appearance captivate Su-Cheol, who, we learn later, is alone, having
lost his entire family. In the course of the story, Su-Cheol's deep
affection for Seong-Gu grows into trust. When he is injured
and transported to hospital, he is no longer over-protective of
Seong-Gu, instead fully trusting Seong-Gu's courage and feeling confident that Seong-Gu will fight in his place. By way of
contrast, as I have written extensively elsewhere (Ryang 2009),
in *Yonggwangro*, even a married couple is connected via each
other's love for the Great Leader, and there is no room for desires other than those related to dedication to the Great Leader.
This is quite different in the case of the male friendship between
Su-Cheol and Seong-Gu, whose mutual support and caring
Yun depicts in detail in this short story. In so doing, Yun is not
constrained by a need to construct these affectionate feelings
between the two men on the basis of their dedication and
loyalty toward the Great Leader. Indeed, the Great Leader is

only mentioned twice in an indirect manner, throughout the entire 26 pages of the story. Considering that this work was written in 1952 at the height of the Korean War, it is interesting that it contains far fewer references, and more pedestrian ones at that, of Kim Il Sung than later examples of North Korean literature, where he appears in a much more centralized and standardized manner.

We can summarize our findings from war stories written prior to the 1970s, including "Bultaneun bam," "Byeoldeuri heureunda," and "Kudaewongwa sindaewon" as follows. First, what I have called "love's perpetual triangle" in the previous chapter, love between two individuals achieved through each other's loyalty to Kim Il Sung, does not appear as such in these early war stories. Yeong-Ok's sorrow at losing her husband, Song-Ryeon's love for her husband and her husband's final love letter, and the two soldiers' strong friendship — in none of these cases do we find this triangular form of love with Kim Il Sung at its apex. Rather, in these early works, individuals find worth in each other, in loving and caring about others and being cared for by others. This contrasts with later, post-1970s novels, where love between individuals is first and foremost predicated upon the supervisory gaze of the Great Leader and the loyalty they show to him in return. In these works, individuals find worth in each other because of their love for the leader, not for each other. Secondly, and in close connection with the first point, Kim Il Sung's deep penetration into the personal lives of individuals is not quite as prominent in the early stories, even in a state of emergency where the survival of the nation is at stake, such as war.

In terms of thematic motifs, the early wartime stories present an unexpectedly interesting and broad spectrum of possibilities, precisely because they encompass terrain unknown to the younger, postwar generations of North Koreans. The period commencing in September 1950 is not well known or talked about in North Korea today. This was when the NKPA retreated, American forces occupied the North, and the fight began to recapture lost territory, with the dividing line being pushed back to the middle of the peninsula with the help of Chinese volunteers. During the war, there was contact between Northerners and Southerners, and between soldiers and civilians. These were fellow countrymen and women, having only been cut off from each other in an artificial and abrupt fashion for the five-year period commencing in 1945—in many ways, Northerners and Southerners therefore together constituted one common Korean people. Encounters between Northerners and Southerners, and between soldiers and civilians, created new romances and alliances. Song-Ryeon's arduous trek with an NKPA unit is a depiction of such an event. People also found new friends and companions during the war while serving in the army, as seen in the story of Seong-Gu and Su-Cheol. Beyond the North-South divide, people met, fell in love, and became friends amidst the tensions and chaos of war. These kinds of human flow became much rarer for later generations of North Koreans, even within the confines of its national borders, as party control over domestic travel, school placement, and office assignment steadily increased, creating the unitary, immobile society we know today. In a paradoxical way, the Korean peninsula during the Korean War may be understood as a time-space of adventure and excitement as well.

In connection to this, then, we have an interesting time gap. In North Korea today, the state claims that it is engaged in an ongoing war with the United States (as argued at the beginning of this chapter). During the Korean War, however, such a consciousness had not yet formed, being a product of the postwar decades, when Kim Il Sung became elevated to a position of absolute authority. This did not happen in a day. In other words, it became the mission of the 1970s and 1980s discourses to turn Kim into a uniquely immortal figure. Ironically, however, this endeavor saw the setting of the Korean War itself become an exception, due to the penetration of the North by the South and vice versa, involving the mixing of soldiers and civilians on one hand, and Northerners, Southerners, and Americans on the other. During this chaotic period, the immortal image of Kim Il Sung as sacred leader cannot be located. Thus, when Kim Il Sung appears in wartime stories, it is usually in a secluded setting shielded from direct contact with enemy elements: in *Mirupeol jeonseol*, he is seen among North Korean farmers in a farming community deep in the mountains, away from alien elements, while in "Pyong-yangeun noraehanda" he is placed at a headquarters in an unknown location, surrounded by his confidants and guards. The chaos of war, direct contact with the enemy, and the blood, sweat, and filth of battle are not for Kim Il Sung: he is not to come into contact with such things.

The sanitization of Kim Il Sung, or more precisely, the sanitization of Kim's existence is closely connected to the way in which North Korea came to perceive itself as a warring nation with a keen need to preserve the absolute nature of its leader — as I shall argue in the final segment of this chapter. Here, I will restrict myself to registering that it was not during the Korean War that the state of emergency as we know it today emerged in North Korea, but after the ceasefire, when the idea of an ongoing war had become consolidated. As far as the Korean War itself as literary motif is concerned, the frequency of direct contacts with the enemy makes it a uniquely chaotic and therefore lively setting for North Korean stories, with themes that differ significantly from those set during the postwar years. This can be seen more clearly in the epic series of stories and films known as *Ireumeomneun yeongungdeul* (Unsung Heroes). In these works, enemy forces (both American and South Korean) are fully embodied as concrete characters. This practice both humanizes and exoticizes the enemy, providing North Koreans with a great source of entertainment. Such depictions contrast fundamentally with the abstract conceptual and discursive forms used in North Korean discourse today to represent its enemy, the United States.

Unsung Heroes (I)

Produced and released in the years 1978 through 1981, the twenty-part series of films collectively entitled *Ireumeomneun yeongungdeul* captured the imagination of the North Korean people unlike any other. Until that time, no other film had attracted so many viewers in North Korea—and repeat viewers at that. Whenever a new episode was released, movie theatres were packed and lines for the next showing would start forming halfway through the previous one. Here and there, not only in Pyongyang but also in suburban towns, wherever one could find a movie theatre, one would encounter moviegoers filled with a feverish passion for this series.

The series is also well-known today in U.S. military intelligence circles due to the inclusion in its cast of former deserters Charles Robert Jenkins and James Joseph Dresnok. The former left North Korea to be reunited with his wife, a Japanese woman who had been kidnapped by North Korean agents during the bout of abductions in the late 1970s and early 1980s, and their children, and now lives in Japan. The latter still lives in North Korea with his family, his life being made into a documentary movie entitled *Crossing the Line,* where he calls Kim Il Sung the Great Leader (see *Crossing the Line,* a documentary made about his life; Gordon 2007). Appearing in *Ireumeomneun yeongungdeul* as American characters, they became popular figures on the streets of Pyongyang. The movie production remains loyal to the original script, using the same title as the screenplay by Li Jin-U (1981). Publication of the two-volume film script postdates the production of the films by three years, since a new episode of the movie was made as the author produced a new segment of the story. (Although written as a film script, Li's work will henceforth be referenced as a novel for the sake of simplicity.)

Set in the period between October 1952 and July 1953, that is, during the nine months leading up to the Korean War ceasefire, the *Ireumeomneun yeongungdeul* series undoubtedly ranks among the most cosmopolitan and international of North Korean novels or films produced to this day. No other novel or film matches it in terms of the diversity of its protagonists, politically, ethnically, and in terms of their characteristics and no other novel compares to this one in terms of its breadth of references to Western culture, from jazz to classical music, from "God Save the Queen" to "La Paloma," and from Lord Byron to Heinrich Heine, embellished as it is with faux leather jackets, tight mini-skirts, Burberry coats, Harris tweed, and Grace Kelly handbags. The multiple national borders crossed by its protagonists, the use of non-Korean actors, and the variety of human connections, emotions, and intrigue on display is exceptional when compared with North Korean novels produced in earlier times or later.

The story opens on October 8, 1952 in Panmunjeom, the site of ceasefire negotiations. Action soon shifts to the streets of Paris. Here, Yu Rim, the hero of the story and a native of Pyongyang in his early 30s, who is a North Korean secret agent with British nationality with the codename "Tumangang" or Tuman River, receives an order to make contact with another agent, Rim Hong-Sik, in Seoul. Hong-Sik is a widower whose only son is studying at a boarding school in Pyongyang specially set up for the children of North Korean agents. Headquarters tells him, "We will meet again in Pyongyang after the war victory." Yu Rim's footprints are depicted on a map of the world: Paris, Istanbul, New Delhi, Hong Kong, Tokyo, and then, to Seoul, his destination. Yu Rim is a Cambridge graduate. Under Japanese colonial rule, he was conscripted while at college in Seoul and sent to the South Pacific with the Imperial Japanese Army, but on his way back, deserted in Hong Kong and saved the life of a British POW. This happened to be the son of a prominent British educator, who later became a Member of Parliament. Considering that Yu Rim had saved his son's life, he thereafter became Yu Rim's benefactor, financially supporting his education while he studied at Cambridge. Yu Rim is now a well-known journalist for the United Nations, stationed in Paris.

In Seoul, Yu Rim meets a Cambridge college-mate by the name of Pak Mu who is a press officer for the South Korean Army. They are having drinks celebrating their reunion. Their exchange is somewhat awkward, however, since their relationship has never been free of tension since their Cambridge days, due mainly to differences in personality. Pak Mu is also

curious about Yu Rim's return to Korea in the middle of the
Korean War, and develops a suspicion that he is a "red spy."
In the bar, Yu Rim recognizes Janet, the wife of Dr. Kelton,
mastermind of the U.S. military's Korean War operations and
Yu Rim's archenemy. Yu Rim is also aware that Janet is a niece
of the British benefactor who took him under his wings and
provided him with the scholarship to Cambridge. Soon, a military vehicle belonging to Colonel Klaus, an American officer,
parks outside. A group of United States Counter Intelligence
Corps (hereafter, CIC) officers emerges from the car. Yu Rim
is taken by surprise at the sight of one of them, a beautiful
Korean woman in an American uniform. It is Sun-Hui, the
daughter of Yu Rim's old professor. Yu Rim tries to calm himself down, hiding his surprise, quietly asking Pak Mu what
her role is. "That's Miss Sun-Hui. She is the assistant officer to
Colonel Klaus. An amazing woman. She was decorated [by
the U.S. Army] recently" (Li Jin-U 1981a, 19). Pak Mu requests
a dance with Sun-Hui.

Watching them dance, Yu Rim reminisces. Sun-Hui's father
was Yu Rim's professor when he attended university in Seoul
while it was under Japanese colonial rule. The professor loved
Yu Rim for his knowledge and intelligence. As Yu Rim was
very poor, the professor often invited him over to his house
for meals. While frequenting the professor's house, he got to
know Sun-Hui and they fell in love. When Yu-Rim was conscripted by the Japanese and sent to the Pacific Front, they
parted in tears, promising to meet again. It was 1942. Ten
years later, Yu Rim has shockingly discovered that Sun-Hui,
now in her late twenties and radiantly beautiful, has become
a CIC lieutenant at the frontline of U.S. counterintelligence
activities.

Immediately and instinctively, Klaus also develops suspi-
cions about Yu Rim and becomes alerted after learning that
Janet has invited Yu Rim to her house a few days later. As
Janet is waiting for Yu Rim's visit, Colonel Klaus invites him-
self over to Janet's house. Before Yu Rim appears, Klaus warns
Janet not to reveal details of Dr. Kelton's whereabouts or

schedule. Yu Rim arrives and, politely ignoring Klaus, he begins a conversation with Janet, making references to Janet's uncle and Yu Rim's benefactor, now a Member of Parliament. Yu Rim comments that when he speaks in Parliament, even Prime Minister Churchill has to listen to him very carefully. Janet is happy to hear the news from London. When Janet happens to mention where her husband Dr. Kelton has gone, Klaus rudely interferes, calling "Madam!" Yu Rim clearly registers the potential danger that Klaus poses to his operation. Indeed, throughout the entire twenty chapters of the story, Klaus and Yu Rim are in constant conflict.

In the meantime, Pak Mu is conspiring with other young officers to take advantage of the chaos of war to overthrow South Korean president, Syngman Rhee, as they are frustrated at his old-fashioned style of government and that of senior military leaders trained under the Japanese during the colonial period. Pak Mu is the son of a large landowner in southwestern Korea, this implying that he comes from a lineage of national traitors who profited from the colonization of Korea by collaborating with the Japanese. Throughout the movie and the story, Pak Mu and Klaus are both depicted as personifications of the worst possible form of evil. However, unlike Klaus, who is American and by extension seen as naturally evil, Pak Mu is Korean. As such, as the story unfolds, his crimes are seen as being even more unforgivable. When I watched this series in Pyongyang in 1980, North Korean viewers booed whenever Pak Mo appeared on the screen.

Yu Rim and Sun-Hui meet one-on-one for the first time in Sun-Hui's office: Yu Rim needs her clearance to make a reporting trip to Keumhwa, where a battle has broke out between the NKPA and the United Nations forces. Since it is part of Sun-Hui's duties to examine any new arrivals, Sun-Hui invites Yu Rim to her office, but Sun-Hui obviously wants to talk to him and find out what has happened since they parted ten years earlier. They greet each other warmly. Yu Rim quietly tells her: "Well, I'm not sure how to start this, but I've always been satisfied with life, except for one thought that has both-

ered me all of this time." He tells her that it is the thought of
Sun-Hui, and continues: "Remember, when we were young,
you told me once that even if ten years or twenty years were
to pass, we must not change." Sun-Hui smiles coldly and answers: "I don't remember. Too many years have passed," and
follows up by stating: "Our love is gone forever, like a wave
in the ocean—it came and it went. I hope you will understand.
I hear you have family in Istanbul?" "That is right," answers
Yu Rim.

Yu Rim and Pak Mu are later riding in a jeep toward Keumhwa. Quickly alternating scenes capture how Sun-Hui established herself as a trustworthy military officer for the U.S.
Army during the Korean War. One scene shows that she is
an outstanding shooter, proficient in the use of all kinds of
weapon, including rifles, handguns, and submachine guns. Pak
Mu can testify to this, since they were classmates at a training
camp for a special unit of the South Korean Army. Once they
have arrived at Keumhwa, Yu Rim is introduced to Pak's superior, Sin Jae-Seon. Sin is the leader of the group, which includes Pak Mu and other young officers, that is secretly plot-
ting to undermine the current government and older military
factions of South Korea. After asking some roundabout questions, Sin asks Yu Rim directly: "Now, let's be frank. [. . .] What
do you think about this war?" Yu Rim, displaying a gentlemanly English type of detachment, answers that he does not
have any conflict of interest, but that, objectively speaking,
Syngman Rhee is incompetent. This pleases Sin. After the meeting, Sin is convinced that Yu Rim will be a useful person in
the context of his subversion and encourages Pak Mu to approach Yu Rim.

Right after this, Yu Rim finally makes contact with Rim
Hong-Sik, a North Korean agent who has successfully penetrated the South Korean system in the guise of a printing factory owner. They find each other by using a pre-arranged secret code printed in a daily newspaper. It turns out that Yu
Rim and Rim Hong-Sik were both conscripted into the Imperial Japanese army and sent to the South Pacific together. They

meet at a secret spot, and warmly embrace each other. Hong-Sik opens a picnic hamper full of traditional Korean delicacies prepared by a woman he says he somehow knows, alluding to the fact that this woman is a special person to him. (This woman is Ms. Suk-Yeong, who will play an important role in the story.) The two men are ecstatic to be reunited.

But, soon, Hong-Sik's cover is revealed by none other than Sun-Hui. In a chase through the streets of Seoul, Hong-Sik is surrounded by military police. Yu Rim happens to pass the scene and shudders. He recognizes a woman, the owner of Café Madonna whom he met briefly when he and Hong-Sik were exchanging information there. This is Suk-Yeong, the widow of a prominent military man, who is now singlehandedly raising her daughter Yun-Mi and is Hong-Sik's lover. (At this point, Yu Rim does not know this.) As Yu Rim and Suk-Yeong look on in anguish, Sun-Hui's sharp voice rings out: "Don't kill [him]. Capture him alive!" But a military policeman shoots Hong-Sik, killing him on the spot. Yu Rim and Suk-Yeong both tremble with rage at Sun-Hui, and are overwhelmed with shock at having lost Hong-Sik. Later, when Yu Rim comes to pay a visit to Hong-Sik's grave, he recognizes Suk-Yeong from a distance and realizes that the Café Madonna owner is the one that Hong-Sik alluded to as being someone special.

Yu Rim faces difficulties after the death of Hong-Sik, as he is now alone in enemy territory without a wireless dispatcher. He travels to Hong Kong to receive his directives. According to Headquarters, arrangements have been made for him to make contact with a North Korean agent known by the codename "Paekma" or White Horse. Colonel Klaus's men have already executed the real White Horse, however, and installed an imposter. North Korean Headquarters is not aware of this. Yu Rim has been given the information that White Horse is left-handed. When Yu Rim cautiously approaches the meeting spot from a distance, a man stands up, throwing a cigarette lighter high up in the air and catching it with his left hand. Yu Rim immediately becomes suspicious, since his experience tells him that no real agent would show off a hidden characteristic in such a manner. He abandons making contact and returns to his hotel without meeting White Horse.

Klaus is all worked up, because he was certain that this rendezvous with the fake White Horse would have provided a decisive lead in shutting down the North Korean espionage network, which his headquarters had long suspected of working very effectively south of the 38th parallel. He gives the fake White Horse a sharp dressing-down, the latter leaving his office on foot. Yu Rim's car passes him. Right after this, another car runs down White Horse. Yu Rim, shocked, makes a U-turn and recognizes that the victim is White Horse. At this point, he is not completely convinced that this White Horse is an imposter. Consequently he feels disturbed, as this may well mean that there are other forces that know something about White Horse, forces that have just done away with him.

The very next day, Sun-Hui appears on Yu Rim's doorstep, requesting his company on a visit to CIC headquarters. Yu Rim is ushered into an interview room, where he finds Lieutenant Martin standing. Martin is content and confident, since he has obtained information about irregularities in Yu Rim's bank account and is ready to question him.

"Mr. Yu Rim, where were you last night?" Martin begins. "You are very interested in my personal life, are you not?" "No, not really. But I still need to know." "I was at a night club. Until 9:00 PM, I was with a female friend. Ah, I suppose you would need her address too?" "Of course." [. . .]"I'm afraid I'm unable to give you that in order to defend that lady's honor." Martin gets irritated, "You mean Mrs. Kelton, right?" "It could be her." [. . .] Martin says, "You're very popular with women, and very rich too. You have bank accounts in London and Switzerland." [. . .] "How much do you have [in these accounts]?" "I have 12,600 pounds in a London bank and 28,000 francs in Switzerland." "You are amazing. I have requested your bank statements and that is exactly what I have here. These are not small amounts for personal accounts." "If you wish, I could lend you some. . ." Martin tries to hide his anger and continues, "Ah, you're funny. Your wife is in Istanbul?" "Yes." "Do you love her?" "Of course I do." "She's also rich?" "No she is not." "Then, it's strange. According to my source, you are not sending a penny to her. [This "wife" of Yu Rim in Istanbul is a cover.] "Mr. Yu Rim, I'm waiting for your answer!" "She did not want any." "Why?" "Why don't you ask her?" "According to the Istanbul police, there is no such woman living at the address you gave us." "She has left for a place where no police can reach her." [. . .] "Where?" "She has passed on and is buried in a cemetery in an Istanbul suburb." Martin completely loses his self-control and strikes the desk, screaming at Yu Rim: "Get rid of that English smugness!" Yu Rim stands up and firmly states, "You are insulting Her Majesty's citizen. How would you like it if an international newspaper carried an article on a CIC officer in Seoul excessively interested in the wife of a British journalist?" (Li Jin-U 1981a, 162–65)

The story is now showing a complex interpenetration of North Korean, South Korean (subdivided into old and young factions), and American elements, in addition to the minor role played by a British officer–turned–MI5 agent, who is secretly helping Yu Rim. The crux of the story involves Yu Rim finding out in advance what the Americans are planning behind the diplomacy of the ceasefire, how the South Korean military is moving around in relation to it, burdened by its own internecine animosities, and, to a lesser degree, the role played by the British government. In this complex environment, Yu Rim is in desperate need of another local agent.

This is the third Wednesday that Yu Rim is supposed to receive his directives via a broadcast from Pyongyang. As he listens to the answers for a high school math test, a series of numbers is read out: 28, 32, 76, 123, 17, 89, 104, 38, 19, 25. . . . These numbers are decoded into a directive from Headquarters which reads: "To Tuman River. At Café Madonna. Number 5 table. Seek Diamond. Wear a diamond ring. Code 15, 17. Diamond is a brilliant agent, recently decorated with the North Korean title of Hero."

The next day, Yu Rim goes to Café Madonna. Suk-Yeong greets him and he asks for the Number 5 table. Suk-Yeong points him to it. There is a woman sitting there, but Yu Rim cannot see her face, as it is hidden behind the newspaper she is reading. Yu Rim requests Beethoven's symphony number 5. Yu Rim approaches the table against the backdrop of this grand orchestral piece. He recognizes that the woman is wearing a

diamond ring. Yu Rim speaks to her, "Hello." She raises her
face—it is Sun-Hui! Sun-Hui, initially assuming that Yu Rim
has happened upon her accidentally, shows a slight awkwardness and returns his hello. Yu Rim sits down. "I have nothing
to do today, it seems," Yu Rim says. "Well, I'm . . ." Sun-Hui
muddles her words. Yu Rim places his hand on the table. Sun-
Hui recognizes the diamond ring. Yu Rim also looks at Sun-
Hui's hand on the table, with its diamond ring. The eyes of the
two meet, overwhelmed with emotion. Yu Rim quietly asks, "Is
this today's paper?" "No, today's papers are all gone. This is
[from] the seventeenth. How about that one over there, is that
today's?" "No, it is [from] the fifteenth." Thus both recognize
that each other knows the code correctly. They look at each
other, trying not to reveal their elation and excitement. After a
little while, Sun-Hui stands up and leaves in silence. Later, back
in her apartment, Sun-Hui cries hard in her room, unable to
overcome her joy, her surprise, and all of the other emotions
that she has just experienced. "These two people, despite their
separation for ten years, have been together in their devotion to
the beloved fatherland. Today, they are reunited on their road
to revolution" (Li Jin-U 1981a, 217). Yu Rim comes to understand that White Horse was an enemy agent and that it was
Sun-Hui who executed him that night.

Yu Rim successfully communicates to Suk-Yeong that he
is a North Korean agent, as was the now departed Hong-Sik,
and that Hong-Sik had told him about her. Suk-Yeong, a beautiful and noble-natured woman with remarkable integrity, is
inducted into the North Korean espionage network due to her
loyalty to the deceased Hong-Sik. Yu Rim plays a voice
recording by Hong-Sik's son, who is living and studying in
Pyongyang. The boy's voice calls her Yun-Mi's mother and
asks her to avenge the death of his father, Hong-Sik. At this
point, it is important to remember that Suk-Yeong has not
been informed of the truth about Sun-Hui. Therefore, she still
believes that Sun-Hui is the one responsible for Hong-Sik's
death (despite the fact that Sun-Hui, in order to save Hong-
Sik, ordered that he be captured alive). The CIC obtains infor-

mation that Suk-Yeong was closely involved with the shot North Korean agent, Hong-Sik, and summons her for an interview. Here, she confronts Sun-Hui who, in order to maintain her cover, deals with her in a ruthless fashion, but never uses force. When she is summoned for a second interview, she is beaten badly by Martin. After she is released, she sits with her daughter Yun-Mi on a bench in a park. On the other side of the square, a young woman is sitting on a bench. Yun-Mi innocently approaches her. The woman is very gentle and loving toward Yun-Mi and gives her a bar of chocolate. Yun-Mi returns to her mother and Suk-Yeong, in order to thank her, looks over at the woman, recognizing that it is Sun-Hui. Changing her tone of voice, Suk-Yeong sternly tells Yun-Mi to return the chocolate to Sun-Hui, telling her that that she is an evil woman. Yun-Mi returns to Sun-Hui and throws the bar at her. Mother and daughter leave, while Sun-Hui tries to hide her tears. One day, Suk-Yeong is approached by an unknown gentleman who pretends to have known Hong-Sik. Elated, she commits an error by not exchanging the agreed code: the gentleman is a CIC cover. Lewis, a British agent who is helping Yu Rim and Sun-Hui, happens to be there and immediately reports this to Sun-Hui. Sun-Hui arrives at lightning speed and arrests the gentleman under the pretext that his papers are not in order: Sun-Hui thus rescues Suk-Yeong, while Suk-Yeong has no idea, mistakenly believing that Sun-Hui is again trying to capture good people. Outraged, Suk-Yeong slaps Sun-Hui's face. Sun-Hui leaves the scene quietly, yet without losing the superficial arrogance of a CIC officer.

Inside the military, preparations are being made for Operation Jeonghyeong: the American and South Korean armies are giving out an unusually high number of permits to foreign journalists to accompany them for the attack on Jeonghyeong Hill where, according to their intelligence, only one small unit of the NKPA is stationed. The U.S. Army and their South Korean allies calculate that they will be able to engineer a major defeat of NKPA forces. Yu Rim, however, has already found out this information through Pak Mu, and an additional 120 cannons have been added to the NKPA arsenal. The Americans and South Koreans thus end up suffering grave losses and ultimate defeat at Jeonghyeong, all in full view of foreign journalists. Pak Mu's suspicions about Yu Rim become unshakeable. As far as he can recall, Yu Rim is the only non-military person to whom he mentioned this information in advance. When confronted by Pak Mu, Yu Rim convincingly argues that he is not to be suspected. Pak Mu superficially accepts this explanation. But, as the narration continues: "Their smiles were false. It is now clear to Pak Mu that Yu Rim is his enemy. Yu Rim also now knows that Pak Mu distrusts him. He feels instinctively that it will be necessary to eliminate him" (Li Jin-U 1981a, 243). Shortly after this meeting, Pak Mu shoots Yu Rim while in disguise, endangering his life. He needs an operation that will require 5 million yen. Pak Mu is hoping that no one will be able to pay such an amount. At this point, Sin Jae-Seon, the leading conspirator among the young officers, orders Pak Mu to allocate the money from his fund as Sin has become fond of Yu Rim. This makes things worse for Pak Mu. In the end, the surgery is arranged, but Yu Rim will need some time to recover.

In the meantime, Sun-Hui tries to direct the CIC's attention to Pak Mu as someone who has leaked top-secret information. Klaus is not so easily influenced, however, and Martin, Sun-Hui's equal, is filled with a sense of rivalry toward her. Moreover, Martin has a long-term ambition to get rid of Klaus and become a colonel himself. Sun-Hui is also successful in tipping off one of the top officers in the old faction of the army, Kim Chang-Ryong. Kim, who used to be Sun-Hui's superior in the South Korean army, is more easily influenced by her than is Klaus. Eventually, Pak Mu is captured by Kim's men on suspicion of betraying the military. Pak Mu is dragged to an execution site. Then, a jeep pulls up and Martin jumps out. "Release this man," says Martin to Kim's men. "This is Colonel Klaus's order." This takes Pak Mu himself by surprise. Martin continues: "You are under arrest by the CIC. Let's go." The jeep disappears into the smoke.

This is the end of the first volume. By now, the reader has become absorbed by the story's quick-paced, well thought-out, and sophisticated turns, and has also become concerned for the safety of Yu Rim and Sun-Hui, knowing that Pak Mu has not actually been eliminated. The fact that the CIC has now seized Pak Mu is a curiosity, making the reader instantly worried about Sun-Hui's well-being, given that she has penetrated the CIC so deeply. Here, we find the only mention of the Supreme Commander in the entire volume, in the form of a newspaper quotation, although Kim Il Sung's name itself does not appear:

The "Workers' Newspaper" [North Korean paper] is carrying a communiqué by the government of the Democratic People's Republic of Korea. [. . .] The U.S. Pacific Fleet has been mobilized. The soldiers of the NKPA are strengthening their coastal defenses.

As soon as the U.S. imperialists realized that its allies would not support land attacks, they [. . .] schemed surprise attacks on both the eastern and western coastlines of Korea. Our Respected and Beloved Leader and Supreme Commander already knew this in advance, ordering the NKPA to strengthen coastal defenses and sending all party units and members a secret letter from the Party Central Committee mobilizing our people and soldiers for a deadly battle [in response to] new attacks by the enemy. (Li Jin-U 1981a, 419)

Unsung Heroes (II)

Volume 2 starts with Yu Rim facing a crisis: he is arrested by the CIC, or more precisely, by Colonel Klaus. Wracked by worry about his arrest and the failed execution of Pak Mu after his last-minute rescue by the CIC, Sun-Hui is in an extremely tormented state. The CIC suspects Yu Rim knows something about the murder of White Horse. Yu Rim is told that they have detected the tire marks of two vehicles: one set matches those of his vehicle and the other is unknown. Yu Rim is disturbed, aware that the other set of marks should surely match those of Sun-Hui's vehicle, although he is not certain whether they also know this. In the meantime, Suk-Yeong is also arrested. She is not only detained, but subjected to severe torture

by Martin. Sun-Hui arrives at CIC headquarters. In front of
Klaus, Sun-Hui and Martin argue, with Sun-Hui denouncing
Martin for having consistently undermined her as a result of
his jealousy. Sun-Hui reveals that Martin has commented in
the past that he would like to eventually eliminate Klaus and
take his place. Martin declares her a liar, while Sun-Hui shrugs
off his threat, saying that she has his words recorded on tape.
This upsets Martin. Klaus, however, decides that it is time that
he gave Sun-Hui a test. He sends her off to Tokyo under the
pretext of her having to attend a seminar.

Upon arrival in Tokyo, however, she is kidnapped by an
unknown group of masked men. Handcuffed and blindfolded,
Sun-Hui cannot figure out where she is being taken. The group
eventually reaches Hokkaido, Japan's northernmost island. In
the meantime, Yu Rim is released, following diplomatic pres-
sure from the British government. Suk-Yeong is also released,
but she has been badly beaten and is injured. The CIC is hoping
that, by releasing her, she will make contact with agents of
the North that Rim Hong-Sik, her deceased lover, had planted
within or close to the CIC. Yu Rim visits Suk-Yeong, and the
two gently exchange words.

"What would you like to do, Ms. Suk-Yeong, once the war is over?"
Yu Rim asks. "I have no special talents. I'll simply raise my daughter
Yun-Mi and Yeong-Jae [Hong-Sik's bereaved son]. [. . .] You may
criticize me, since I don't seem to have a noble frame of mind [neces-
sary] to sacrifice myself for the fatherland." Yu Rim smiles and says,
"But of course, you are already helping our fatherland." Suk-Yeong
hesitantly asks, "Are you afraid, sometimes?" "How do you mean?"
"I mean, for example . . . if you could not see the day of our victory..."
Yu Rim slowly speaks, "Yes, I think about that often. But, humans
are not afraid when they die for [the benefit of] future generations.
In fact, they become braver than ever." (Li Jin-U 1981b, 71–72)

Later, Yu Rim learns that Sun-Hui has been kidnapped by
an unknown group in Japan. This kidnapping has been staged
by Klaus, as stated above. He wants to secure proof of a connection between Yu Rim and Sun-Hui that extends beyond
their old friendship. So, he has sent fake communists to kidnap

Sun-Hui. After Yu Rim has learned of the news, Klaus sends a certain woman to him as a messenger. But Yu Rim sees through the irregularity of this contact and takes no action, even though it is supposed to have as its objective the rescue of Sun-Hui. In the meantime, after much hard analysis, Sun-Hui figures out that these so-called Japanese communists are not communists; although she is not certain who sent them to kidnap her, she decides that no secret will be given to them. During a moment when the kidnappers have let their guard down, Sun-Hui grabs a handgun and manages to escape from their hiding place, killing a few of her former captors in the process. This is announced in newspapers throughout East Asia as a praise-worthy act of courage on the part of Sun-Hui and Yu Rim thus comes to know that she is free and safe. Yu Rim flies to Tokyo and the two make brief contact.

Yu Rim returns to Korea to face the news of a POW riot on Keoje Island. Foreign journalists decide to make a field trip to the island. There, Yu Rim witnesses the courageous resistance of NKPA soldiers and officers in the face of their brutal treat-ment at the POW facilities run by the United States and South Korea. Unexpectedly, he recognizes a childhood friend among the POWs, Chil-Seong from Pyongyang. He is embarrassed, since he assumes that Chil-Seong will also recognize him and see that he is now a foreign journalist, having deserted his fatherland. Later that night, as the riots and commotion rage on, he receives two secret visitors in his hotel room. He is con-cerned, but receives them cordially. One of them asks him: "Your home is Pyongyang, right?" Yu Rim asks him how he knows this. The other answers: "When your car drove past our prison cell, our captain [presumably Chil-Seong] recognized you. The captain was executed [afterwards]. We came here for something that the captain asked us [to get]." The man takes out a sheet of paper, smeared with bloody letters, and says to Yu Rim: "This is written with our blood. A total of 7,402 of us have signed it. Could you please send it back to our father-land?" Yu Rim is skeptical. The man assures him: "Our cap-tain asked us right before he was executed. He said you would do this for us." Yu Rim agonizes in his mind, but says: "I'm sorry, but I'm a British journalist. I do not wish to be involved in this kind of matter." Then, the two sense that someone is approaching them. They leave the sheet of paper with Yu Rim anyway. Yu Rim thinks about it very carefully.

Let's think about it. . . . This is serious. Chil-Seong said something about me? Already ten years have passed since we parted, and I appeared in front of his eyes as a bourgeois Western journalist who had deserted our fatherland and my own mother. That's why he was looking at me with hatred. But, how come now I'm receiving this kind of material? If Chil-Seong was really executed, then he could not have had such a moment with his comrades, telling them about me. This must be a trap.

Yu Rim is correct. Klaus has arranged it in order to see if Yu Rim might reveal who he is. Thus, Yu Rim takes the sheet to the South Korean officers, presenting it as a warning about some kind of insurgency.

Back in Seoul, Suk-Yeong and Yu Rim make contact. Yu Rim is surprised to hear that Pak Mu has told Suk-Yeong that Yu Rim and Sun-Hui are lovers. Suk-Yeong cannot believe this and confronts Yu Rim. Yu Rim, with grace, accepts this confrontation. The two are talking in her establishment, Café Madonna.

Suk-Yeong makes coffee for Yu Rim. "Please," she offers it [to him]. "You are thinking deeply about something, Ms. Suk-Yeong. If you take me as your friend, please tell me what is bothering you." "I did take you as my friend. Until now, there were only three individuals in this world that treated me lovingly: my mother, Hong-Sik, and you. But . . ." Suk-Yeong is unable to continue. Yu Rim encourages her. "Please tell me." Suk-Yeong looks down at the floor and quietly mumbles, "Who is Kim Sun-Hui?" Yu Rim is taken by surprise, and unable to utter a word. Suk-Yeong quietly continues, "Please do not misunderstand. I still love Hong-Sik truly. But, precisely because of that, it pains me that you love that woman, that enemy." Yu Rim cannot say anything. Suk-Yeong resentfully continues, "Who *are* you? I don't understand. How can you love our enemy?" After silence, Yu Rim quietly answers, "She is not our enemy." Suk-Yeong cannot contain her anger. "How can she not be our enemy? Surely, you know that she murdered Hong-Sik." [. . .] "I'll have to tell you everything. [. . .] You must be surprised. But Sun-Hui tried her best until the last minute to keep Hong-Sik alive. But, Hong-Sik tried to protect me and that's how he became the target. Just as you, madam, cannot forget Hong-Sik, I cannot ever forget him [either]." [. . .] "Sun-Hui has protected us undercover. [. . .] No one knows who she is. [. . .] Do you remember you denounced her in the park? She suffered from that. She cried, when you slapped her face." Suk-Yeong begins to sob. "But, Comrade Sun-Hui asked me to tell you only when the time is right and tell you that she has always loved you very much. She really wants to call you *eonni* [older sister] and wants to nurture friendship [between you]." Suk-Yeong raises her face. "Why are you telling me this now?" Yu Rim quietly answers. "Now I feel I can tell you everything. I trust you. We trust you. You are our comrade in the revolution. The name 'comrade' captures the loftiest trust between humans. Ms. Suk-Yeong, you have a great comrade named Sun-Hui." (Li Jin-U 1981b, 185–87)

Several days later, Suk-Yeong and Sun-Hui secretively embrace each other in tears. Soon after this, however, Suk-Yeong is captured and tortured to death by Pak Mu. Her daughter, Yun-Mi, is also kidnapped by Pak Mu. Yu Rim, Sun-Hui, and the other North Korean agents bitterly regret not having eliminated Pak Mu earlier.

For some time, the CIC officers have been plagued by the North Korean wireless dispatcher who has resumed operations—obviously, someone has replaced the deceased Hong-Sik. This is true: his name is Tu-Jin. Sun-Hui and Yu Rim have successfully smuggled Tu-Jin into the south of the 38th parallel a while ago. So far, they have been able to protect Tu-Jin's identity. Unfortunately, however, the CIC officers finally figure out the location of the dispatcher. Now, Tu-Jin is in danger. Tipped off about the CIC's approach, Tu-Jin escapes in time, but is unable to gather up his forged identification and other personal records prior to his departure. Klaus examines Tu-Jin's identification, which states he is a high-ranking South Korean officer. Something clicks in Klaus's head—he remembers that one day, Yu Rim made contact with such an officer in a hotel lobby, and that his men have the encounter on videotape. Klaus summons Sun-Hui, Martin, and other officers to his room and begins to show them the tape. Yu Rim appears on the screen. The next moment, he throws away a cigarette butt. Someone bends over and picks it up. But before his face is shown, the screen abruptly goes blank: Sun-Hui has managed to destroy the part which shows Tu-Jin's face. Sun-Hui is fully aware that this will attract grave suspicion toward her, but decides she has no choice. Klaus is confident that finally, he has tracked down the underground network of North Korean agents that includes Sun-Hui. But, upon running a fingerprint check on the video, the person who tampered with the film turns out to be one of Martin's own men. Martin is doomed, and Klaus, while knowing full well that Martin has been framed by Sun-Hui, decides to choose her over him. Staring at Sun-Hui from behind, Klaus makes up his mind to eliminate her one way or the other. He remembers that Yu Rim has always wanted to know the whereabouts of Dr. Kelton, Janet's husband. He approaches Janet and warns her about Yu Rim's true identity. In the meantime, Sun-Hui decides to give Yu Rim crucial information about Dr. Kelton. She tells him that Dr. Kelton will appear in his church in Seoul in a few days. Intrigued, Yu Rim asks why. Sun-Hui "looks lovingly at Yu Rim, as if to remember his face forever" (Li Jin-U 1981b, 369) and shakes her head, saying she does not know why. Still, she asks Yu Rim to get hold of Kelton.

The next day, Sun-Hui appears unannounced on Janet's doorstep, asking her to accompany her to the CIC. Janet is curious, but goes along. In the jeep, Sun-Hui threatens Janet at gunpoint while driving swiftly through town toward the suburbs. She notices a vehicle is following hers—it is Pak Mu. She decides to confront him. First, she terminates Janet—it is her plan to kill her, so that her husband, Dr. Kelton, will have to appear in public for her funeral at the church. After eliminating several of Pak Mu's men, she is fatally shot by him. In the streets of Seoul, newspaper extras are printed carrying news of the death of a beautiful Korean woman lieutenant killed in a battle against communist guerrillas: Klaus has decided to depict Sun-Hui's death in this way. Yu Rim looks at the posters, which are getting soaked and destroyed in the pouring rain. Later, in private, he reads Sun-Hui's last letter. "Comrade Yu Rim. My plan is to kill Janet, so Dr. Kelton will have to come to her funeral. This is my last service to you and the fatherland. I would have really liked to join you in Pyongyang. Please do not forget one young woman who dedicated everything, including her youth, for the sake of the fatherland. Stay well, my love!" (Li Jin-U 1981b, 377). Yu Rim understands it is Pak Mu that is behind her murder. He locates Pak Mu in a hiding place and executes him. In the meantime, Tu-Jin, Yu Rim's radio communication assistant, successfully escapes north of the 38th parallel, taking with him Yun-Mi, Suk-Yeong's bereaved daughter, who had been kidnapped by Pak Mu but was later rescued by Yu Rim.

Kelton is indeed present at Janet's funeral. By this time, the world has increasingly come to the realization that a ceasefire will be reached in the Korean War, American and South Korean armies having failed to invade and conquer North Korea. Afterwards, Yu Rim locates Kelton and has a private conversation with him. Yu Rim instigates a sense of crisis in Kelton, reminding him that Klaus is willing to blame Kelton for the Korean War ending in a ceasefire, an embarrassing outcome for the United States. Klaus and Kelton later meet. Each of them blames the other for the American failure. Yu Rim is getting ready to fly back to the United Kingdom via Hong Kong, although the plan is for him to be repatriated in secret from Hong Kong to North Korea. He holds one last meeting with Klaus, denouncing him for having written Sun-Hui's obituary as a U.S. officer, knowing full well that she was a North Korean agent and his comrade. Klaus realizes that Yu Rim could kill him there and then. Yu Rim continues: "If everything [about Sun-Hui] is passed on to the CIA, you understand what's going to happen to you. There are many witnesses willing to implicate you, including Martin. I am not going to kill you now, today, this day of joy [at news of the ceasefire]. Colonel Klaus, live long." Yu Rim departs for the airport. Klaus is despondent, understanding that his career and life are both over. In the last scene, Yu Rim is sitting in an aircraft seat. Against a background of white clouds, the narration goes: "Since that time, many moons have passed. The world has changed and so have people. But, our fatherland will eternally remember the dedication of unsung heroes who walked the path of stern trials in order to safeguard our Great Leader and our Party" (Li Jin-U 1981b, 414). Again, Volume 2 does not once mention Kim Il Sung by name.

The Significance of Ireumeomneun yeongungdeul

No literary creation in North Korea, either before or since *Ireumeomneun yeongungdeul*, has placed the activities of its protagonists on such a broad, global canvas. A simple count of locations mentioned in the novel yields London, Tokyo, Istanbul, Paris, Seoul, Singapore, Pyongyang, Los Angeles, Taipei, Yokohama, New Delhi, Cambridge, Panmunjeom, Hong Kong, Macau, Manila, and so forth. The distances traveled by protagonists are remarkably long, with travel frequently involving multiple crossings of national borders. To my knowledge, no other North Korean novel adopts this kind of setting. Furthermore, Western elements are not always taken to be bad or negative: English snobbery is praised and European upper-class taste admired. In the depiction of Yu Rim's relationship with his international colleagues, the work presents a Hong Kong singer who is also a friend of North Korea (who makes only a brief appearance in Volume 1), for example, showing to North Korean readers that humanly connections are possible outside the boundaries of the North Korean state and outside the Great Leader's circle of followers. In its depiction of one British agent who helps Yu Rim and Sun-Hui throughout the novel, in both overt and covert ways, the story teaches North Korean readers that friends for North Koreans do exist in the outside world. Importantly, whereas North Korean state media is saturated with official news of gift presentations and offerings of praise toward Kim Il Sung and North Korea by their allies—mostly in Africa, nowadays—no literary and audiovisual products until

Ireumeomneun yeongungdeul depicted foreign friends of North Korea with concrete, if fictional, personifications.

The personalities in this novel take on unprecedented characterizations. Yu Rim is cool, collected, and never loses his head. A well-educated gentleman, he is popular with women, both Korean and Western, married and unmarried. He is thoroughly gentle with women and never violates gentlemanly codes, always treating them with respect. The only person he kills in the story is Pak Mu, the archenemy of Yu Rim, Sun-Hui, Suk-Yeong, Hong-Sik, and by extension, all North Koreans. He owes his sophistication to his Cambridge education, an unprecedented attribute in North Korean literature. He is extremely well connected throughout Western establishments, his contacts including a British Member of Parliament, powerful newspaper publishers, and high-ranked officers in the United Nations. Considering that at this point, the beginning of the 1980s, North Korea was refusing to join the United Nations, maintaining that the body was a lackey of the United States (although it revised this stance a few years later), the use of the United Nations as Yu Rim's base in the story is remarkable.

His elegance is contrasted with the enigmatic, yet ultimately determined strength of Sun-Hui. An exceptional beauty, she is a first-class pianist and at the same time, a first-class marksman, extremely skilled in precision shooting, especially when it comes to moving targets. In the story, she executes many evildoers, but also accidentally lets some good guys get killed as well. Most of the bloody work in this story is performed by Sun-Hui, rather than Yu Rim, while most of the men in the story find her attractive and irresistible. She is sharp, curt, and intimidating, yet has all the attributes of a femme fatale. Extremely intelligent and quick-thinking, she usually snaps at people using a minimum of words. This contrasts with Yu Rim, who is consistently softly-spoken and elaborate in his speech. This type of female character is new to North Korean novels and films.

Sun-Hui's female opposite is Suk-Yeong, portrayed as a gentle, affectionate, and warm soul. She is noble-minded with elegant manners, resilient behind a soft façade. She is sensitive, vulnerable, and deeply emotional, yet she is capable of suppressing her feelings, and restricts herself to portraying a graceful presence. Her grace is admired by men and also by Sun-Hui, who longs to be embraced by her as a younger sister, a wish granted only once before Suk-Yeong is brutally murdered by Pak Mu.

Pak Mu is the exemplar of evil in the story, not only because of his nature, but also because he is Korean. As noted above, unlike in the cases of "evil" Americans such as Colonel Klaus and Martin, Pak Mu's crimes are inexcusable; whereas Americans are simply true to their brutal and cruel natures, Pak Mu's evilness is augmented and portrayed as extreme due to his being a Korean. Also educated at Cambridge, he comes from a wealthy landholding background, which implies that he belongs in the class of exploitative and pro-Japanese national traitors of the colonial era, rendering him as both a class enemy as well as a national enemy. Nevertheless, he is thoroughly depicted as Korean—exemplifying the existence of evil among fellow Koreans. Pak Mu also appears as a maverick, not quite belonging to the traditional older faction of the South Korean military and eventually expelled by the young officers' group as well (although this is the result of a successful plot by Sun-Hui). Pak Mu is a loner and a loser, but he does not just end his life: until the last moment, he tenaciously resists, continuing to harm the good guys. The last person he murders is Sun-Hui. Thus, Pak Mu's killing by Yu Rim is to avenge all of the good people the former had brutally killed, including Sun-Hui and Suk-Yeong. Whereas Klaus and Martin do not kill anyone in particular, murder scenes in which Pak Mu is the perpetrator are captured repeatedly, both in the novel and the movie.

Of course, as far as the plausibility of the story is concerned, all of this is highly improbable. It is difficult to imagine that a North Korean spy had penetrated deep into South Korean and U.S. military circles and was operating successfully at the end of 1952. Neither was it possible for someone like Sun-Hui to have been a decorated officer in the U.S. military. Considering that during the Korean War, women's participation in the U.S. military was largely limited to navy nurses, for a Korean woman who was not an American citizen to be ranked as an intelligence officer in the U.S. Army is a far-fetched idea. What is indisputable, though, is that it was radically new for a North Korean novel or film to portray a good Korean protagonist deep inside the enemy den, with constant close physical contact with the enemy. As stated, this novel was simultaneously made into a film and enjoyed incredible popularity among North Korean viewers during the late 1970s and early 1980s.

It is interesting to note that, in the context of postwar film production in the Korean peninsula, it was precisely around this time that movie director Sin Sang-Ok and his wife, lead actress Choe Eun-Hui, the acclaimed South Korean film-making couple, were kidnapped by North Korean agents. After a long period of incarceration, they were ordered to produce a new type of cinema in North Korea (Choe and Sin 1988; Chung 2009). According to their memoir, it was through Kim Jong Il's personal intervention that a new age of North Korean cinema emerged around the late 1970s. It is unclear whether Sin and Choe had anything to do with the production of the *Ireumeomneun yeongungdeul* series. Considering, however, that there was a spirit in North Korea at the time to create new kinds of cinema and educate and enlighten the masses through the use of cinematic representation, it would be fair to infer that their kidnapping and the production of such movies were ultimately the product of a new political culture emerging in North Korea at the time.

Espionage is nothing new in North Korea, which has consistently conducted coastal and cross-border espionage operations in relation to South Korea since national partition (and South Korea has done the same vis-à-vis the North). But, from the late 1970s on, a new strategy emerged involving the kidnapping of Japanese citizens to provide native teachers of Japanese language and culture. As was revealed in 2002 by Kim Jong Il himself to then–Prime Minister Koizumi Jun'ichirō,

North Korean secret agents kidnapped Japanese citizens from Japan's shores from the late 1970s through to the early 1980s — precisely during the period when *Ireumeomneun yeongungdeul* was being written and adapted to film. Mutual reinforcement between the active use of spy operations and popular cultural productions in which espionage plays a significant role cannot be entirely discounted.

Above all, however, *Ireumeomneun yeongungdeul* is most striking in its depiction of love, or more precisely, love at a time of war. Unlike the other novels that I introduced in the previous chapter and the preceding part of this chapter, this novel does not construct individual love relationships with love for the Great Leader as the immovable center. The camaraderie between Hong-Sik, Yu Rim, Sun-Hui, and Suk-Yeong is portrayed in multiple flows, almost suggesting that their coupling is not so important as the overall connection shared between them. Yu Rim and Sun-Hui are presented as lovers, but this is not always clear. For example, note the scene where Suk-Yeong confronts Yu Rim about Sun-Hui. She states that so far there have been only three people that have loved her: Hong-Sik, her mother, and Yu Rim himself. Her sense of betrayal and of being spurned is painfully clear in her controlled, concise wording. But once Yu Rim reveals that Sun-Hui is in fact their comrade and not Hong-Sik's murderer and she tried to protect Hong-Sik until the last moment, though unsuccessfully, Suk-Yeong quickly dismisses her feelings of hatred and is filled with love for Sun-Hui. Sun-Hui on the other hand, asks Yu Rim to tell Suk-Yeong one day how much she loved Suk-Yeong and the reader recognizes that sisterly affection between Sun-Hui and Suk-Yeong has quickly formed. In these exchanges, the Korean word *sarang* (love) is used in an unqualified way, as if to suggest that there is no difference between Sun-Hui's *sarang* toward Yu Rim and that of Suk-Yeong toward him. This also crisscrosses with Sun-Hui's *sarang* for Suk-Yeong and Suk-Yeong's newly acquired deep affection for Sun-Hui. Recall the warm and deeply affectionate embrace between Hong-Sik and Yu-Rim early in the novel. *Sarang* as such flows through these individuals almost without any distinction being made between romantic love and friendship and regardless of gender. Time and again in the story, the camaraderie among the revolutionaries is referred to as the noblest form of love—beyond romantic love and friendship. Given that the story is set against a background of war and espionage, it is understandable that the utmost trust between the comrades carries the most weight. What is interesting is that Kim Il Sung the sacred being is absent from these this-worldly human connections.

Unlike in other North Korean novels, where the anchoring point connecting multiple flows of camaraderie is usually the Great Leader, here it is *choguk* or the fatherland. The Great Leader is mentioned once in each volume, right at the end, but the name Kim Il Sung is never used in either volume. Throughout the novel, it is the fatherland that unifies the loyalty and commitment of all the personalities. In Sun-Hui's final letter to Yu Rim, she pleads with him to remember that there was a girl who dedicated everything to her fatherland, closing the letter by calling Yu Rim her love. Here, her love for Yu Rim and her love for *choguk* overlap. In admittedly odd ways, *Ireumeomneun yeongungdeul* resembles the earlier wartime stories that were written during the actual war, including "Byeoldeuri heureunda" (discussed earlier in this chapter). But the fundamental difference is that while in the earlier wartime stories, the enemy does not appear with any real humanity, in *Ireumeomneun yeongungdeul*, enemies are concrete individuals with particular temperaments, emotions, and other human characteristics. Precisely because of this, Kim is absent from the novel—as he was being elevated into a sacred being, his co-presence with enemy characters would have polluted him.

The Emergence of Exception

By the time *Ireumeomneun yeongungdeul* was published, the Korean War was only a memory in North Korea: a child born in 1953, the year of armistice, would have been 28 years old when the print version was published in 1981. Not only that, it had become a national memory worthy of romanticizing. Romantic liaisons between spies and the tensions of war are intertwined in this novel. Furthermore, for later generations of North Koreans born and raised after 1953, the war has been less a memory than a cultural construction. If that is so, why do I say that North Korea still regards itself to be at war with the United States? If the Korean War is so remote from the national imagination, its imagery that of a romantic, exciting, and suspense-filled spy movie, how can I claim that tense, martial law–like conditions continue to exist in North Korea today due to the unfinished nature of the Korean War? This, I argue, is based on a historical shift in the image of war, or more precisely, the image of the enemy in North Korea.

Ever since 1950, North Korea has consistently professed to be at war with the United States, although the exact nature of this "state of war" has changed over time. During the 1950s and 1960s, war existed in the context of the national economy, and was closely associated with the postwar reconstruction of all sectors of the economy. These were the years of the *cheollima* movement, which had as its goal the manifestation of real-life miracles, borrowing the name of a mythical horse (*cheollima*) that could fly a thousand *ri* (approximately 400 kilometers) in one sweep. Then, in the 1970s and 1980s, war manifested itself in the context of ideological struggle, which basically came down to Kim Il Sung's victory in the domestic ideological war against his opponents by declaring himself the nation's heart and mind, his ideas the only ideas available to the nation. Kim Il Sung's ideas, collectively known as *juche* (see the Introduction to this volume), were adopted as the sole national ideology. One of the most cherished slogans of the day went: "Let us make ourselves into revolutionaries whose bodies are filled with *juche*-type blood!" This is different from the later period: from the late 1980s on, war in North Korea was squarely placed as a national security issue. With Kim Jong Il emerging more prominently as a military leader, rather than the cultural producer he had been styled as during the previous decade, North Korea began developing its nuclear weapons programs and, more importantly, dealing directly with the United States (if not always in an amicable or effective manner) in diverse diplomatic arenas. A notable culmination of the efforts made in this period was the 2000 visit by Madeleine Albright, then U.S. Secretary of State and the highest-ranking U.S. official so far to have visited North Korea. Further, after Kim Il Sung's death in 1994, national defense and security came to be perceived in tandem with celebrations of Kim Il Sung's eternal life (as I argued in the Introduction to this volume).

Having stated the above, I must hasten to emphasize that in North Korea, the term *mije* or U.S. imperialism has always existed as a synonym for the enemy. *Mije* indeed is *the* enemy. It was *nalgangdo mije* or "evil, thieving U.S. imperialism" that divided the Korean peninsula after World War II and unjustifiably captured Korea's southern half for itself. It was *chimryakja mije* or "invading U.S. imperialism" that violated the North during the Korean War, threatening North Korea with extermination. It was *seungnyangi mije* or the "U.S. imperialist wolves" that brutally ravaged and destroyed North Korea during the Korean War occupation. It is *wonssu mije* or the "cursed enemy, U.S. imperialism" that continues to occupy South Korea to this day and is drooling over any opportunity to reinvade the North at any time, according to North Korean public discourse.

The image of *mije* prior to *Ireumeomneun yeongungdeul* was abstract, a picture-perfect poster child, usually adorned with military headgear, khaki uniforms, and a long, crooked, and pointy nose. Hardly any human attributes were assigned to this image, and it was rarely found outside of propaganda contexts, such as in the North Korean slogan: "Let us tear the *mije* into a thousand pieces" (*Mijeui kageul tteuja*). Prior to this novel, it was unheard of to have an American protagonist in human form. In *Ireumeomneun yeongungdeul*, Americans such as Colonel Klaus and Martin appear with emotions and idiosyncrasies and with greater or lesser amounts of intelligence, strength, humor, anger, or evilness. If Klaus is a big, smart, evil character, Martin is a petty coward. Both, nevertheless, are captured as humans, not simply as things or icons. Prior to this time, enemies routinely bore generic attributes with no unique personalities. The reason why the United States did not appear at the forefront of public displays prior to the late 1970s and early 1980s can be attributed to the aforementioned historical shift in notions of war and the enemy in North Korea, a shift from an abstract, monstrous evil to a concrete evil that had a human form.

During the decade of the 1960s, once postwar economic reconstruction efforts had achieved certain results (with major assistance from the Soviet Union), North Korea began constructing its own ideological heritage, which its state called *hyeongmyeongjeontong* (revolutionary tradition). At the heart of this campaign was an emphasis on learning from the exemplary loyalty displayed by participants in the anti-Japanese guerrilla war. As noted in the Introduction to this volume, former guerrilla veterans wrote their life histories, which the general public was required to read and learn from. Thus, during the 1950s and 1960s, novels and fictional works were not the primary source of ideological education for the masses. During the 1970s, as I also stated in the Introduction, as Kim Il Sung's teachings became a sacrosanct form of gospel and the ability to recite them by heart became a measure of the loyalty of North Koreans, concrete imagery of the enemy once again faded into the background. Also, due to the extreme elevation of Kim Il Sung's position vis-à-vis the people, novels depicted Kim as a noble, perfect, and all-loving character.

By the late 1970s and early 1980s, North Korea was different. It was coming into direct contact with the outside world, albeit in very limited ways, through international collaborative ventures. More importantly, Korean residents in Japan began visiting their repatriated families in North Korea on a massive scale from around 1981, bringing with them Japanese- and Western-made goods (as described in the Introduction). Indeed, it was a popular pastime each year for thousands of Korean visitors from Japan to watch *Ireumeomneun yeongungdeul* at their hotels during their stays in North Korea. This was also popular among hotel employees as well: my Pyongyang hotel was rendered nearly deserted whenever screenings were held, since all workers—cleaners, room maids, waitresses, even chefs—abandoned their duties and rushed into the auditorium. They would laugh and cry as one scene after another of the film unfolded: when Sun-Hui was killed, they would cry their eyes out; when Pak Mu was finally executed, they would applaud and let out loud swear words. Works of fiction and film in 1980s North Korea were turning into mass entertainment or, more precisely, educational entertainment. In this sense, it is important to emphasize that the post–Korean War state of exception emerged in rather a pleasurable shape, that of entertainment. Yet, such a plot as *Ireumeomneun yeongungdeul* was rendered possible and successful in popularity precisely because of the historically sustained discourse of North Korea being at war against the United States ever since 1950. This changed again in more recent decades, when North Korea faced economic sanctions due to its incompliance regarding its nuclear weapons program: *migungnom* or "American wretches" were to blame for shortages in food and energy. Through shifts and transformations, nevertheless, it has remained a consistent and constant historic reality for North Koreans that they are and have been at war against the United States and they are and have been living under wartime tension and emergency.

The Camp

To return to Agamben's idea of the camp, he writes of it as a space in which "human beings could have been so completely deprived of their rights and prerogatives to the point that committing any act toward them would no longer appear as a crime" (Agamben 2000, 41). Let us look at the army "comfort stations" instituted by the Japanese military during the Pacific War. Hundreds of women, the majority of them Korean, were forced into sexual slavery by the army. These women, euphemistically referred to as *ianfu* or "comfort women," were taken

from one battleground to another as military possessions. They
were given one room each with a small door, in front of which
soldiers lined up with one condom each—condom use was
mandatory. Often, because of time constraints, soldiers had
sex with women without even bothering to close the door,
while the next man stood waiting outside the room. Even in
this extremely dehumanizing context, however, rules existed.
Apart from the aforementioned compulsory use of condoms,
soldiers were not allowed to consume alcohol with the women.
Neither violent nor abusive behavior toward the women per-
mitted. Such rules derived from the logic that the "comfort
women" were a gift from the emperor. My purpose here is
not to inquire as to whether these rules were followed or not.
Rather, I am simply pointing out that even in a context such
as an army camp "comfort station," a form of logic existed—
the logic of exceptionality in the name of the emperor, the war,
and the national emergency. There was, as it were, a certain set
of rules, no matter how exceptional and precarious the situation may have been. And yet, it is here, precisely because of
the fundamental logic of exception and emergency, that uniformed officers and officials, representing authority, were able
to use the rules arbitrarily—such is the paradoxical logic of
the camp.

Since 1950, North Korea has maintained a public discourse
based on the national security emergency resulting from the
unfinished war. This does not mean that North Korean society became one savage pit where anything goes. This long-
sustained national emergency was accompanied by all of the
paraphernalia of everyday life—romance, marriage, family,
children, schools, jobs, kinship, jokes, comedy, joy, anger, and
fun. This is not hard to understand: even amidst the post-9/11
national security hype in the United States, and even after the
American invasion of Iraq in 2003, Americans continued with
their day-to-day activities. What made this period different
for the United States, however, was that a legal and political
mechanism was introduced allowing the President the power
to make exceptions—exceptions from the Geneva Convention,

exceptions from the Universal Declaration of Human Rights, exceptions from the Constitution, and so on, in the name of war and the national emergency. Thus, under the Bush administration (2001–2009), POWs in Guantanamo were detained more or less indefinitely without legal representation, the National Security Agency was allowed to randomly wiretap the telephones of American citizens, and the war against terror was declared to be neverending. (Unfortunately, many of these activities appear to continue unhindered even today.)

In North Korea, this mechanism exists as a part of everyday life, has existed for more than 50 years, and will continue to exist in future as long as the current state structure is maintained. So, even though the imagery of the American enemy has shifted from decade to decade, as I have shown in this chapter using literary sources, the ultimate logic of the national emergency has been consistently kept intact. Furthermore, in North Korea, the man who was granted the most power to declare an emergency, to make exceptions, and to turn exceptional situations into normal ones, was Kim Il Sung. His death in 1994 seemingly resulted in the transfer of his power to his son, Kim Jong Il, but as I argued in the Introduction, Kim Jong Il's existence did not represent or replace Kim Il Sung's authority; only Kim Il Sung himself represents his own authority, as Kim Il Sung has now been declared to be the Eternal President who lives with North Koreans forever. In this cosmology, while people live or continue to live with this eternal being, the nation never dies.

It is ironic that North Korea's ontological foundations are so deeply connected with the logic of the national emergency that it has become difficult for North Koreans to imagine life without emergency, without the national enemy. When the electricity occasionally goes off in North Korea's towns and villages, it is because of U.S. imperialism; when there is not enough rainfall, causing drought, it is because of U.S. imperialism; when people starve to death, it is because of U.S. imperialism.

Let me reiterate: this does not mean North Korea is in chaos. Far from it: just like in the Japanese army "comfort stations,"

rules exist, and are strenuously enforced. It is the use of authority in the name of the emergency that can strip one of humanity,
however. For example, a CNN production on North Korea,
Undercover in the Secret State (first aired on November 13, 2005),
shows a brief encounter between a young female transportation officer and two middle-aged women passengers on a train.
When the officer checks their papers — no North Korean citizen
is allowed to travel from one town to another without a written
permit from the authorities — the women's permits turns out to
be not in order. The officer hysterically orders them out, but the
train is moving. Realizing that, despite her repeated demands,
the women are dragging their feet, the officer begins pulling at
their bags, possibly trying to throw them off the train. But these
bags are presumably filled with food and other necessities
purchased from the other town that they will need in order to
guarantee the basic survival of their families. The women, perhaps the age of the officer's mother, exhausted and emaciated,
desperately hold on to their bags, each covering their face with
one hand and quietly sobbing, submissively asking the officer
why she is treating them in this way. The officer begins hitting
the women on their heads and slapping their faces, while the
women submit without protest.

The arbitrary exercise of authority by this young railroad
worker, who spontaneously grants authorization to herself to
use violence against the female passengers, is symptomatic of
the camp-like nature of this society. Despite the ground rules,
or precisely because of the ground rules, uniformed officers
grant themselves authority in the name of the national emergency. Similarly, in such an "emergency nation," entertainment
goes on, with many visual media products, including films
(like *Ireumeomneun yeongungdeul*) and children's cartoon shows,
built around themes of war, hatred, and contempt for American imperialism. When we bear this in mind, the ongoing performance of mass games by million-strong groups in North
Korea makes sense: these, too, are portrayed and perceived
as a type of battleground against the forces of imperialism.
Men and women participating in these games are routinely told

that if they are to succeed in acting and moving together as one body, it will make the imperialist wolves tremble with fear. What would be a more appropriate celebration gift for Kim Il Sung's eternal life than victory over the enemy? Pleasure, pain, achievement, disillusionment, suffering, hope, distress, pride, rage, success—these things occur every day in North Korea, just as in the United States and elsewhere. However, as can be seen in the stories introduced in this chapter, the framework of war and the framework of the emergency ultimately have an influence on all of the above instances of everyday life. In North Korea today, the emergency continues, in large measure, to underpin its cultural logic.

THREE

Self

This chapter follows the movement of the self in North Korean literature and attempts to understand and interpret its behavior. As stated in the Introduction, the self plays a crucial role in North Korea: it is an entity that needs to be killed through sacrifice for the Great Leader, but it first needs to be identified before it can be killed. As with love, the killing of the self is not forced, but is the result of a choice made by the actor himself or herself. Either way, it is imperative to recognize that North Koreans must have a secure and solid consciousness of self in order to operate according to a principle of devotion to the Great Leader. In doing so, we will see that, in a similar way to the two bodies of the Tudor kings, North Koreans aspire to have two lives: one physical and the other political. Literature plays an important role in furnishing people's everyday lives with the discourse necessary for the latter: for political life.

In his *History of Sexuality: Care for the Self,* Michel Foucault provides an important clue that we may use in understanding how the self is born in North Korea. Listing diverse societies in which the individual self is prominent yet nevertheless displays different efficacies and contours, he states:

Finally, there are societies or groups in which the relation to self is intensified and developed without this resulting, as if by necessity, in a strengthening of the values of individualism or of private life.

The Christian ascetic movement of the first centuries presented itself as an extremely strong accentuation of the relations of oneself to oneself, but in the form of a disqualification of the values of private life. (Foucault 1986, 43)

This is as close as we can get to a description of the self in the context of North Korean society, where one's relationship with oneself is strongly emphasized, but where, at the same time, one's private life is suppressed. Here, selves exist publicly. How does this occur? According to Foucault, it occurs by the "intensity of the relations to self, that is, of the forms in which one is called upon to take oneself as an object of knowledge and a field of action, so as to transform, correct, and purify oneself, and find salvation" (Foucault 1986, 42).

A constant and recurring theme in the stories introduced in this chapter is how protagonists carry out purification, correction, and transformation of the self. In the North Korean perception of self, one is wholly and solely responsible for one's own improvement. This is, moreover, a spiritual discipline that everyone in North Korea is supposed to practice every day, especially at the end of each day, week, month, year, or other significant period of time (for example, following one's completion of studies at college). These exercises are called *chonghwa* or total (self) review. What is important here is one's ability to reflect upon and reveal one's own shortcomings, backwardness (in terms of ideology), and weaknesses (vis-à-vis malignant and undesirable influences). This is akin to what Foucault called the technology of self with the focus on self-knowledge. He asks: "How have certain kinds of interdictions required the price of certain kinds of knowledge about oneself? What must one know about oneself in order to be willing to renounce anything?" (Foucault 1988, 17). *Chonghwa* is the venue in which individuals strive for attaining the eventual perfection in purifying their loyalty toward the Great Leader. As the term's totality implies, *chonghwa* demands individuals to look back into the most remote and hidden corners of themselves, reveal their shortcomings publically, and gratefully receive public criticism. As such, through recurrent *chonghwa*—and literally, hundreds of such occasions—North Koreans learn to acquire certain conduct, ways of speech, posture, tone of voice, and, along with these, beliefs.

Typically, in North Korea, every unit (for example, a work group or a classroom) begins a *chonghwa* review session by firstly calling on each member to publicly present the results of his or her own respective self-review, with each presentation followed by the critical responses of other group members. This practice is normally referred to as *bipangwa jagibipan*, or criticism and self-criticism. In North Korea, no review is complete without mutual criticism. In regular reviews, public criticism would simply follow after one has presented self-criticism. But in more important, milestone reviews, such as completing one's college study, or on the occasion that one has committed an act worthy of criticism, after presenting self-criticism, the person would be asked to leave the room, while the rest of the unit members discuss how best to help this person overcome his or her shortcomings and prevent them from corrupting him or her again. After a little while, the person would be called into the room, where he or she would receive others' criticism in orderly manner.

Greater emphasis, however, is placed on one's own self-criticism. The ability to reflect upon one's own weaknesses is seen as a virtue, being able to reveal one's cowardice in public is seen as an example of courage, and being able to demonstrate sincere regret and remorse for one's wrongdoings—all are seen as transformational skills. Thus, as in Foucault's words, selves in North Korea are first and foremost closely related to themselves. The direction toward which these relationships point is, however, unquestionably clear: loyalty toward the Great Leader.

Many institutions in North Korea are often explained in terms of a combination of the legacy of Japanese colonialism and postwar Soviet influences (see Armstrong 2004). I do not disagree with such views, but I would like to consider the North Korean institution of self-criticism in comparison to a somewhat unexpected entity: the practice of confession in

Christianity. My focus, however, will be less on the purification of the believer's sins through his or her absolution by a priest (as found in Catholicism) than on the spiritual development of the believer (as found in Eastern Orthodox Christianity). More precisely, it is serious contemplation upon the self, as seen in St. Augustine's *Confessions* (1998), that is the kind of model that North Korean self-criticism sessions hope to achieve. Written in the fourth century CE, *Confessions* is accentuated with episodes that highlight the renewal of the author's piety. Of these, one of the most important must be the one in which he falls down on his knees, overcome by the tearful recognition of his insignificance in the presence of a greater being, later hearing children's voices telling him to read the gospel. Following his conversion (and baptism by Ambrose), Augustine gives up debauchery, possessions, and money, leaving only his house, which he plans to convert into a monastic institution. *Confessions* is filled with sagas in which his deep piety and devotion win out, and in which victorious outcomes are derived from self-contemplation in a state in which he feels the presence of God and proximity to this supreme being.

In each self-criticism session, North Koreans are expected to take one step closer to the Great Leader. The process of eliminating one's impurities — by way of self-criticism — is a process by which one reduces and eventually eliminates one's distance from the great being, in order finally to be fully accepted by this being. (Chapter 1 discusses this logic of moving closer to Kim Il Sung, the sacred being, in the context of love.) It would be much more helpful to understand the North Korean institution of self-criticism in this way, that is to say, not as a form of punishment for the sinful soul as such, but rather as an occasion for achieving self-improvement and self-elevation as one becomes closer to the Great Leader. Just as St. Augustine wrote his *Confessions* for God, North Korean self-criticism and the language used therein are produced for and dedicated to the Great Leader.

With this background discussion in mind, I propose to closely examine two stories in this chapter: *Yonghaegongdeul*

(The Ironworkers) by Li Taek-Jin and *Seongjangui bom* (A Spring of Growth) by Kim Sam-Bok, both published in 1982. North Korea's official publisher, Munye chulpansa, classifies both as *jungpyeon soseol,* medium-length novels. I have chosen to examine works in this medium for several reasons. The production of longer novels, known as *jangpyeon soseol,* is typically assigned by the state to more experienced and politically privileged writers (and often to a group of writers as a collective). Often consisting of revolutionary epics, they are, therefore, read by citizens as part of their political studies in their respective work units. The same is the case for *tanpyeon soseol,* short novels, but for different reasons: these are more likely to be used by work units as collective reading material in ideological education, since their shorter length permits unit members to finish a story in one meeting. *Jungpyeon soseol,* or medium-length novels, are usually read by citizens as a voluntary form of time-killing entertainment. Again, this puts *jungpyeon soseol* in a slightly more private (to the extent that we can use this term in the North Korean context) category, compared to others.

Yonghaegongdeul is set in an industrial site, whereas *Seongjangui bom* has an agricultural setting. Both are tales of economic struggle, so to speak, and both involve protagonists dealing with personal and familial contradictions. In the context of these two stories, the self, or more precisely, the language of the self in North Korea, will be revealed as belonging to the realm of the gods and spoken for the benefit of the Great Leader. Risking a contradiction in terms, I propose that in North Korea, as far as I can determine from its literature, selves exist by way of public or formulaic language, as it is at the level of the self that loyalty and dedication to the leadership and the nation are publicly proven. At the same time, each self exists as an individual domain, as in Foucault's depiction, one having to face oneself in a vacuum occupied only by oneself. Paradoxically, in this type of contemplation, selves have no language of themselves. The language of the self exists in an opaque, impoverished, and repetitive vocabulary, one that resembles mantras, prayers, chants, or other kinds of formulaic discourse. I shall attempt to substantiate this argument below.

The Ironworkers

The novel *Yonghaegongdeul* is set in an industrial town, the entire identity of which is built around its iron works. The Great Leader visited the town's facility right after the Korean War, and today, several decades after that visit, its workers are striving to come up with more energy-efficient and cost-effective ways to produce iron. The story opens with work unit captain Hyeon Dae-Heung returning from a six-month period of re-education classes. In his 50s, Hyeon is a dedicated worker and is now even prouder that his son, Seok, has just joined his hometown's iron works as chief engineer after graduating from the Engineering University in Pyongyang and completing his graduate studies. His wife, Sun-Deok, whom he married prior to the liberation of Korea in 1945 following the traditional matchmaking process, warmly welcomes him back to their house and shows him his newly re-arranged study. Hyeon learns that his son Seok and daughter Ok have worked together to make the room look this nice. He cannot, however, find his old metal ashtray, instead finding a nice stainless steel one sitting on his desk. Sun-Deok explains to him—in an old-fashioned speech form—that Seok has replaced it with a new one that he bought in Pyongyang. Showing mild impatience, yet refusing to get upset, Hyeon demands that his old ashtray be put back in its original place.

Hyeon's family does not know the importance of the metal ashtray. He reminisces that it was made for him by his fellow ironworkers right after the visit by the Great Leader following the Korean War. During that visit, the Great Leader called him *tongmu* (comrade) and held his hands warmly. Encouraged, Hyeon always led in the production competition at the works. As a prize, his fellow workers made this ashtray from leftover pieces of metal. Thus, for Hyeon, the ashtray represented a symbol of his loyalty toward the Great Leader and his dedication toward his fatherland. Hyeon murmurs to himself: "Well, that son of mine does not know how this ashtray came into being. So, it's alright, it's great he bought a new one for me, but he can use it himself. That does not kill his piety . . ." (Li Taek-Jin 1982, 7). As Hyeon takes the new ashtray upstairs to his son's room, his friend Choe Kap-Su comes to pay a visit and soon afterwards, his son Seok returns home.

As the three converse, Kap-Su, who is older and more experienced than Hyeon, informs the latter that the Party Committee chairman has told him that, following his re-education, Hyeon would be elevated from his current position as work unit captain to a management role. Hyeon resists, stating: "Listen, older brother, I don't understand what the chairman is trying to do. I've just taken classes and that does not mean that all of a sudden I've become better qualified. All I want is to return the love of the Party that allowed me to study at this age. And in order to do that well, I should just stick with what I have done all my life: work, and not administration or any other new job . . ." (Li Taek-Jin 1982, 9). Listening to the two, Seok, Hyeon's son, is relieved, since he feels it would be too much of a burden for his father, who is in his mid-50s, to have to learn something new, such as managerial skills. This opening alludes to the story that will unfold as we turn the pages, a story of conflict between a son who, out of intense love for his father and a desire to protect him, somehow ends up trying to curtail his father's enthusiasm, and a father willing to move ahead, no matter what, in order to fulfill the expectations placed upon his shoulders by the Party.

As the three men continue chatting over the drinks that Sun-Deok serves them, two girls come into the scene: Hyeon's daughter, Ok, and Eun-Ha, an engineer. Eun-Ha and Seok have known each other well since their college days. Not only is Eun-Ha familiar with Seok's graduate dissertation research, but the pair has also kept in touch by mail over the past few years. During this period, Seok was completing his graduate work in Pyongyang, while Eun-Ha was assigned to his town as an engineer. Eun-Ha has come to congratulate work unit captain Hyeon for successfully completing his re-education classes.

Seok's parents, especially his mother, are fervently hoping that the affectionate relationship between Seok and Eun-Ha will result in marriage. Seok walks Eun-Ha to the women's dormitory. (In North Korea, unmarried workers from other areas, who do not have family members with whom to live, reside in gender-segregated dormitories.) They talk to each other affectionately.

Eun-Ha walked alongside Seok. It was in the depths of the winter and New Year's Day was near. But, the cold air felt as if it was intended to make the two walk closer. The evening streets were beautiful. With their lights, the farmhouse windows looked as though they were smiling. Only a cold winter night could offer this kind of pristine sensitivity.

"This is a good night." [Eun-Ha said.]

"Yes, I feel great. I always enjoy walking on winter nights like this."

"Why so?"

"After hours of research, it always helps to get some fresh air. I used to walk like this along the Daedong River [in Pyongyang]. Breathing in clean air, it felt as if my mind was being cleansed and I was able to focus better."

"That sounds like the right hobby for a researcher." [. . .]

As they talked, time went by so fast and before they knew it, they were already standing in front of the dormitory building. Eun-Ha turned around to see Hyeon Seok off until he turned the corner. (Li Taek-Jin 1982, 22–23)

The New Year arrives and the factory faces a number of challenges in relation to its iron production. Of prime concern is its aging ventilator, which is slowing down production considerably. Work unit captain Hyeon is concerned about this, while his own son, Seok, is trying to upgrade the ventilator with the help of Eun-Ha. Hyeon, however, finds it difficult to keep quiet on this topic, since, as an experienced veteran iron worker, he knows the facilities and machinery inside out, continuing to find Seok's approach a little too intellectual and one step removed from the realities of the workplace. Hyeon is frustrated. Seok in turn, as a filial son, is worried that his lack of credentials is causing anxiety for his father and tries even harder to apply himself to his research, although he continuously expresses his reservations about his father getting involved — mostly because he is over-protective toward his father and worried about his father possibly losing face if he makes an error.

One day, Seok learns from Eun-Ha that his father has suggested that they resolve the ventilator problem by applying an airtight freezer to the fans. Seok has not been unaware of this possibility, but has remained less than fully convinced. When he learns this news from Eun-Ha, he is hesitant even to talk about it further, suggesting to Eun-Ha, "Let's not talk about it [. . . since] it is an empty dream." According to Seok, the airtight freezer needs to be applied to the ventilator by connecting it to a large-scale generator. The iron works does not have the funding to buy such a freezer, while producing it from the materials on site would be almost impossible. He adds, "It's actually fortuitous that it will not be realized." Eun-Ha asks, "What do you mean?" Seok wants to clarify his position to her:

Comrade Eun-Ha, I've already talked to my father about the lack of possibility of improving productivity by renovating the ventilator. [. . .] I cannot set my father to [carrying out] adventurous and potentially very dangerous work, like experimenting in order to produce a freezer using our own resources. This is going to be a gamble, and while I will do anything to make it happen, I'm unable to involve my father. I cannot involve him. (Li Taek-Jin 1982, 132–33)

Eun-Ha asks:

"I think I understand what you mean, but why would you presuppose that our work will be a failure even before we do anything?"

"I accept that criticism. However, when it comes to a matter that involves my own father, I cannot bear putting his reputation at risk."

Eun-Ha became quiet. She understood Seok's feelings toward his father, his protectiveness, and filial piety. But how about Captain Hyeon himself and his [own] passion? Hyeon would not accept such "protection." He once told Eun-Ha that there was a portion of work for a son and another for a father and that neither could take over the other's portion. [. . .] Wasn't Seok in fact disregarding his father's [own] passion, his father's entire world, Eun-Ha wondered. [. . .]

"I'm humbled by your dedication to your father. But, I also worry that your caution is actually undermining your father's position. Look, your father is actively coming forward with his own ideas and suggestions. He, too, knows how you feel about his doing so, but he is still trying to play an active role. If you are genuinely concerned about your father, genuinely wishing the best for him, shouldn't you in fact be supporting your father's efforts? [. . .]"

Seok felt Eun-Ha's words were justified. Yet, still, he insisted: "Of course, I have no [way of] refuting your words. But, engineering requires planning and order. I cannot just put this idea [of the airtight freezer] into practice, simply because it is my father who suggested it."

"Fine. I will take care of it in your place. I will be responsible for the entire experiment. I'll even find out whether there could be some other method. . . ." [. . .]

"Comrade Eun-Ha, are you suggesting that we should involve my father in the experiment?"

"No. Not simply involve him, I think we must place him high up in a leadership [role]."

"Very well. You are simply insisting on principles, because you don't have any personal investment here." [. . .]

Seok was perplexed. He understood that now that the idea of the airtight freezer was on the table, someone had to pursue it, and it was going to have to be Eun-Ha. But, then, what would happen to their personal relationship? Why should the two lovers stand in opposing positions toward each other? Seok was saddened. (Li Taek-Jin 1982, 133–34)

After this exchange, Eun-Ha returns to her dormitory room at around midnight, exhausted and distressed.

Her roommate Ryeon-A [a workplace doctor who later plays an important role] got up and asked, "Oh, why are you so late coming home?" Then, Ryeon-A was taken aback by Eun-Ha's pale face. "What happened? Are you all right?" "Well, I've just been working hard today, I think. Don't worry." Eun-Ha and Ryeon-A were very close, but Eun-Ha did not feel like telling her what had happened that night between Seok and herself. Ryeon-A had brought dinner from the canteen for Eun-Ha, but Eun-Ha said, "Thank you, but I'm not hungry. I'll go to bed." Eun-Ha buried her face under her quilt. Tears welled up. "Comrade Eun-Ha, we do not know each other very well, it seems." Seok's parting words came back to her. Those words summarized their relationship so far and declared an unfortunate ending. [. . .] Eun-Ha could not help but find Seok bureaucratic. This was a betrayal of her original image of him: she had thought him to be a pioneering engineer, audacious and courageous in applying new technologies and implementing new experiments. But no, today, Seok appeared to her as someone who was pedantic, unimaginative, defensive, and above all, lacking in passion. [. . .] "Who was it that was standing in front of me?" Eun-Ha asked herself — "Is he truly a *juche* scientist, or is he an imposter?" In front of the two different men that Seok had presented to her tonight, her love was at stake — "Is this the pain that love gives one?" she pondered, confused and upset. "I must not see him ever again! I will do my best to help Captain Hyeon even at the cost of using an imported freezer. I will make it happen!" Eun-Ha made her mind up. Her temple throbbed with pain. (Li Taek-Jin 1982, 135–37)

Eun-Ha stops accepting invitations to Hyeon's house after this falling-out. Hyeon and his wife Sun-Deok cannot avoid noticing that something has happened between their son and his lover. Seok has been sleeping in his office lately, in order to devote more time to his research. One day, his mother pays him a surprise visit and warmly yet persuasively argues that he should try working things out with Eun-Ha and at the same time, try to be a little more tolerant of his father's involvement in technical matters. In the meantime, Hyeon himself approaches Eun-Ha, asking whether she fought with his son over his own involvement in the freezer renovation. Eun-Ha denies this, but Hyeon understands, and tells her:

I can see he is giving you a lot of pain. He treats me, his own father, the same way. He says he is considerate toward me, but on the contrary, he often gets on my nerves, with that attitude that only he can resolve the most complex technical matters. It's alright to be self-confident, but he has a long way [to go] to actually know how hot the iron is when it comes out of the furnace. I proposed the airtight freezer device in part because I wanted to teach him a lesson. But, in

the meantime, I'd be very grateful if you could support his work. . . .
(Li Taek-Jin 1982, 145)

Eun-Ha is deeply touched by Hyeon's words. Of Eun-Ha's
parents, only her mother is alive, her father having been killed
during the Korean War. Her mother lives far away in her
hometown. For this reason, she particularly appreciates her
close relationship with Seok's parents. She renews her determination to successfully complete the device that will allow
the use of an airtight freezer for the ventilator fans.

Soon after this, Seok finally returns home to have dinner
with his family. He has made good progress in his research
lately, and has therefore decided to allow himself this luxury.
When he enters the house, he realizes that his father is asleep
in his chair. He looks at him affectionately — the silver streaks
in his hair, the deeply carved wrinkles . . . all signs of his hard
work and determination. Then, he notices his father's notebook lying on the table in front of him. He is drawn to its
pages and realizes that his father has been putting an enormous effort into research and experimentation. He is overwhelmed by a sense of guilt and humbled by his father's endless devotion to his work. After placing a blanket over his
father's back, he grabs the notebook and begins examining it,
page by page. He is impressed and then astonished by the
incredible detail of the ideas sketched out by his father in its
pages. After his father wakes up, Seok and his father make
peace and decide that Seok will follow up on the ideas that his
father has devised in his notebook and bring them to fruition
(Li Taek-Jin 1982, 147–55).

Once this father-son collaboration has been agreed upon,
the project comes to be surrounded by an air of excitement,
everyone full of hope and energy. With hard work and devotion, the workers manage to produce the airtight freezer and
the day for the test run has come. Everyone is hopeful. When
the switch is turned on, the freezer starts to respond. Hopes
rise. But, after a little while, a fan breaks with a sharp cracking
sound. The experiment is a failure. Everyone is shocked and
disappointed. Seok is the most disappointed of all and feels

responsible. In his agony, he even entertains the possibility of leaving town and applying for other positions. His relationship with Eun-Ha continues to be sour and awkward, and he thinks there is not much left for him to achieve by remaining in town. But, faced with the continued passion and determination of the workers, Seok decides to stay on, albeit with a half-hearted sense of commitment.

Ever since the test failure, Seok, Eun-Ha, and the other members of the technical team have been staying in their office at the worksite, devoting their evenings to research so as to resolve the problems with the project as soon as possible. One day, Sun-Deok comes to visit Seok and finds Eun-Ha. She is as warm as ever, asking Eun-Ha why she has not been to see them. Overcome by emotion, Eun-Ha bursts into tears, realizing that the end of her relationship with Seok has also cut off her access to this warm-hearted and gracious woman. Seok happens to pass the hallway and takes a glimpse at two women. Witnessing Eun-Ha's tears, Seok is reminded of Eun-Ha's delicate side, which contrasts with the consistently determined and decisive manner she displays at work. He is deeply saddened at this scene and also by his own lack of control of the situation, and sinks deep into self-contemplation. He questions his mental purity, carefully assesses the strength of his loyalty to the cause and examines his sincerity toward Eun-Ha. After serious self-examination, he realizes that not only in love but also in work, he has been a coward—his commitment has been lukewarm and not determined enough. Through self-examination, he rediscovers his own qualities as a revolutionary engineer and his true self, the self that stands in front of the Party, his work, and Eun-Ha. From that day forward, Seok devotes his entire energy to his research (Li Taek-Jin 1982, 223–32).

One day, after weeks of sleepless devotion, Seok finally succeeds in testing an airtight freezer for the ventilator fans. Hearing this news, everyone congratulates him, but he firmly responds: "No, this is not my success. It is your success . . . all of you, the workers!" (Li Taek-Jin 1982, 231). He realizes at this point that science for the sake of science is of no use and begins work on real-life applications for the new device. The workers and members of the technical team face a few difficulties, but eventually reach the point where they are able to conduct another test run. Switches are turned on and machines begin to operate. The next moment, Seok recognizes that the gauge is fractionally off. He keeps watching, but it continues to be slightly off the mark. In order to rectify this problem at this point, someone has to go inside the gas furnace and adjust the needle. He realizes there is no time to look for experienced workers. With determination, he climbs up a ladder and then descends another one inside the entrance to the furnace. As soon as he has adjusted the needle, a small explosion occurs and he loses consciousness. His vision blurred, he makes out his father's voice. The next moment, he wakes up to find himself in his father's arms. Everyone is anxiously looking into his face. He remembers that there was an explosion. He feels weak, but also knows that he is all right. "Father, I'm embarrassed. I could not figure out . . . ," Seok starts to apologize to his father. His father cuts him short, saying, "No, don't apologize. You — you are truly my son, the son of an ironworker [*yonghaegongui adeul*]!" Warm tears stream down Hyeon's cheeks. Everyone is overcome by emotion at this scene of honesty and trust between father and son. At this moment, someone yells from the direction of the furnace: "Comrades! Success! It is working!" and everyone cheers the victory. Amongst them is Eun-Ha, who is gently smiling. "Comrade Eun-Ha! You saved me. You make me truly so happy." "I, too, am so happy. Ah, I will never be able to leave this workplace." The two decide to climb up the central control tower in order to have a panoramic view of the iron works. The morning sun is rising. "Comrade Eun-Ha, our motherland has invited us to [enjoy] such a beautiful morning." "Really, could there be any happier morning than this?" Eun-Ha and Seok embrace each other (Li Taek-Jin 1982, 304–11).

The novel closes with a scene in which Hyeon is boarding an airplane sent by the Great Leader. He is traveling to Pyongyang in order to participate in the New Year's state feast, to which select dignitaries are invited. Hyeon is being sent off by his loved ones, including Seok and Eun-Ha. He has been invited to the feast because, thanks to the technological innovation implemented by Seok and Eun-Ha, his iron works has been successful in producing 27 tons of iron using facilities designated for the production of only 19 tons. Climbing up the red-carpeted steps to the plane, he is overcome by immense love for the Great Leader: "Truly, how can I repay this much love?" he asks himself. The plane disappears into a silver sky.

A Spring of Growth

The heroine of *Seongjangui bom*, Yu-Yeong, is an agricultural college student and a Three Revolutions team member who has been assigned to consult with, engage with, and mobilize agricultural workers in a cooperative farm. Coined in the 1960s, the Three Revolutions concept refers to ideological, technological, and cultural revolutions. From 1973, the North Korean ruling party officially began assigning young college students and graduates to factories and agricultural cooperatives as Three Revolutions team members to work with workers and farmers, respectively. Unlike in the case of the Cultural Revolution in China, however, this was a benign initiative implemented without excessive force or abuse of power. In North Korea, Three Revolutions team members played a liaison role between leaders and assembly line workers at workplaces and between the members of the agricultural cooperative cadre and farmers. The North Korean state, unlike its Chinese counterpart, was not successful in completely dismantling the culture of seniority in which deference must be shown to elders. Thus, although in theory, these young men and women were sent to act as leaders, their actual roles were typically obscure and low-profile ones. Basically propaganda campaigners rather than technical or technological innovators, they remained supportive toward the workers' own initiatives, as opposed to their Chinese counterparts, who often overruled existing workplace hierarchies and disrupted human relations by severely and publicly criticizing older and more experienced personnel. To my knowledge, few bitter memories, indeed few memories at all, remain of the Three Revolutions in North Korea today. By the late 1980s, no one, including official party organs, was talking about the Three Revolutions any longer. However, the unusual nature of the Three Revolutions program, as featured in *Seongjangui bom*, in which designated outsiders visited work-sites and became regular members of particular work teams, makes this novel more complex and intriguing than other novels of this period.

The novel starts with a scene featuring Yu-Yeong knocking on the office door of the main protagonist, Kang Du-Jin, one snowy night. Kang, the work unit leader and a seasoned farmer, opens the door and hurriedly takes Yu-Yeong in, asking why she has come all the way on foot on a night like this.

"Come in now, hurry! Your hands are freezing!" [Kang asked Yu-Yeong where the rest of the team members are.] "I came alone. They will all arrive here tomorrow morning by bus." [. . .] "So, why did you come walking all the way for twenty miles or so?" "Since it has been snowing from early on, I just got worried about the *mopan* [seedbed for infant rice plants]." [. . .]

Although it had snowed, that did not mean that the *mopan* had been destroyed, and having one Three Revolutions team member on site would not have changed anything anyway. But, for Kang Du-Jin, Yu-Yeong's pure sincerity was precious. He could not help feeling deep affection toward this young college student. [. . .]

Farming had been his life, his entire life. Kang Du-Jin was born in this village [named Ryongho] before Liberation [of Korea from Japanese colonial rule in 1945]. For him, Yu-Yeong was only a little girl, just like his own daughter. Even before she was born, Kang Du-Jin had received land for cultivation thanks to the Great Leader's land reform [in 1946] and had truly experienced all sorts of ups and downs [. . . in his struggle to farm the land]. Ryongho's every hill, every stream bore his sweat and blood. Thanks to [. . .] the productive labor of agricultural workers like Kang Du-Jin, new generations, including Yu-Yeong, were born and raised happily on this land. Yet, tonight, finding this young girl right outside his office door in the snow left a deep impression on him. He felt she had something very pure and untainted inside her. (Kim Sam-Bok 1982, 4–6)

The prologue suffices in introducing Yu-Yeong's sincerity and devotion and Kang's broad-mindedness and personal warmth. A little later on, the novel touches more specifically upon Yu-Yeong's character.

Yu-Yeong was a young woman who was just like a frail, graceful flower. She knew nothing about life's difficulties. She could only see surface realities. To her, slogans such as "Happiness means struggle" meant poetic verse. So, Yu-Yeong made a conscious decision to join the Three Revolutions team in order to discipline herself further in the realities of the everyday revolutionary struggle. That snowy night, too, she consciously pushed herself out of her dormitory room door to make the twenty-mile trek in order to test her own strength. (Kim Sam-Bok 1982, 12)

Among the *nongjangwondeul* (agricultural cooperative workers) with whom Yu-Yeong has direct dealings as a Three Revolutions team member is a 26-year-old man by the name of O Hong-Bong (who used to work in a factory, but volunteered to work at this cooperative farm), a middle-ranking production team leader called Kang Su-Il, his younger sister, kindergarten teacher Kang Su-Ok, quiet yet sturdy veteran farmer Pak Chang-Gu, and the Three Revolutions team district leader Choe Gwan-U, among others. Yu-Yeong has a long-distance lover, Kim Gi-Cheol, who does not play a substantial role, except in a couple of scenes where he appears as a graduate research student in engineering who supports her with regular correspondence. Later in the novel, his research will play some role, but overall, the technical details are not important (as the reader will have also noticed in *Yonghaegongdeul* — I will discuss this more extensively below).

O Hong-Bong is characterized as an unruly person, an odd man out, viewed with a mixture of suspicion and ridicule by the other farmers. This is in part due to his working-class industrial origins and in part due to his explosive temperament and careless manner of speaking. Rumor has it that the reason O Hong-Bong has not left the Ryongho agricultural cooperative is because of the romantic ambitions he holds toward Su-Il's younger sister, Su-Ok. Su-Il, a very capable work team leader who was handpicked by the previous generation of cooperative workers to be a thoroughbred agricultural cadre, does not trust Hong-Bong.

One day, Hong-Bong approaches Yu-Yeong with his suggestion for improvement of the farm's irrigation system. At this time, his sub-unit is receiving its supply of water only after all of the other sub-units have received theirs, as there is only one channel for all of the sub-units to use. According to Hong-Bong, however (and Yu-Yeong is inclined to agree with him here), if one were to look at the way the sub-units were spread out, one would see that they formed a triangle, not a direct line. Therefore, rather than leaving his sub-unit at the end of the supply pipeline, a new and shorter channel should be built from the source directly to his sub-unit, simultaneously delivering water to his sub-unit as well as to the rest of the sub-units. Agreeing that this makes sense, Yu-Yeong asks Hong-Bong why no one is talking about this. Hong-Bong replies that Su-Il is adamantly against it (Kim Sam-Bok 1982, 17–19).

Later, toward the end of the workday, Yu-Yeong runs into Su-Il and brings up the topic of irrigation improvement. Su-Il is full of venom, calling Hong-Bong a grumpy cancer in the unit who complains about almost anything. Su-Il further complains to Yu-Yeong that Hong-Bong cannot stick to one task and that he is now also sticking his nose into chemical experiments regarding fertilizers and growth stimulants. Yu-Yeong gently suggests that the idea of irrigation improvement does not strike her as totally misguided. Su-Il decisively declares that while it may seem like a good idea on paper or in words, in actual farming, such a thing would require an enormous investment of human labor and other resources, causing delays in the production cycle and endangering the current water supply, as it would involve tearing off parts of the existing channel. Yu-Yeong is at a loss, faced with two resolutely opposing views (Kim Sam-Bok 1982, 23–25).

After this discussion, realizing how late in the day it now is, Su-Il arranges for a tractor driver to give Yu-Yeong a ride back to the Three Revolution team headquarters twenty miles away. Yu-Yeong flatly refuses this offer, but Su-Il persuades her, telling her that the tractor is bound to be delivered to town the following day anyway and that it will not make any difference to the cooperative whether it is moved that night or the next day. Upon this explanation, though still with hesitation, Yu-Yeong gratefully accepts the offer (Kim Sam-Bok 1982, 25–26). Back at the headquarters of the Three Revolutions team, Yu-Yeong reports on the situation to her director. The director tells her to watch the two very carefully while not being partial to either (Kim Sam-Bok 1982, 27–28).

Right after this, Yu-Yeong has an opportunity to walk with Kang Du-Jin: both are headed for the county office, and so they walk there together, chatting away. Du-Jin tells Yu-Yeong some old stories of the cooperative:

Kang Du-Jin, Kang Deok-Man [Kang Su-Il's father], and Pak Seong-Gap [Pak Chang-Gu's father] were exemplary farmers and best friends since pre-Liberation days. [. . .] These fathers first built socialist cooperative farms, and their sons, Kang Su-Il and Pak Chang-Gu and others, who, thanks to the Great Leader, received a high school education, are now running this cooperative. [. . .]

"Regrettably, Kang Deok-Man passed away due to injuries received during the war [the Korean War]. So, the Party consciously elevated Su-Il to [the position of] cooperative cadre. [. . .] He is extremely dependable and truly ready to take on a rank higher than the one he is in now, but we are giving him a few more years to work on the land. You see, a genuine agricultural worker must know what the land wants, how to communicate with the land, and you can only do that when you have spent sufficient time together with the land." [Kang Du-Jin goes on, recounting to Yu-Yeong a series of heroic deeds performed by Kang Su-Il. Yu-Yeong is deeply impressed, as this image of Su-Il contrasts starkly with that of O Hong-Bong, whose grumbling, behind-the-back slandering of Yu-Yeong herself reached her ears a couple of days earlier.] (Li Taek-Jin 1982, 40–42)

From this time on, O Hong-Bong is unhappy. He thinks Yu-Yeong is showing favoritism toward Su-Il as Su-Il is using his influence to ensure she understands she is receiving special treatment as a guest. Hong-Bong is even less happy because his romantic designs for Su-Ok are being jeopardized. Not only is Su-Ok rather distanced from him, she is also at a loss how to deal with him, as he is in constant conflict with her brother, Su-Il. One day, Hong-Bong is driving a tractor along a paddy when he catches a glimpse of Su-Ok, who is walking along the paddy with her kindergarten pupils. He loses focus for a second, his mind straying into fanciful thoughts about Su-Ok, and the next moment he is running his tractor right into a herd of goats. The elderly goat herder, Kang Chil-Seong, is speechless at this careless behavior by a former industrial worker. Hong-Bong is now sent to the Socialist Working Youth League unit for criticism and self-criticism sessions. Yu-Yeong, as the Three Revolutions team member in charge of Hong-Bong's work unit, is required to accompany him (Kim Sam-Bok 1982, 60–68).

Yu-Yeong listened to the League members' criticism of Hong-Bong very carefully. One young man criticized Hong-Bong a bit too excessively, Yu-Yeong thought, while another man was trying to help Hong-Bong in a roundabout way; one woman would not say anything about Hong-Bong, only talking about herself. In sum, it could be summarized that Hong-Bong was arrogant, impulsive, and unable to control himself in important situations. Furthermore, everyone seemed to agree that Hong-Bong's weakness was *kaeinyeongungjuui* or egotistic heroism. It was fortunate that Old Man Kang [the goat herder] had not been hurt. Nevertheless, Hong-Bong's careless driving had potentially endangered him. The League members wanted Hong-Bong to realize the seriousness of his deed. Yu-Yeong, too, hoped that Hong-Bong would reflect deeply and seriously on his action. Hong-Bong, however, was silent, his head lowered. His self-criticism was ambivalent: it could have been interpreted that he did [indeed] realize his weakness, but it could have also been superficial.

"Comrade Hong-Bong," Yu-Yeong asked after the meeting, "Do you find the criticisms you've received unsatisfactory?" Hong-Bong turned his head away from her and said, "No." "Well, don't just be like that. Tell me if you found something wrong in the criticisms." Yu-Yeong was unable to understand why Hong-Bong was making this situation so difficult for himself, and she continued: "It frustrates me. I think of you very highly in light of your courageous act of volunteering to work in the agricultural sector [since everyone knows that it is much harder work and given less recognition than industrial labor in North Korea], yet it frustrates me that people in the unit do not have favorable opinions of you. I think the criticisms you have received today have some truth in them. Can you accept them sincerely?"

Hong-Bong looked at Yu-Yeong. His eyes changed color with anger. "Look, I know they were all correct. And I know that I was completely wrong. I'll make up for it, I'll be a different man. I have to go. Good bye!" Hong-Bong was so angry that his hands were shaking. [. . .] Yu-Yeong stood there in shock. (Kim Sam-Bok 1982, 70–71)

By this time, Yu-Yeong's disappointment in Hong-Bong is nearly complete. Then, an incident happens that will turn her view around. Her Three Revolutions team leader, Choe Gwan-U, comes to see her. He breaks the news to her that Hong-Bong left the village the night before in order to obtain fertilizer or some kind of chemical and has not returned for the last 24 hours. Kang Su-Il believes he has left the cooperative for good, because of the recent series of notorious errors for which he has been criticized. Yu-Yeong feels responsible for this since, as a Three Revolutions team member, she should have more carefully grasped the human relations in this workplace. Choe then asks how Yu-Yeong has decided to deal with Hong-Bong's suggestion about irrigation improvement. Relying on Kang Su-Il's interpretation, Yu-Yeong answers that Hong-Bong's idea is premature. Choe cautiously starts:

"I am hearing that, in your unit, Kang Su-Il is giving you special treatment. On one evening, he even arranged a tractor to give you a ride home. And, O Hong-Bong is feeling quite a grudge against that. He is said to be going around telling people that the team member [i.e. Yu-Yeong] listens to everything Kang Su-Il says, because Kang is treating her like a princess." Yu-Yeong was disgusted, and stood up in indignation. Choe calmly said: "Sit down, please. Now, calm down and listen." Yu-Yeong sat down, trying to quell her anger. Choe continued: "I did not want to tell you this, but I think it would be helpful after all to let you know what I think is going on. First, I have no criticism toward you. So, please know that. But remember, when *tangjungang* [the Party Center: Kim Jong Il was referred to in this way during the 1980s—see the Introduction to this volume] sent us to workplaces, we were told to share every bit of life with the workers and farmers and never to regard ourselves as someone special. This means that even though the farmers want you to receive their gratitude, sometimes you must decline. I know full well that you would never have taken the offer, had you known that Kang Su-Il had made up the excuse that the tractor had to be sent to the town anyway, as he was worried about sending you back to town in the dark all alone. Now, why do you think O Hong-Bong is so upset? Everyone, including even Hong-Bong, cares about you, and they go out of their way to help [you in] your work. Then, why is he so angry? I think there is some more depth to human minds than what meets the eye." [. . .]

Yu-Yeong was always mindful of her own lack of a "real" life, but it is true that for young women like Yu-Yeong who had grown up knowing only the convenience of the city and the privilege of the learned [. . .], tasks such as the Three Revolutions [project] could easily be taken as romantic dreams. [. . .] When Yu-Yeong and her college classmates first heard about the Three Revolutions teams, they were so excited that they went to the beach and sang songs of joy. [. . .] Walking along the wavy seashore, Yu-Yeong and her classmates talked about how they would contribute to national mobilization [efforts] such as the Three Revolutions [project]. With excitement, everyone, including Yu-Yeong, left college [and headed] in all directions—north, south, east, and west—to work as Three Revolutions team members. [. . .]

Yu-Yeong wondered: (I still have a long way to go. I'm still lacking something important and fundamental. How can people be so superficial toward me? How can they treat me like this? But wait, how did I treat them first? Did I always approach them with the utmost honesty and sincerity? Did I even understand what it means to be a farmer? Right. It was I. I was the one that did not relate to them as they deserved. I must, must give them my entire heart). In this way, Yu-Yeong carefully and severely reflected on her own self and lifestyle since arriving at the Ryongho cooperative. (Kim Sam-Bok 1982, 72–77)

Thus, Yu-Yeong contemplates her own self. She carefully traces back how she started her work as a Three Revolutions team member, how she related to the cooperative members, and how she in fact missed so many clues about the complexity of human relations at the farm. She realizes, through careful self-examination, that her lack of leadership is responsible for many of the problems created on the farm.

That evening, Yu-Yeong is determined to locate O Hong-Bong. She takes a freight truck to XX Chemical Factory, arriving there at 11:00 PM. The workers are still on the job. Yu-Yeong asks for a farmer named O Hong-Bong from Ryongho village. Hong-Bong comes out with a Three Revolutions team member from the factory. Yu-Yeong is overcome by complex emotions. "Let's, let's go home. Everyone's waiting for you." "Now?" Hong-Bong answers awkwardly, "No, I cannot leave now." "Very well," Yu-Yeong calmly answers, "I shall wait for you right here until you come out with your stuff." Hong-Bong will not move. The Three Revolutions team member from the factory cannot keep his silence any longer. Stepping in, he says: "I'm sorry to interfere, without knowing the background, but Comrade O, isn't it a bit too much, when someone from the cooperative has come to get you this late. On top of that, it's raining outside. Shouldn't you be more considerate?" Ignoring this advice, Hong-Bong walks back along the hallway. Yu-Yeong asks the factory team member to leave Hong-Bong and her alone. He leaves and Yu-Yeong catches Hong-Bong before he goes inside the work room. Hong-Bong asks, "Where's your truck?" "It's at the railway station, unloading the packages." "I'll walk with you to the station." "Are you kidding me?!" Yu-Yeong is livid. "No, I am not. I never say anything dishonest and when I make my mind up on something, I always see it through to completion." Yu-Yeong glares at him in rage. "Are you, are you so concerned about your own pride?" "No." "So, then, you are trying to be 'manly' or something? You are a coward." "Am I a coward?" "Yes, you are. You did not come to the cooperative because you wanted to help the agricultural sector; you came there just because you fancied Comrade Su-Ok. That is why you never earned the trust of everyone there. And look, in the end, you went running away from us. What happened to your initial determination to support agriculture? How can you possibly even say that you never changed your mind?" "You know nothing about me!" Hong-Bong's eyes are burning with flames of anger. "Are you saying I ran away from agriculture?" "If that's not acceptable, I can reword [this] and say that you have come back to your old comfort zone, the factory. Comrade O Hong-Bong, I am embarrassed for you. It is shameful. I will not beg you to come back with me to the village, but I am ashamed of you as a member of the same young generation. How can you indulge yourself in this way in the sweat and blood of previous generations?" Hong-Bong maintains his silence. [. . .] They reach the railway station. The truck driver has been waiting for Yu-Yeong. Yu-Yeong quietly leaves Hong-Bong, without a farewell, and gets into her seat. The driver recognizes Hong-Bong and does not know what to do—whether to leave now or not. Then, the next moment, Hong-Bong comes running toward the truck and opens the door, saying "Comrade team member, I am not a coward. I just cannot leave this place just yet. But tomorrow! I promise. Tomorrow I will be back. I am never a quitter." He slams the door shut and runs toward the direction of the factory (Kim Sam-Bok 1982, 78–82).

When Yu-Yeong returns to her dormitory, she receives a note from her lover, Kim Gi-Cheol. Gi-Cheol had come to see Yu-Yeong and waited for her, but had had to leave before her return in order to catch his last train back. Yu-Yeong reads the letter with joy, learning that Gi-Cheol has finished his studies and has been assigned to work at XX Steel Mill as an engineer. To Yu-Yeong's surprise, Gi-Cheol mentions O Hong-Bong, telling her that they are old acquaintances. Yu-Yeong is overcome by affection for Gi-Cheol and sorry that she has missed him (Kim Sam-Bok 1982, 83-84).

After work the next day, Yu-Yeong is waiting for Hong-Bong on a hilltop. Pak Chang-Gu notices her. He tells her that it is getting chilly and windy out and suggests that they wait inside the office. Yu-Yeong thanks him for his kind suggestion, but insists that she would rather see Hong-Bong right there. Pak Chang-Gu mumbles: "If he really intended to come, he would have already been here. . . ." Yu-Yeong is nervous: "Will he not come, do you think? I don't know, really. . . ." It is getting quite dark. They stand there, Chang-Gu with feelings of doubt, Yu-Yeong with a certain amount of hope. Then, Yu-Yeong screams: "Look, there's a light!" True, a tiny dot of light can be seen in the distance, and it is approaching. Chang-Gu thinks to himself: "O Hong-Bong is really a nasty guy. How can he give a team member [i.e. Yu-Yeong] this much pain?" Then, without thinking much, Yu-Yeong screams, "Comrade O Hong-Bong! Hong-Bo-oong!!" No answer. She continues, "Comrade O, is that you?" Then, both Yu-Yeong and Chang-Gu hear: "Yes, it is! Is that you, Comrade team member?" "Ah! Finally! I'm so glad!" Yu-Yeong is elated. Pak Chang-Gu is relieved, not because Hong-Bong has made it, but because Yu-Yeong's anxiety and pain are over. Chang-Gu approaches Hong-Bong first, saying: "Look, you troublemaker. How can you do this to Comrade team member? If I were her, I would first criticize you in public, but she has been waiting for you, worried sick!" (Kim Sam-Bok 1982, 95–98)

Hong-Bong chokes up, overcome by emotion. "Comrade team member, I am sorry, so sorry. I thought you had decided to 'educate' me. I thought you had labeled me as a cancer in the unit. So, I was overly defensive and failed to accept your sincerity. Please forgive me." Due to his previous distrust of Yu-Yeong, Hong-Bong has not told her what he has been up to at the XX Chemical Factory. He has been experimenting with growth stimulant for the rice paddies. Hong-Bong used to work at a chemical factory and, thus, knows quite a bit about fertilizers and growth stimulants for use in agricultural production. He realized that the use of a substance named B acid would enhance productivity. He even knew where to obtain materials to be used in experiments for the production of B acid — usually from a steel mill. The reason Gi-Cheol knew Hong-Bong was because Gi-Cheol's XX Steel Mill was right next to XX Chemical Factory: Hong-Bong met with him and explained what kind of experiments he was conducting. Gi-Cheol was supportive, seeing strong potential in Hong-Bong's theory about B acid. Hong-Bong tells Yu-Yeong all about this, and continues: "I thought you were the same as Comrade Su-Il. So, I did not tell you anything about B acid." "Why are you talking about Su-Il in such a light?" "When I first approached him with this idea of B acid, he completely dismissed me." "But I would understand that, because you did make an error in another experiment last year, correct?" "That is correct. But, one mistake! One mistake cannot determine the future. About this one, I was confident. [. . .]" Yu-Yeong does not want to slander Su-Il behind his back like this. So, she changes the topic. "So, tell me more about your experiment" (Kim Sam-Bok 1982, 99–101).

Hong-Bong suggests that Yu-Yeong come to his house and see what kind of projects he has been working on. As they enter the small yard of a bungalow, Yu-Yeong cannot believe what she sees. The yard is full of test *mopan*, seedbeds with infant plants of various kinds. And the inside of the house looks like one massive laboratory. Hong-Bong patiently explains to Yu-Yeong how his industrial background made him realize that with a little bit of chemical input, current productivity could be multiplied. Hong-Bong shows her volumes of his notebooks containing equations and other theories. Yu-Yeong is deeply impressed. At the same time, her suspicions about Kang Su-Il are deepening. Inside her head, she murmurs: "Why does Su-Il refuse to listen to Hong-Bong, when Hong-Bong has such solid grounds for his proposition? Is Su-Il narrow-minded and myopic?" Hong-Bong tells Yu-Yeong that XX Steel Mill engineer Kim Gi-Cheol supports his experiment but that he is overloaded with his own assignments. Therefore, he stresses, Yu-Yeong is the only one he can rely on. Yu-Yeong now understands how Gi-Cheol and Hong-Bong are connected. Yu-Yeong is overcome with joy, the joy of getting to know this truthful man, O Hong-Bong (Kim Sam-Bok 1982, 103–7).

The next day, Yu-Yeong confronts Kang Su-Il. Upon being questioned as to why Su-Il has not only consistently failed to support Hong-Bong but also at times placed obstacles in the way of Hong-Bong's experiments, Su-Il gets agitated. "How can you accuse me of that?" "Well, you should have been the first person to support Comrade Hong-Bong's experiment. But on the contrary, you dismissed him categorically, and so Comrade Hong-Bong even had to lie to us to get B acid from the factory." "Why should I give *him* special treatment?" "I don't mean that. But, if you had understood Hong-Bong's intention to radically raise productivity in our cooperative, you would not have behaved in that way. You did not pay sufficient attention to Comrade Hong-Bong. Even though Hong-Bong might not succeed in the end, I think we must still support his experiment." Yu-Yeong concludes her criticism by telling him how sorry she is to see this. Kang Su-Il does not respond, smoking in silence (Kim Sam-Bok 1982, 107–9).

The day after, Kang Du-Jin visits Su-Il's unit. "I hear Hong-Bong's back," Du-Jin starts. Su-Il is nervous, thinking to himself: "What did Yu-Yeong tell this man?" A moment later, Yu-Yeong comes into the office and tells Du-Jin in detail about what Hong-Bong has been up to. Du-Jin gently turns to Su-Il and says: "Is that right? That guy is pretty all right. [. . .] Su-Il, you were mistaken, right?" Su-Il blushes and keeps his silence. Du-Jin continues: "Well, this is a different story than the one you told me, Su-Il. We must help with Hong-Bong's experiment. This could be a great step forward." "I sure will," Su-Il says, looking unhappy. Yu-Yeong is hopeful that finally the cooperative members are coming together as one. But Kang Su-Il is thinking something quite different. He is depressed and feeling very unhappy about Hong-Bong getting ahead of him as the object of Yu-Yeong's attention and, more importantly, that of Du-Jin (Kim Sam-Bok 1982, 109–10). Later, Hong-Bong's B acid formula is sent to the agricultural science academy for verification. The academy is to examine it and respond with suggestions.

One morning, Yu-Yeong's Team leader, Choe Gwan-U, receives an urgent phone call from Kang Su-Il, letting Choe know that B acid is killing the rice plants. Choe asks: "Who is responsible? Who put B acid on the plants?" "That is, of course," answers Su-Il, "that O Hong-Bong." Yu-Yeong is walking toward her work unit and comes to a halt at the sight of O Hong-Bong, who is standing on the edge of the paddies,

Fig. 3 Illustration from *Seongjangeui bom* (A Spring of Growth). The rice plants are dying and Yu-Yeong tries to collect herself. Illustration by Kim Yong-Gwang.

saddened and disappointed. Yu-Yeong smiles at him and asks what the matter is. Hong-Bong greets her, but his face is dark. Hong-Bong tells her: "On the fourth and fifth of June, we spread comprehensive growth stimulant, but only the field that received it on the fifth is showing some weird [signs of] damage." Yu-Yeong assumes a serious face and asks: "But, it's not just our unit that used the stimulant, right?" "Right. And that is why it is strange that only this particular field is suffering from damage." The two hurry toward the paddy that Hong-Bong is talking about and Yu-Yeong sees it: the rice plants are dying! Trying to collect herself, Yu-Yeong asks Hong-Bong: "What do you think happened?" "I'm not sure. Fertilizer and weed-killer were administered as usual, except. . . ." "Except, what?" "I mixed 0.003 percent B acid with the stimulant." "No! How could you?" Yu-Yeong is shocked, because such acts are not acceptable without going through the vehicle of collective team discussion. "I am so sorry. My ideological weakness has caused this, but I saw that the plants in that field were showing strange [signs of] damage, and having seen that, I thought I should try B acid," Hong-Bong apologizes. Yu-Yeong is despondent, as strong doubts about the B acid experiment have crawled into her mind (Kim Sam-Bok 1982, 176–82). (At this point Yu-Yeong and Hong-Bong are still waiting to hear from the agricultural science academy about Hong-Bong's formula.).

Having made the phone call, Kang Su-Il is not comfortable. He is aware that this particular paddy required extra treatment by letting the cold water out, and he did not do that. In some ways, this is a more serious oversight than the simple addition of a miniscule amount of B acid. Based on his long-term experience, he of all people can tell that the dying plants are showing signs of retaining too much cold water. But Su-Il is adamant that he will not even reveal that fact. This is why he has proactively made a phone call to the Three Revolutions team district leader Choe, informing him that Hong-Bong's B acid experiment is causing severe damage to the cooperative's production. Everyone is disappointed and inclined to blame O Hong-Bong and, indirectly, Yu-Yeong. Later in the evening, Pak Chang-Gu comes to see Su-Il at home. Chang-Gu, unlike his usual self, is angry:

"Didn't I always suggest that that particular paddy required more control of cold water? That field always caused us problems. I don't think it was B acid or Hong-Bong. I think it was you who neglected the treatment. Hong-Bong is a clean man. He did not hesitate in accepting every responsibility. But you, look at you! You are a coward. You are the one who is truly guilty here." Kang Su-Il looked like a corpse, colorless. He felt as if someone had shot him right through the heart. He was hoping that no one would talk about the cold water, but Pak Chang-Gu, who was as experienced as himself in farming, would not overlook it. But Su-Il did not want to give in. [. . .] "No, it was Hong-Bong's fault. He used B acid without permission. That's why the plants are dying." Chang-Gu yelled: "How can you be so pig-headed?! You know better than anyone else that it was your fault. If you're not willing to publicly apologize, I will on your behalf." "Stop it! Mind your own business." Chang-Gu calmed down, as if he was giving up, and said: "I've said what I needed to say, for your own sake. If that's such a problem for you, then you do whatever you like." [. . .] The door of the upstairs room opened and Su-Ok, who had been listening to their exchange, cried out in a tearful voice: "Brother, I . . .

I did not know you were such a human being. You are no longer the brother whom I respected. How can you not listen to Comrade Pak Chang-Gu? I don't want to live here any longer. I am, I am so sad." [. . .] Angered, Su-Il stood up and left home. (Kim Sam-Bok 1982, 192–94)

A couple of days later, Yu-Yeong hears that Su-Ok has left her home and is living in a dormitory due to the conflict with her brother. Yu-Yeong had also heard a little while earlier that Kang Su-Il has spread the rumor that Yu-Yeong was supportive of Hong-Bong because of Kim Gi-Cheol's involvement with the B acid experiment. Yu-Yeong concludes that the time has come for her to travel to the agricultural science academy to seek expert advice. At the academy, she learns that not only is the B acid formula that Hong-Bong has experimented with useful for increasing productivity, but that it also needs to be applied at the ratio of 0.003 percent, that is, exactly what Hong-Bong has done. Yu-Yeong comes home with this great news, firstly telling Kang Du-Jin. Du-Jin is overcome by a sense of guilt, due to his lack of trust in Hong-Bong and his excessive dependence on Su-Il. Upon Du-Jin's initiative, the Party district is conducting a review of Kang Su-Il's life and work. After public criticism and self-criticism, Su-Il is deeply reflective of his own shortcomings, but still struggling to come to terms with his own weaknesses. After a heartfelt exchange with Kang Du-Jin, Su-Il finally comes clean and truly begs for the forgiveness of the cooperative, the Party, and the fatherland. The closing scene of this novel is embellished with the warmth that Yu-Yeong and Su-Il generate as they recover their mutual respect (Kim Sam-Bok 1982, 199–203, 218–28).

The Mundane

Both *Yonghaegongdeul* and *Seongjangui bom* have "side" love stories that represent the realm of the mundane: whereas the primary revolutionary saga weaves through the main body of each of these novels, mundane love stories or what we might also call secondary stories are often utilized in order to animate the novels and help emphasize their messages. In *Yong-*

haegongdeul, it is the romance between Ryeon-A, the workplace physician, and Ho-Cheol, the son of a legendary ironworker who died during the Korean War, although he does not clarify who his father was at the beginning of the story. Ho-Cheol initially appears brusque and gruff, lacking in sophistication. These characteristics quickly turn out to be likable and even admirable, as he reveals his fundamental solidness as an ironworker. Seok's father, work unit captain Hyeon, takes a particular liking to him. This is because Ho-Cheol's rawness and energy somehow stand in contrast with the characteristics of his own son, Seok, who is a little too intellectual for Hyeon to deal with, especially at the beginning of the novel.

Ho-Cheol and Ryeon-A start off on rough footing because Ho-Cheol, too preoccupied with exceeding his labor quota, has forgotten to receive an immunization shot and becomes seriously ill. As a result, Ryeon-A's fellow health workers criticize her, and it is therefore with feelings of resentment that she visits Ho-Cheol in his dormitory room to give him his injection. Their encounter is a bitter and awkward one, although both register something special about the other in their own ways. Ryeon-A was raised by a single mother who used to own a small shop in town. After the socialist reform of commercial activities, her mother applied for a managerial position in a provincial government-owned hotel. She is a very capable woman with a quick wit and a sharp tongue. She has always planned for Ryeon-A to marry a physician in Pyongyang. Her older daughter is married to an engineer and lives in Pyongyang. Through this connection, Ryeon-A's mother has already established a hopeful suitor for Ryeon-A.

Ryeon-A, according to the author, unlike her mother (and by implication her sister), is not interested in living a life of luxury—living standards and lifestyles in Pyongyang stand out among all of the cities and towns of North Korea. Ryeon-A is not only content with her assignment to a rural industrial town as a doctor taking care of the health of the ironworkers there, but also proud of her work. Her mother does not approve of this and is waiting for the perfect occasion to send Ryeon-A to Pyongyang.

In the meantime, Ho-Cheol and Ryeon-A begin developing romantic feelings toward each other. Hyeon, who is fond of Ho-Cheol, is a reliable source of moral support. One day, it turns out that Ryeon-A is leaving for Pyongyang to attend a conference on Eastern medicine. A couple of days prior to Ryeon-A's departure, Ryeon-A's mother comes to visit Ho-Cheol. She tells him that, seizing upon this opportunity for Ryeon-A to go to Pyongyang, she has arranged a meeting between Ryeon-A and a doctor in Pyongyang and she is hoping that they will eventually be married. After this meeting, Ho-Cheol is livid, confessing to Hyeon that he will completely sever his relationship with Ryeon-A. Ryeon-A herself has already departed for Pyongyang and, therefore, there is no way to verify her knowledge of her mother's plan through her own words. Hyeon tries to persuade Ho-Cheol:

Look, if you really love her, then you must trust her. You just heard this story from her mother, and did not confirm it with the doctor herself. That's not like an ironworker [*yonghaegongdapchiana*]. To love is to believe. To trust human beings is a fundamental quality of the working class. I know nothing about new [forms of] love under socialism. All I really know is that I trust my wife and my wife trusts me. That's all. It doesn't matter if you're lovers or friends or neighbors. Trust is the most important thing between humans. Without trust, [there is] no love, you know. Of course, sometimes in life, one faces betrayal. But, the one that betrays will lose, because that is the law of life. [. . .] Unless the person belongs in the category of enemies, we must trust everyone and that to me is the heart [i.e. the core characteristic] of being an ironworker! (Li Taek-Jin 1982, 255).

Hearing Hyeon's words, Ho-Cheol is deeply reflective, and realizes that he has been too shallow in relating to Ryeon-A. Hyeon, on the other hand, decides to go meet with Ryeon-A's mother on behalf of Ho-Cheol, without telling him he is going to do so. When Hyeon encounters Ryeon-A's mother, things unexpectedly get out of his control:

The woman somehow guessed why this guest had come to see her, yet she asked: "How may I help you?" Actually, the woman looked likable, at least more so than Hyeon had imagined. She even looked almost graceful and obviously much more sophisticated than did regular housewives. "I understand you came to see Ho-Cheol, one of our ironworkers, the other day," Hyeon said, opening the conversation. "Sure, I met with him briefly," answered the woman. "So, what do you think of him as Ryeon-A's future husband?" "What are you talking about? I just went to see him for some business," answered the woman with an obviously fake smile. "So, you don't want to talk about it straightforwardly, Madam? Why are you trying to interfere with young people's relationships? I cannot accept your attitude toward this ironworker. He is just like my son." Hyeon became very mad as he blurted out these words. "Wh. . . what is it?" The woman gave a sharp look and became very rigid. Hyeon continued: "You must not. If you are a mother, be a good one." The woman was taken aback, but only for an instant, and the next moment, she resumed her posture and quietly opened her mouth. "I am not appreciating you getting worked up [about this matter], but I understand how so many people appreciate what a good woman my daughter is. That actually pleases me." In this way, the woman successfully turned Hyeon's anger to her advantage. "I am not talking about your daughter. I am criticizing your attitude toward Ho-Cheol. You are very arrogant toward him." "Oh, am I? Very well. If so, maybe we can arrange a meeting between Ho-Cheol and my daughter." The woman took the complete upper hand. Hyeon resisted: "This nation cherishes ironworkers. How can you treat our worker like that? Your ideology is problematic." "Mister, I *am* the manager of this government-run hotel. I, too, have received a political education. I don't look lightly upon ironworkers. However, if you had a daughter, you would know that as a parent, one has to wish the best for one's child, and especially a daughter. I see nothing wrong in trying to marry my daughter well."(Li Taek-Jin 1982, 260–62)

After this disastrous meeting, Hyeon keeps quiet around Ho-Cheol. As Ho-Cheol waits patiently for Ryeon-A's return from Pyongyang, he receives a state invitation to join a revolutionary pilgrimage tour, the standard tour that exemplary workers are invited to participate in as a reward for their hard

Fig. 4   Illustration from *Yonghaegongdeul* (The Ironworkers). Artist unknown.

work, which includes visits to places such as Kim Il Sung's birth place near Pyongyang, Mount Baekdu, and other examples of what North Koreans call *hyeongmyeong jeonjeokji* or places of revolutionary footprints. After this wonderful tour, Ho-Cheol's train pulls into his hometown railway station. It is raining cats and dogs. As he descends from the train, an umbrella appears, and then, from underneath it, Ryeon-A's lovely face. He is elated, but not sure why she is here . . . because of him . . . is she here to meet him? Ryeon-A greets Ho-Cheol warmly and tells him that she has learned the news about his return this evening from work unit captain Hyeon. Ho-Cheol is happy, and the two walk in the pouring rain, chatting softly under their one umbrella. Both are convinced that they have found their respective loves (Li Taek-Jin 1982, 289–93).

After this, Ryeon-A's mother comes to Hyeon's house to seek a meeting with him. She starts, "Mister, I am sorry to visit

you this late." "Why do you want to see me, Madam?" The
truth is that Ryeon-A's arrangement in Pyongyang did not
work out. Once she reached Pyongyang, she told her sister that
she was not interested in getting married yet. Hyeon continues:
"Well, if your daughter herself says so, then. . . ." "No, Mister,"
Ryeon-A's mother cuts him short, "it is no doubt because of
that Ho-Cheol. You know that. He must be influencing her."
"Madam, what influence? Why do you underestimate your
own daughter, who is a trustworthy health worker of our nation? Ho-Cheol is a great young man," Hyeon answers angrily.
"You are always exaggerating about that young man. I don't
know. Either way, it is no use. I already knew you'd be on
Ho-Cheol's side." Hyeon this time quietly asks her: "What
do you really think of him? Is he so bad?" "Well, of course he
is a fine young man." Ryeon-A's mother continues, "But I don't
like the situation, that is, that he is an ironworker, while my
daughter is a highly educated physician. This would not be
a good match." Hyeon follows up: "So, what is a good match
for you?" "That doctor in Pyongyang is often sent abroad by
the government. He is a rare find, one in one thousand. I
don't understand my daughter. He is quite keen on meeting
my daughter and is saying that he would wait for the next opportunity. Mister, please, could you persuade that young man
[Ho-Cheol] to leave my daughter alone?" Hyeon replies: "I'm
unable to do anything like that. [. . .] Your daughter fell
in love with a man, not with all these so-called conditions.
How can you even imagine that your daughter would give up
Ho-Cheol for some 'conditions?'" (Li Taek-Jin 1982, 297–301).
After this meeting, Ryeon-A's mother leaves them alone, and
Ho-Cheol and Ryeon-A, along with the other couple, Seok
and Eun-Ha, stand together on the front line of revolutionary
construction efforts.

Seongjangui bom also includes a romantic side story between
O Hong-Bong and Kang Su-Ok. However, this romance plays
a more central role in the overall plot of the novel than the one
between Ho-Cheol and Ryeon-A in *Yonghaegongdeul*. Nevertheless, the novel does not pretend to be a love story: it main-

tains its goal of depicting the complexity of human relationships at a production site, with romantic endeavors playing a
secondary role. Hong-Bong, as I stated in an earlier section,
is rumored to have volunteered to work at an agricultural cooperative in Ryongho village because he is in love with Su-Ok.
Indeed, a tantalizing scene involving Su-Ok and Hong-Bong
can be found early on in the novel. Hong-Bong follows Su-Ok
on their way back to the cooperative from an unspecified location. Giggling, Su-Ok refuses to walk with him. As Su-Ok
continues to refuse Hong-Bong, they reach a river, and Hong-
Bong makes an exaggerated gesture, ending up jumping into
the river. This entire scene is witnessed by Yu-Yeong.

Throughout the story, Su-Ok agonizes, caught between
Hong Bong's passionate feelings and the antagonism of her
brother, Su-Il, who has taken a strong dislike toward him, as
we saw. Hong-Bong's courtship is always out of the ordinary,
but he is usually unsuccessful in attracting Su-Ok's full attention. For example, one day, Su-Ok is leading a group of kindergarten pupils up a hill. Wearing her flowery printed skirt
and red sweater, Su-Ok looks as pretty as a gerbera daisy.
Hong-Bong suddenly appears from the roadside and asks:
"Let's go over the fence for a second. I need to talk to you."
Su-Ok hesitates. "Why? What's the worry?" asks Hong-Bong.
"Well, my brother . . ." Upon hearing this, Hong-Bong nearly
explodes: "What about your brother!" "Well, really . . ." Su-Ok
quickly escorts the children back to the kindergarten and then
unhappily joins Hong-Bong. "Let's sit down," suggests Hong-
Bong. Standing still, Su-Ok asks: "So, what is it about? I don't
have much time." Hong-Bong tells her that he is aware that
her brother does not like the idea that Hong-Bong and Su-Ok
may become closer. Su-Ok tries to protect her brother, saying
she respects him and, while saying so, begins to cry. She finds
it very difficult to be placed between the two men, both of
whom she cares about very much. Su-Ok pleads with Hong-
Bong to reconcile with her brother, Su-Il. Similar scenes appear
a couple more times in the story.

In this situation, Su-Ok naturally turns to Yu-Yeong, who is a couple of years older than her and from an urban, sophisticated setting such as college. This becomes, in fact, a matter of urgent necessity: Su-Ok's kindergarten pupils have won at county level in a Korean traditional dance contest, and Su-Ok is now taking them all the way to the provincial capital for the next round. Su-Ok embarking on this kind of exciting adventure only augments Hong-Bong's anxieties. To make matters worse, a rumor is spreading throughout the cooperative, a rumor that Su-Il has already arranged a suitor for Su-Ok in the provincial capital, and that they will be meeting up while Su-Ok is in the capital for her kindergarten pupils' dance competition. Hong-Bong is hysterical. Agitated, he ends up repeatedly giving Su-Ok a hard time. The curiosity of other cooperative members does not help, either. Some are angry with Su-Ok, believing that she has already agreed to her brother's arrangement, while others insist that she deserves a gentler and more sophisticated husband than Hong-Bong would be. Amidst this confusion, Yu-Yeong tries to help Su-Ok. They sit down on a river bank.

Su-Ok began telling Yu-Yeong about the relations between her brother and Hong-Bong. Her voice trembled. Let us say O Hong-Bong was right and her brother was wrong. But, that did not mean that Su-Ok could simply stop respecting and loving her own brother. [. . .] There was no other choice for Su-Ok than hoping that the two men would reconcile and become friends [again — they used to be closer]. In this situation, that false rumor began circulating. Su-Ok was truly in difficulty, since O Hong-Bong would surely misunderstand her. [. . .]

Yu-Yeong pondered in her mind. How should she help Su-Ok? How *could* she, indeed? Let me talk to O Hong-Bong, Yu-Yeong thought, and try to explain the situation. [. . .] But she shook her head from side to side, thinking that such an intervention would only worsen the situation after superficially remedying [it]. [. . .] In Yu-Yeong's mind, happiness for Hong-Bong and Su-Ok depended on Kang Su-Il, his generosity and his changing his mind about Hong-Bong. In other words, Yu-Yeong knew that it was Kang Su-Il's pride and selfishness that had undermined O Hong-Bong's position vis-à-vis Su-Ok. The more Yu-Yeong cared about Su-Ok, the more she became disgusted with Su-Il. [. . .]

Yu-Yeong began: "We humans are so easily ruled by our environment. But, we must not be simply ruled by it. If you truly love Comrade O Hong-Bong, then no one should be able to stand in your way. That is something like the law of life. [. . .] Don't you think that true love and respect must not be blind? Whoever the person may be, once you find a noble character within him, he will be lovable. And, by the same token, whoever that person may be, if you find him not to be truthful, then you must help him change and improve [himself]. This is what true love does. [. . .] I wish you were a woman who could take the initiative in your own life. That's all I want!" (Kim Sam-Bok 1982, 171–73)

In the end, as we have seen, Su-Ok's romance is achieved as Su-Il realizes his own shortcomings and the cooperative members recognize Hong-Bong's personal qualities, revolutionary determination, and truthfulness.

These two "side" love stories embedded in the above two novels represent the mundane in North Korea. Unlike the main plots (which I will explore in the following section), these subplots are about "average Joes" and their daily lives, about people caught in conundrums involving social relations. Upon closer examination, the two stories also present different aspects of the mundane, involving industrial and agricultural settings respectively. Ryeon-A, a physician at the iron works, smoothly dodges the marriage arrangements her mother has made for her and pursues her own romance with Ho-Cheol. Village kindergarten teacher Su-Ok, on the other hand, is in a weaker position, in that she has to face her brother and Hong-Bong everyday in a small village setting and agonizes constantly, torn between different kinds of love for each man. Her love for her brother is based on the same kind of indebtedness that any child might hold toward his or her parents. Given that she and her brother lost their father right after the Korean War and, I would assume from the total absence of any mention of their mother, that they grew up motherless, Su-Ok is obliged to repay her brother for caring for her through all those years since their father's death. The main reason why

Kang Du-Jin and the other older-generation cooperative members love Su-Il is due to the legacy of his deceased father. From this, also, I would assume that the village itself more or less collectively raised brother and sister as the bereaved children of their fellow farmer. We can infer that human relations among the residents of Ryongho village are of a particularly close-knit nature.

The rumor plays a significant role in the village. Once Su-Ok's kindergarten pupils are selected to compete in the provincial capital, speculation begins to form in relation to Su-Ok's trip. In addition, it being public knowledge in the village that Su-Il dislikes Hong-Bong, when there is a hint that Su-Ok might possibly meet a suitor in the provincial capital during her stay there, this becomes more or less everyone's emotional concern. In the end, no such possibility actually existed. On the contrary, once in the capital, Su-Ok is fully reminded of the sincerity of Hong-Bong's feelings toward her. Witnessing the sophisticated beauty of the young city girls, Su-Ok feels a little embarrassed. Watched by the smartly dressed store attendants as she leaves a store, carrying bags filled with lots of supplies for the village kindergarten, she feels very self-conscious, knowing that she looks like a country bumpkin hoarding urban goods not available in the countryside (Kim Sam-Bok 1982, 142–43). This makes her realize that the good-looking Hong-Bong could have gotten any of these beautiful and sophisticated city girls, but chose to stay in the village for her. It is rare in North Korean novels to see such a depiction of a country girl's perspective. This is partly due to the fact that North Korea insists that the difference in the living standard between cities and the countryside has been minimized. Although as a kindergarten teacher, Su-Ok is one of the better-educated women in the village, she is made to feel quite clearly that, despite her beauty, she remains just a little country girl, unable to compete with the city girls.

In contrast with the emotionally torn Su-Ok, Ryeon-A is in good control of her fate and her romance. She is a physician and, although raised by a single mother, would be able to marry well — if she so wished — due to her mother's relatively powerful position and her sister being married to someone who holds a position in Pyongyang (by default meaning a much better-paid and better-recognized job). Instead, however, she exercises her own choice and decides to explore a future with Ho-Cheol, a man who, according to her mother, is inferior groom material when compared with the doctor who lives in Pyongyang and frequently travels overseas. Unlike Su-Ok, who is burdened by her concern for her brother's satisfaction, Ryeon-A does not pay excessive attention to how her mother feels. It is quite possible to infer that she is aware of what her mother is up to, but she shrugs her shoulders and does not even meet the doctor in Pyongyang. Furthermore, rather than risking confrontation with her mother head on, she asks her sister to write a letter to their mother on her behalf. Her mother, thus, is forced to seek help from work unit captain Hyeon, with the results that we saw earlier in this section. Whereas Su-Ok is frequently seen in tears throughout the novel *Seongjangui bom,* Ryeon-A cries only once in *Yonghae-gongdeul,* in the scene where she failed to provide the correct medical treatment to Ho-Cheol. These two women, both in their early twenties in early-1980s North Korea, thus represent rather different lifestyles.

Interesting and intricate human connections in mundane settings are also presented in encounters between different generations in two different contexts, one industrial and the other agricultural. In *Yonghaegongdeul,* the main protagonist, Hyeon Dae-Heung, is at times torn between his deep love for his son and problematic feelings toward him. His son, Seok, in turn, deeply respects his father. Both men, however, display awkwardness toward each other until their last moment of reconciliation, when Hyeon Dae-Heung declares Seok to be his true son. Friction develops between these two men throughout the novel, partly as a result of their deep love for one another and partly due to their rather different outlooks on life. Seok is too protective of his father, simply wanting him to retire and enjoy a peaceful, leisurely old age. His father is frustrated in the face of Seok's excessive concern and somewhat burden-some love and constantly wonders why Seok cannot trust his father to choose his own path in life. In the meantime, Hyeon's affections drift toward Ho-Cheol, the bereaved son of a legendary ironworker. While rather unsophisticated and gruff, Ho-Cheol appears to be a genuine ironworker in the eyes of veteran Hyeon. By contrast, his own son appears to be overly intellectual and slightly superficial in his approach toward work. Throughout the novel, Hyeon is torn, agonizing over not being able to love his son more fully.

The case of Kang Du-Jin and Kang Su-Il in *Seongjangeui bom* is the mirror opposite of the above. Du-Jin already trusted Su-Il, perhaps too much. Therefore, when he felt he had been mistaken, his sense of betrayal was profound. Su-Il was, in fact, not the perfect farmer that Du-Jin had hoped him to be, since Su-Il's personal antagonism toward Hong-Bong led him to deliberately disrupt the B acid experiment. In the end, Su-Il's self-centered style of leadership meant that he neglected the fields and caused problems for the cooperative. Yet, Su-Il made it look like it was Hong-Bong's fault. Du-Jin was deeply disappointed, not only at Su-Il's cowardly act, but also at his own misplaced trust. Like everyone else in the cooperative (except for Yu-Yeong), Du-Jin had also been viewing Hong-Bong with slight suspicion, and had failed to take his commitment to agriculture seriously. Through Hong-Bong's example, Du-Jin realized that he had been captive to an old-fashioned idea of what farmers are supposed to look like and he subsequently revised his very understanding of farming in the context of North Korean socialism.

Through the two meetings between generations discussed above, we learn that North Korean socialism is facing a generational shift, and also that this shift is not a simple or easy one to achieve. The same goes for what I have called the "side" romances in each of the two novels referred to here: in both cases, we learn that in North Korea, just like anywhere else, human relations, gender relations, and friendships are formed through a complex web of connections and disconnections,

alliances and disputes, agreements and disagreements. While
many of these clashes are caused by personal characteristics
and qualities, such as Hong-Bong's hot-headedness, Seok's
aloofness and self-centered intellectual snobbery, or Su-Il's selfishness and arrogance, what underpins these are in fact the
political aspects of life and, notably, the political aspect of the
self. I shall now expand further on this argument, focusing on
Seok on the one hand and Yu-Yeong on the other.

Cultivation of the Self

Early on in this chapter, I stated that the language of the self in
North Korea was public. What I meant was that the language
individuals use to reflect upon their selves does not, paradoxically, belong to them: they do not possess it—it is, as strange
as it may sound, possessed by the Great Leader. In the final
segment of this chapter, I shall explore this point through a
discussion of the selves of Seok and Yu-Yeong, keeping a particularly close eye on the ways in which they refer to their
inner selves and their transformation. Through this exercise,
I hope to show the reader that the self in North Korea can only
be political, since—as tautologous as it may sound—only political life allows individuals to have a self. There is no self or
self-consciousness in life external to the political.

By the above statement, however, I do not mean that individuals in North Korea are not mutually related or connected.
Both Seok in *Yonghaegongdeul* and Yu-Yeong in *Seongjangui bom*
closely interact with the other protagonists, including their co-
workers, family members, friends, and respective lovers. But
the allegory of self-cultivation that these stories offer, as I shall
argue, asserts that the isolated space occupied by the self alone
is that which matters most in the context of self-formation and
self-discipline in North Korea: this space is needed as a precondition for a person—purified and most humbled, naked and
most unadorned—to face the Great Leader.

Seok is tormented by his protectiveness toward his father
and his father's audacious style of work. There is no doubt
that Seok loves his father dearly. He is proud of his father's

achievements and understands how highly his father is regarded by his fellow workers. He appreciates that it is thanks
to the trust that his father enjoys from the Party and from his
co-workers that Seok himself has had the privilege of studying
at college and graduate school. He is, therefore, determined to
repay his debts, both to the Party and to his father, by achieving
a groundbreaking technical innovation. In the process of doing
so, he finds his father's enthusiasm for his work bothersome,
as he has mentally consigned his father, again out of a sense
of protectiveness, to honorary retirement. This gets on Hyeon
Dae-Heung's nerves in a big way, and he increasingly finds his
son too bookish and out of touch with the realities of iron production. At the same time, he is strongly attracted to Ho-Cheol,
the bereaved son of a legendary ironworker killed during the
Korean War. Hyeon even secretively volunteers to protect Ho-
Cheol's honor by seeking a meeting with Ryeon-A's mother,
thus putting himself in an awkward position. Hyeon offers Ho-
Cheol advice in relation to the latter's romantic passion for
Ryeon-A, stating that an ironworker must trust other humans
with the utmost heartfelt sincerity. But Hyeon himself is unable
to trust his own son. In his mind, as the reader is led to believe
on a number of occasions, Seok is not quite worthy of being
called an ironworker's son.

Throughout the novel, despite confrontations occurring in
other relationships — between Seok and Eun-Ha, and between
Hyeon and Ryeon-A's mother, for example — none takes place
between Hyeon and Seok as father and son. While Hyeon critically comments on Seok behind his back, there is no tearful
catharsis or heart-warming confession session between the two.
The story reaches its climax when Hyeon declares Seok to be
the genuine son of an ironworker without much moving encounters between father and son. What brings about this outcome is Seok's self-examination. When Seok witnesses Eun-
Ha's tearful interaction with his mother, he sinks deeply into
self-examination, contemplating who he truly is and realizing
that he has been a coward in both work and love. After this
realization, he becomes a reformed man in his attitudes to-

ward work, Eun-Ha, his father, and above all, himself, finally becoming a man who is truly loyal to the Great Leader (Li Taek-Jin 1982, 223–32).

Contemplation of the self is an essential element in Yu-Yeong's own growth—as alluded to in the novel's title itself, *Seongjangui bom* (A Spring of Growth), the term "growth" here containing a double meaning, referring to both crop production and Yu-Yeong's personal development. Throughout the story, Yu-Yeong makes a number of errors when assessing the qualities of others. She trusts Kang Su-Il much too easily, allowing him to let her ride the cooperative's tractor without realizing that this constitutes an example of receiving special treatment. She dislikes and distrusts Hong-Bong, primarily due to his gruff attitude and abrupt manner. Although she has initially felt that Hong-Bong had a point with regard to irrigation improvement, Kang Su-Il is able to turn her opinion against him. Her Three Revolutions team supervisor Choe notices this weakness of Yu-Yeong (namely, believing others too readily and being unable to see the complex side of human nature), but lets her carry on her own journey of self-discovery. One day, Choe talks to her, emphasizing that he has no criticism of her, but that she must understand that humans have complex dimensions beyond the surface level of external presentation. With this cue, Yu-Yeong, just like Seok, enters into deep self-contemplation. Unlike Seok, however, Yu-Yeong initially resists, asking how others can treat her so heartlessly. As she carefully examines herself, however, she realizes that she herself has failed to understand the subtle connections and disconnections inside the cooperative and that her own lack of sophistication in dealing with diverse human characteristics has created a variety of problems, both small and large (Kim Sam-Bok 1982, 72–77).

Neither Seok nor Yu-Yeong seem counter-revolutionary or even remotely lacking in revolutionary passion or commitment. On the contrary, both individuals are presented as devoted, sincere, and hardworking young North Koreans. Yet, the stories require them to go farther—not simply in terms of workplace achievement, but more importantly in terms of self-cultivation. And, in fact, the latter is the condition for the former: only when one constantly engages in self-cultivation can one achieve higher goals in one's work, study, creative endeavors, and so on. In this process of contemplating one's own self, others (including one's family members or lover) are not important. What counts is understanding who one truly is.

But this exercise is not merely self-gratification. It has a clear goal and a set direction in the North Korean context: to elevate oneself, building a self that is more loyal, devoted, and committed to the Great Leader. For this reason, self-cultivation in North Korea is not a private, but a public endeavor.

What does this mean—to say that the cultivation of the self can only be public? First and foremost, the language used in relation to self-cultivation in North Korea does not deviate from the formula. While novels depict self-examination as the monologue of a given protagonist, in actual North Korean work units and school classrooms, self-contemplation is required to be conducted in public. As I stated at the beginning of this chapter, regular reviews (*bipangwa jagibipan*) are mandatory in North Korean life. From around age eight, all children are required to join the Young Pioneers; when they reach fifteen, they join the Socialist Youth League; when they join the workforce, each factory, agricultural cooperative, or other office setting has its own politico-organizational unit, or a small group of co-workers that form a review unit. (Such a unit would be called a cell in the case of the Workers' Party of Korea.) In these units, men and women are disciplined to reflect upon themselves—publicly revealing their weaknesses, analyzing them, and renewing their pledge to work toward a purer, stronger, and better self that is more devoted to the Great Leader.

While mutual criticism is offered to each worker by his or her co-workers inside the review unit, the most important element in this exercise is self-criticism. It is important to bear in mind that words used by an individual to criticize him or herself are not offered primarily to the unit, but to the Great

Leader. In other words, a renewed pledge to improve oneself is constantly offered to the Great Leader. Thus, North Korean criticism sessions (where the deeper self is revealed) are public displays of one's relationship with oneself in one's journey toward the cultivation of loyalty and purity in the eyes of Kim Il Sung. Individuals are supposed to feel the presence of the sacred being in order to reveal to this great entity every shortcoming that they happen to possess, so as to attain self-improvement. The tools deployed by those engaged in self-criticism (in other words, the language of self-criticism) cannot be invented by the critics themselves—such acts could be regarded as transgressions and become the object of criticism themselves. So, for example, if one were to simply repeat what was said to one by co-workers during a criticism session, such an act would be regarded as lacking in truthfulness. Words used in self-criticism come from North Korea's official publications, such as the works of Kim Il Sung and also its literary output. Years of criticism and self-criticism exercises give one the skills necessary for presenting the contents of one's private self-contemplation sessions in public in a form deemed to be proper and appropriate. Without this mutation, that is, turning private contemplation into public presentation, no true self-criticism can be attained in the North Korean context.

In this endeavor, the most important social value is the political. All other values—such as economic, ethical, cultural—are subordinate to the political. So, for example, love (both romantic and familial) is important only when it is politicized. Seok's realization that he has been a coward in both love and work carries meaning only because it is a reflection of the self's political unpreparedness. Yu-Yeong's anger toward Hong-Bong is relevant only because it is an example of politicized anger, directly connected to the concern over productivity and morals of the cooperative workers. The self that does not participate in political life has no reason to exist in North Korea. By the same token, the reason why the technical details of the novels that I have introduced in this chapter are not so important derives from this view: these novels are offered to the public not in order to help them understand how iron productivity can be improved or how agricultural cooperatives can more efficiently produce crops, but in order to emphasize that increased productivity or improved work efficiency does not matter unless it is politically meaningful.

The concepts of self and the individual are crucial in North Korea precisely because they are or need to be politicized. Unlike what is usually assumed to be the case in totalitarian societies, North Korean selves are individualized. Not as elements of a collective or group; individuals as individuals are each responsible for their own moral-ideological purity, discipline, and perfection in the eyes of the Great Leader in their journey to attain a political life (*jeongchijeok saengmyeong*). Thus, often, even one's own family members are irrelevant. The most valued and exclusive human connection in North Korean society is that between the individual (each isolated and in separation from the other) and the sovereign leader, Great Leader Kim Il Sung.

"Political life," argued North Korea's literary theorists in the 1980s, is the most decisive factor distinguishing new human beings fit to live in the age of *juche* from all other forms of human existence. As noted earlier in this volume, *juche* is shorthand for the philosophy of Kim Il Sung. Denoting master (*ju*) and body (*che*), the idea of *juche* insists on self-determination and self-reliance. "The age of *juche* is fundamentally distinguished from all historical ages that have preceded it. It posits the historical task of having to clarify the precise directions and methodology of constructing, creating, and developing a literary art that is compatible with the demands of the new age. . . ." (Han and Jeong 1983, 2). In this age of *juche*, a new type of human being is created: "The new human model that fits our time is that of the communistic human of the *juche* type. The *juche*-type communistic human [*juchehyeongui kongsanjuuijeok ingan*] is a passionate revolutionary and an authentic communist that possesses the purest and cleanest [sense of] loyalty and sincerity toward the *suryeong* [the Leader, Kim Il Sung] and the Party" (Han and Jeong 1983, 40).

For this new type of human, the utmost meaning is found in the context of political life: "Humans are social beings and therefore, for them, *jajuseong* [self-mastery] is life. . . . That a human being strives to realize his self-mastery corresponds to . . . enhancing one's political life. For humans, whose life is self-mastery, political and social life is more important than bio-physical life. If a human does not have a socially and politically meaningful life, he has no true life. . . ." (Han and Jeong 1983, 37). How does one obtain such a "political life"? The answer is: "Endless loyalty toward the Great *suryeong* is the most fundamental quality of a communist [of our age]. Only when one is loyal to the *suryeong* does one gain political life [*jeongchijeok saengmyeong*]" (Ryu and Kim 1983, 57).

One gains one's political life by being endlessly loyal (loving) to the *suryeong*, while only the *suryeong* can provide this life—a tautologous self-propagation, so to say: "Bio-physical life is given to humans by their parents, but political life is given to them by the *suryeong* and nurtured by the Party. Just as bio-physical life is unthinkable without parents, we cannot speak of human political life away from the bosom of the Party and the *suryeong*. The political life that our *inmin* [people] possesses today is the most valuable political life that is given by the Great *suryeong* and nurtured by the glorious Party" (Ryu and Kim 1983, 58).

The form of existence that embodies the most valuable form of life for humans, political life, is therefore the Leader, the *suryeong* himself: "The *suryeong* is the heart of the revolution and the brain of the *inmin*. . . . The *suryeong* is the utmost embodiment of the interests of the Party, the revolution, the working class, and the *inmin*, and his ideas are the collective will of the Party, the working class, and the *inmin*" (Han and Jeong 1983, 70). Thus, the *suryeong* is in the hearts and minds of each member of the population, yet at the same time, he leads them:

The *suryeong* is the possessor of the noblest humanity and the embodiment of the most benevolent nature. Because of this, the *suryeong* receives the *inmin*'s endless respect and reverence, its absolute trust

and support. . . . Our respected and beloved *suryeong*, Comrade Kim
Il Sung, embodies the greatest human qualities, equipped with the
warmest love and majestic revolutionary camaraderie for the *inmin*,
the biggest heart and capacity to tolerate and accept [anyone], endless
modesty and the simplest grace. Our respected and beloved *suryeong*
has attained the noblest [form of] communistic human love, [one]
never before attained by any other human. . . ." (Han and Jeong 1983,
86)

What we can see from the above discussion is biopolitics at
its apex in North Korea, where it is implied, paradoxically,
that one has to die loyally in order to live loyally for the Great
Leader. Put simply, since political life or *jeongchijeok saengmyeong* can only be proven by way of dying and at the same
time living forever—just like the Great Leader himself, who
now lives eternally because he is dead—one has to die in order
to show the utmost loyalty; in other words, the most valuable
political life is attained through death. This is the highest political goal to which selves in North Korea are supposed to
aspire. Yet, each individual is the only one capable of handing
down the final judgment on his or her own performance: ultimately, one is the only judge of one's own eternal political
life.

We can conclude that a highly sophisticated principle gov-
erns selves in North Korea without allowing them to deviate
from the path that they are supposed to follow constantly and
consistently. If, at the end of every day, one were to ask oneself whether one had conducted oneself during that day in a
responsible manner appropriate to an eternally loyal subject
of the Great Leader, thereby asking oneself whether one had
taken one more step closer to one's eternal political life/death,
every day would bring one yet another day closer to the end
of one's life. On the one hand, here is a brilliant governing
principle that keeps the population concerned about how to
die; on the other, the Great Leader is provided with a boundless *raison d'être* to exist for the sake of his own existence—
a sovereign being, as explained in the Introduction to this volume. Thus, the self's devotion to the task of becoming the best,

the purest, and the strongest in the eyes of the Great Leader perpetuates both the population and the Great Leader. It is neither coercion nor law enforcement, neither enslavement nor physical exploitation that directly enables North Korea to continue to exist today, but rather the way North Korean selves exist in relation to the Great Leader that eternally locks them in a perpetual cycle of self-examination.

CONCLUSION

On the Social and the Political

Eternal Winter of Festivity

As referred to in the Introduction, the Eskimo studied by Marcel Mauss lived two distinct forms of life—a dual morphology, to use his term, between the nomadic lifestyle of the summer months to the ritual-bound activities of the winter.

This description of the dual form of life followed by the Eskimo opens up an interesting perspective for looking at North Korean society today, although it would be more apt to deploy the concept of the political as opposed to the ritual or the religious. During the Eskimo winter, the social and the ritual closely overlapped. Even small events within the communal compound, such as a girl's menstruation, the conception or birth of a baby, or the death of a person, were now assumed to be public in nature. This contrasted with summertime, when these events were marked in a simple fashion within each nuclear family with minimal religious ceremony. As the nomadic summer gave way to the sedentary winter, and active hunting coming to an end with the onset of cooler weather, communal life came to be dominated less by economic pragmatism than by rituals and events with religious significance.

Drawing on the model described by Mauss, I would argue that North Korean society has entered an eternal "winter" stage. Regardless of economic crises, the political has taken hold of national life, that is to say, the excess of the political—

whether it be nuclear weapons or mass-participation games, it is the political meaning bestowed upon them that supersedes all other concerns in the nation. Deferential rituals accompany political ceremonies. Workers on organized shifts clean the area surrounding Kim Il Sung's gigantic, gilded statue in Pyongyang every day, for example. While cleaning, the workers maintain silence, a solemn countenance, and proper posture, showing the utmost respect toward the Eternal President. His mausoleum, named Geumsusan Memorial Palace, has become the ultimate destination for North Koreans being rewarded for hard work. When visiting, they remain silent and form orderly lines while touring Kim Il Sung's memorabilia, which is serenely exhibited inside the palace. Thus, every day, in a highly choreographed manner, North Koreans perform mortuary rites, which, paradoxically, celebrate Kim Il Sung's immortality.

As mentioned in the Introduction, North Korea is often depicted as a family state based on Confucian or neo-Confucian principles (and I have also noted that I do not concur with this view: see below). Needless to say, North Korea is not the first society to have been thus described. Perhaps the most useful analogy would be prewar Japanese society after the Meiji Restoration of 1868. Here, the emperor assumed a father-like role to the nation, with each and every individual inside the nation supposedly being descended from a single, unbroken, centuries-old imperial lineage (Gluck 1987). Household registration in prewar Japan included the records of multiple generations, not because the registry valued ancestor worship, but because entries served to prove each individual's membership of the larger "household nation" that was headed by the Emperor, the nation's founding father (Anderson 1974). Thus, unlike in Greek antiquity, with its distinction between *polis* and *oikos*, where political life was separated from economic and domestic life, prewar Japan saw even the most extreme aspects of personal life, such as one's marriage, sexual activity, and beliefs or sentiments, supposedly suffused with emperor-focused values. The use of kinship terms, as in references to the emperor as the benevolent father figure of the nation on one hand and to the people as the emperor's babies (*tennō no sekishi*) on the other, was a pronounced feature of this society. There, individuals belonged directly and ultimately to the emperor, bypassing other connections such as families and workplaces.

However, as I stated in the Introduction to this volume, I maintain that North Korea is not a Confucian or neo-Confucian family state. Furthermore, as I shall argue, it is also distinct from the prewar Japanese state. The traditional Korean kinship system, the foundations of which rest firmly on Confucian principles, categorically denies the conflation of the national founder and the ancestor of each lineage. In the case of the father of a royal court official passing away, for example, the official had to suspend his service to the king and perform a mortuary rite for his own father. This contradiction between allegiance to one's lineage and to one's king did not exist in post-Meiji Japan. Japanese family names were seen as gifts bestowed by the emperor, not as having derived from the ancestors and history of each lineage. Thus, ultimately, in prewar Japan, the nation was deemed a blood-related collective; it is not far fetched to think that this conceptual foundation may be correlated to the fact that Japanese traditionally had rather a lax attitude toward first-cousin marriage. By way of contrast, in Korea, marriage between individuals from the same lineage, *bongwan*, is to this day seen as a calamity-inviting taboo, despite the fact that the number of *bongwan* is rather limited. Interestingly, North Korea abolished the lineage system, obscuring everyone's *bongwan* and viewing ancestor worship as old-fashioned and belonging to the pre-revolutionary era. This does not mean, however, that the North Koreans have now entered into one massive form of lineage with Kim Il Sung as the original ancestor. As we saw in Chapter 1 of this book, North Koreans submit to Kim's authority via love for the sacred, not through any sense of obligation to respect a lineage-based hierarchy authority. Although the kinship term is used in North Korea, calling Kim Il Sung the Father, this is close to the religious usage than familiar address. In this case, therefore, the term "father" inspires awe and sacredness rather than familial relation. By way of contrast, in Confucian and other patriarchal and patrilineal kinship systems, one does not have to love the father—filial piety in itself is separate from love. Instead, often the contrary is the case: the father can posit a lethal peril to the son.

In ancient Rome, if a son that had committed a crime were to be executed by his father according to the principle of *patria potestas* that accorded a father certain rights and powers with respect to members of his *familia*, this son was deemed *homo sacer*, a sacred or accursed human. The killing of such a person was not considered as homicide. A *homo sacer* was, therefore, a human, but his status as such was only validated by way of his being killed. In Rome, a guilty son could be turned into *homo sacer* by his father—and by his father alone (Agamben 1998; Frier, McGinn, and Lidov 2003). As sovereign of his household, he was placed in an exceptional position within his *familia*, as no one within the household held the right to kill him.

In the Confucian kinship system, in a similar way to the Roman *familia*, the father has absolute authority. As a classical patriarchal and patrilineal system, the Confucian kinship system justifies the exercise of extreme power on the part of the father. The clearest example would be that of King Yeongjo of Korea (r. 1724–1776), who ordered his son, the then-27-year-old Prince Sado, to enter a rice chest in 1762 and stay in it until he was pronounced dead eight days later (Haboush 1996). If one were not a royal prince, one would have one's own father as well as the king to obey. Such is the Confucian hierarchy. It would be logically impossible to have a Confucian family state, in which there is no clash between the authority of the father and that of the sovereign and the founder of the nation is deemed to be everybody's ancestor. Just as in Rome, the Confucian household has its own private law.

In North Korea, this kind of private father figure is missing: individuals are directly subjected to Kim Il Sung the sovereign. For, he is the one and only being that can truly grant himself an exceptional position. The lack of Confucian patriarchal private law within the household and lineage renders it difficult to deem North Korea Confucian, as such absence of ancestral authority—let alone *patria potestas*—constitutes a fundamental antithesis to Confucianism. Thus, calling North Korea Confucian is based on misunderstanding or incomplete understanding of both Confucianism and North Korean social structure.

If this is the case, why not then call North Korea a family state by equating it with Imperial Japan, where the sacrosanct emperor was the only sovereign/father to whom every individual had to directly submit—that is, bypassing the Roman/Confucian father? Indeed, I have regarded the Japanese emperor as such and, along with what Ruth Benedict largely supposed, I have argued that atrocities and brutalities committed by Japanese soldiers before and during World War II were closely connected with the logic that held the emperor to be the sole holder of national sovereignty: the most heinous crimes against humanity were committed in the name of the emperor as honorable acts to glorify him (Ryang 2006, Chapter 2). In this case, the Japanese emperor appears to come close to Kim Il Sung in that he was a sacrosanct being for the Japanese, just as Kim continues to be for North Koreans. Further, the emperor was regarded as the originator of the Japanese nation, the father to all, and the ancestor to every Japanese. Observing the North Korean reaction to Kim Il Sung's death in 1994, Heonik Kwon writes that: "The death of Kim Il Sung meant the death of a father for many North Koreans, and the drama of collective bereavement [. . . was] in fact, in an important sense, a *family* affair" (2010, 15; emphasis in original). As thousands of citizens rushed to Pyongyang upon hearing the news of Kim's death, many in the West found their public display of devastated grief a bizarre yet powerful phenomenon.

I do not, however, see this as a family matter; rather, the human tide of wailing mourners has more in common with the Pietà, the sorrow of Mary holding Christ's body in her arms. Her sorrow is excruciating. Jesus was her son, who should not have been taken away from her in such a cruel and untimely manner. While Mary and Jesus were mother and

son, their relationship was not merely one based on kinship —
together, they were holy, the source of all beauty, virtue, and
goodness. The picture of wailing North Koreans, lining up
quietly, yet demonstrating the gravest pain and sorrow, was
not comparable to the sight of grieving family members at a
funeral; it was a reenactment of holiness, and if the notion of
family had to be evoked, it would have to be that of a holy
family: this was a mass-scale Pietà. And, just as the Gospels tell
of Jesus rising from the dead three days after crucifixion, Kim
Il Sung rose from the dead on the very day that he had died,
July 8, 1994. Resurrected, he could now assume the office of
Eternal President. Thus, rather than mourning in bereavement,
today, North Koreans are celebrating his eternal life.

No single emperor of Japan was given this kind of reverence.
When the Meiji Emperor died in 1912, he was succeeded by
his heir, the Taishō Emperor. It turned out that this emperor
had a mental illness and was not fit to remain on the throne for
an extended period. After a mere thirteen-year reign, he was
pronounced dead and replaced by the Shōwa Emperor, whose
rule from 1926 to 1989 was the longest in post-Restoration
Japanese history. Emperors are, therefore, replaced one by one,
each completely interchangeable with another. In North Korea,
as I have argued in the Introduction to this book, Kim Jong Il
has not replaced Kim Il Sung. For, Kim Il Sung is the one and
only Eternal President, the supreme, sacred being. As I stated,
the use of kinship terms such as Father Marshal or *abeoji wonsunim* in this sense has more in common with religious practice
than with kinship relations. While Catholic priests are called
Father, they do not replace God the Father. Similarly, while
Kim Jong Il is called *abeoji janggunnim*, Father General, he does
not replace Kim Il Sung the Eternal President. It is certainly
noticeable that elements of Christian fellowship exist in the
way North Koreans aspire to be accepted within Kim Il Sung's
bosom. Ultimately, however, as I have shown in the preceding
pages, North Koreans are alone in their individual struggles
to achieve ideological purity. And unlike Christianity, which
is truly transnational and transcontinental in the context of

today's globalizing world, the notion of Kim Il Sung as a sacred being is only valid within the context of North Korean nationalism. After all, North Koreans do not strive for piety; they strive for a political life through the demonstration of eternal loyalty for the *suryeong*, the Great Leader.

Another important difference between the Japanese emperor and Kim Il Sung can be found in the ethico-ideological foundations respectively underpinning each nation. Whereas post-Meiji Japan was a newly unified polity that emerged unequivocally as one nation, albeit through the tension-ridden and often forceful and unjustifiable annexation of Japan's peripheral territories as well as outcastes and other unprivileged people, to call North Korea one nation would actually contradict its ethico-ideological foundation as a nation—as paradoxical as this may sound. This is related to the ongoing partition of Korea into two nations. Insisting on Kim Il Sung being the national ancestor would forego North Korea's 60-year commitment to national reunification. When one half of its own nation is not recovered, Kim Il Sung cannot be the ancestor of all Koreans: we never find any examples in North Korea's official discourse in which Kim Il Sung is described as such. Kim Il Sung cannot be the ancestor of North Koreans only, either, since this would be equivalent to abandoning the southern half of the nation. When North Koreans call Kim Il Sung *minjogui taeyang* ("sun of the nation"), this includes the entire Korean nation. The establishment of such a nation, however, has yet to be realized. Furthermore, *minjogui taeyang* never implies that Kim Il Sung is the generator of the nation. Instead, its promissory connotation is that he is the sun that will eventually shine on all parts of the Korean peninsula. In the case of prewar Japan, by contrast, there was no need for such a promissory note. Although the reality was different— due to the forced annexation of Okinawa and the unjustifiable treatment of the Ainu, for example—on the level of public discourse, Meiji Japan was able to emerge as one nation, over which the emperor presided as the head of one large household.

Ever since North Korean forces crossed the 38th parallel on June 25, 1950, the nation's *raison d'être* has consistently been identified as the achievement of reunification. The importance of this goal for North Korea should not be underestimated. Unlike in South Korea, where a post-totalitarian, neo-liberal turn more or less removed the concept of reunification from any possible role in its future, in North Korea, national reunification is alive and well as the ultimate existential goal. With this in mind, I would like to reiterate my position: Kim Il Sung is North Korea's sacrosanct sovereign, not its ancestor. Every North Korean is supposed to strive to get closer to him, in mind and body, and to sacrifice oneself if required in order to gain eternal life and join the Eternal President. According to this logic, each individual stands alone, face to face with his own self vis-à-vis the Great Leader. No one, not even one's father, stands between him or her and the great being.

Totalitarianism

In his classic study of totalitarianism, Peter Drucker explores the cases of Italy and Germany as they moved down their respective paths towards fascism and Nazism. Prominent characteristics he cites in distinguishing them from other Western European nations in the post–World War I period include a shared history of what we might call top-down revolution and the fact that both had only recently attained unified nationhood. According to him, therefore, neither Italy nor Germany had a democratic tradition, and democratic values were greatly overshadowed by nationalist tendencies (Drucker 1995, Chapter 5). More or less the same can be said of Japan during the period from the Meiji Restoration until its disastrous defeat in World War II in 1945. A relatively recent national unification, a strong focus on nationalism, and the absence of a mass, grassroots revolution — these are all characteristics that historians of the Meiji Restoration have consistently emphasized.

In a similar way to each of the above three nations, North Korea placed a strong emphasis on nationalism from the first day of its existence. But what fundamentally differentiates it from these other countries is that it was formed when (or because) a line was abruptly and arbitrarily drawn across the Korean peninsula by foreign nations in the wake of World War II. Furthermore, unlike in the cases of Germany, Italy, and Japan, which all suffered devastating defeats at war, North Korea did not participate in World War II as an independent nation. The only war North Korea knows to this day is a civil war that it initiated in 1950, a mere two years after its establishment as a nation-state, with the intention of reunifying the Korean nation. As I argued in Chapter 2, this war and North Korea's self-proclaimed victory (in the sense that American-led South Korean forces could not conquer the North) as well as its material devastation at the hands of the United States, consequentially strengthened, rather than destroyed, North Koreans' fundamental commitment to the leadership of Kim Il Sung.

By far the most important difference between North Korea and classical totalitarian regimes is found in the target of loyalty and commitment. Hannah Arendt writes about totalitarianism as follows:

> The disturbing factor in the success of totalitarianism is rather the true selflessness of its adherents: it may be understandable that a Nazi or Bolshevik will not be shaken in his conviction by crimes against people who do not belong to the movement or are even hostile to it; but the amazing fact is that neither is he likely to waver when the monster begins to devour its own children and not even if he becomes a victim of persecution himself, if he is framed and condemned, if he is purged from the party and sent to a forced-labor or a concentration camp. On the contrary, to the wonder of the whole civilized world, he may even be willing to help in his own prosecution and frame his own death sentence if only his status as a member of the movement is not touched. (1974, 307)

Here, it can be seen that followers are committed to a cause or a movement, not a person, let alone a sacred being. Given our usual understanding of totalitarianism, then, how should we attempt to understand a society such as North Korea? Its ethico-spiritual focus on Kim Il Sung as a sacred being is somewhat different from commitment to a cause, as such.

It is important that we remind ourselves that North Korea started off as a more classical totalitarian state with a whole-hearted commitment to what Slavoj Žižek calls "the emancipatory struggle" (2008, 183). In its aspiration for complete national-territorial integrity, total unification of the Korean people, and the achievement of a genuine unitary national entity, it bore an acute resemblance to pre–World War II Germany and Italy. There was, however, an important difference. Rather than being totalitarian or fascist, imperialist or racially purist, North Korea was born as the offshoot of a Marxist state. Until around 1972, the 60th birthday of Kim Il Sung, North Korea viewed its ideological origins as residing in Marxism, and more precisely, Marxism-Leninism (*Makseu Renin juui*). Oversized portraits of Marx, Engels, Lenin, and Stalin were carried aloft in state-organized parades. During the period from the late 1960s through to the early 1970s, however, all references to Marx, Engels, Lenin, and Stalin, and indeed Marxism itself, disappeared as North Korea refashioned its ideological system as *yuilsasang chegye* (the singular ideological system), based on the *juche* ideology of Kim Il Sung. Just like Mao Zedong, Kim Il Sung reformulated Marxism (or more precisely, the Soviet version of it) as being inadequate to be directly applied to the North Korean revolution. We must not forget that Mao Zedong's refashioning of Marxism was, in the 1960 words of Emmanuel Levinas (quoted in Žižek 2008, 177), "the yellow peril" that involved "a radical strangeness" in historical incidences of Marxist events. The "Asiatic" refashioning of Marxism was strange, unconventional, or maybe even scary for many (on both left and right alike), and North Korea was one example.

So, even as a Marxist national state, North Korea's first steps were seen as strange in the eyes of the outside world. And, after its adoption of *juche* as its sole ideological system, its strangeness stood out even within the Marxist bloc. This system's prioritization of the mental, the spiritual, and the political in the creation of a revolutionary human already represented a mutation from Soviet-brand dialectical materialism.

Define juche

Furthermore, while North Korea initially adopted a Soviet-style planned economy, starting from its post–Korean War three-year plan and moving to five- and seven-year plans, for example, by the mid-1970s, these plans were not acted upon or achieved. By the 1980s, these economic plans became quite irrelevant in North Korea. This was because politics became prioritized over economics, as if putting into practice the Althusserian neo-Marxist notion of overdetermination between the base and superstructure on the national level, prioritizing the superstructure (ideology, politics, and culture, for example) over bread and butter. This type of "end of economics" model is also a prominent characteristic of classical totalitarianism, as can be seen in the very title of Drucker's book, *The End of Economic Man.*

Once North Korea abandoned Marxism-Leninism as its ideological foundation, it became much easier for the world to denounce it as inhumane, weird, and above all, totalitarian. In the center of this, the world finds its sacred treatment of Kim Il Sung as the strangest and most anti-democratic element. It incurs even greater wrath from the West, since this practice resorts to the discourse of love. In the words of Žižek:

Which political regimes in the twentieth century legitimized their power by invoking the people's love for their leader? The so-called "totalitarian" ones. Today, it is only and precisely the North Korean regime which continually invokes the infinite love of the Korean people for Kim Il Sung and Kim Yong Il [*sic*] and, *vice versa*, the radiating love of the Leader for his people, expressed in continuous grace. [. . .] The very fact that we, the subjects of power, are alive is proof of the power's infinite mercy. This is why the more "terroristic" a regime is, the more its leaders are praised for their infinite love, goodness, and mercy. Adorno was right to emphasize that, in politics, love is invoked precisely when another (democratic) legitimization is lacking: loving a leader means you love him for what he is, not for what he does. (Žižek 2010, 98–99)

Aside from the discourse of love, just as in Drucker's depiction of totalitarianism, North Koreans are sometimes rewarded in a this-worldly manner in their struggle to achieve approximation with Kim Il Sung. And such rewards take on distinctly non-economic forms: the honor of being photographed with Kim, for example, or of being invited on an excursion to Mount Baekdu, seen by North Koreans as a sacred site of revolutionary pilgrimage due to its close association with Kim Il Sung's anti-Japanese guerrilla warfare activities and its designation as the birthplace of Kim Jong Il. In previous chapters, we have seen the protagonists in various North Korean fictional works being given this kind of reward: in *Yonghaegongdeul*, the elder protagonist Hyeon was given the honor of attending a national gathering held in Pyongyang as a representative of his factory; in the same novel, Ho-Cheol received a state invitation to participate in a revolutionary pilgrimage tour that included visits to Mount Baekdu and other sacred places touched by the revolutionary footprints of Kim Il Sung (see Chapter 3 above). Today, as mentioned earlier, the most desired reward is a chance to visit Geumsusan Memorial Palace and receive the honor of viewing of the now eternally enshrined Kim Il Sung. This kind of non-economic reward, according to Drucker, is characteristic of totalitarianism. He writes:

It is a moot question whether totalitarianism is capitalist or socialist. It is, of course, neither. Having found both invalid, fascism seeks a society beyond socialism and capitalism that is not based upon economic considerations. Its only economic interest is to keep the machinery of industrial production in good working order. At whose expense and for whose benefit is a subsidiary question; for economic consequences are entirely incidental to the main social task. The apparent contradiction of simultaneous hostility to the capitalist supremacy of private profit as well as to socialism, is, though muddle-headed, a consistent expression of fascism's genuine intentions. [. . .]

Mussolini and Hitler, like so many revolutionary leaders before them, probably neither understand [*sic*] the nature of their revolutions nor ever intended to go beyond denouncing the "abuses" of either side. But [. . .] social necessity forced them to invent new noneconomic satisfactions and distinctions and, finally, to embark upon a social policy which aims at constructing a comprehensive noneconomic society side by side with, and within, an industrial system of production. (1995, 132)

The above passages seem to capture what we have seen above in our examination of North Korean literature. Production is a serious concern, and the men and women in the novels examined in this book are motivated to go above and beyond their job descriptions in order to bring about increased efficiency, output, and abundance. Yet, in the novels above, what fundamentally matters is not the actual outcome of production or cost-effectiveness, but the level of political, mental, and emotional commitment to the Leader and the strengthening of such commitment, which sustains "a comprehensive noneconomic society side by side with, and within, an industrial system of production."

By the same token, punishment in totalitarian society also takes on non-economic forms, most vividly represented in the example of the concentration camp. Concentration camps are fundamentally non-utilitarian in structure, their labor not contributing to construction or production, instead being used purely as a means of politically dominating the punished. Today, the world generally understands that concentration camps exist in North Korea, although little is known of their scale, severity, or the size of the population incarcerated within such establishments. Non-economic rewards and non-utilitarian forms of punishment—do these make North Korea a totalitarian state?

While, on one level, Drucker's description fits North Korean society today, on another, his words are challenged by the complex realities of the present-day world. Today, we have so-called neo-liberal states where, in the name of national security, people with non-conventional religious practices, lifestyles, sexual orientations, or social norms face disturbingly substantial risks and even threats to their individual freedom. Furthermore, this condition is augmented in times of war or when war-like conditions exist. A good example is presented by the war against terror initiated by the Bush-Cheney administration (2001–2009) in the United States. Under the Patriot Act, institutionalized after the attacks on the World Trade Center towers in lower Manhattan by Al Qaeda militants on September 11, 2001, religious and racial minorities in the United States became subjected to closer scrutiny. Subsequently we learned that such scrutiny was not only directed at these so-called minorities, but extended to the entire population, as became clear following the revelation that the National Security Agency had been assigned to randomly wiretap citizens in the name of homeland security. As a result of such actions, people were led to doubt whether the civil liberties, civil rights, and other democratic values that the United States had taken for granted still rested on solid ground. In fact, American democracy proved to be extremely fragile after the 9/11 attacks: not only did the invasion of foreign states by the United States become justified, but the domestic policies of the nation and, indeed, the domestic life of the citizenry came to be placed under the close surveillance of unknowable government agencies. As Žižek remarks, if one of the clearest signs of totalitarianism is a lack of access to others' (and public) knowledge about oneself, the United States under the previous administration seems to fit the bill as comprehensively as might North Korea (2002, 63).

Furthermore, unlike the time Drucker first wrote the above book (1939), industrial capitalism proved to be not as completely utilitarian or single-minded in terms of economic efficiency and productivity as had previously been thought. The market economy appears to be heavily dependent on psychological factors, with rises and falls in the stock market seeming to be as much a product of the sentimental reactions of buyers and sellers to political news items as pragmatic responses to hard economic data, such as figures showing variations in the unemployment rate. After all, while capitalism tries to maintain a distinction between economic and political spheres, this has proven impossible in the past and will continue to be so in the future. In today's globalizing economy, it is becoming increasingly clear that economic rationalism is not the only force driving business. There are other factors in the mix— protectionist tendencies, the desire for political correctness, environmental concerns, and humanitarian considerations, for example—and these work in mutually helpful or antagonistic ways, depending on the particular circumstances, with little centralized orchestration or predictability.

Rather than simply classifying North Korea as a totalitarian society (or otherwise), I therefore propose to adopt a strategy that focuses on the dominant form of social relations in today's North Korea: the political. Moreover, I would argue that in North Korea, the political exercises its dominance by overlapping with the social—in North Korea, there are no social relations that are devoid of political concerns. When studying the culture of the ancient Inca, Maurice Godelier, once counted among the neo-Marxists in French philosophical circles, theorized that given the utmost importance of collective rituals in this culture, the ritual mode was the dominant form of relations in that society (Godelier 1996). Indeed, according to Godelier, ritual constituted the defining factor of Inca social relations. Applying this understanding to Mauss's Eskimo example, we may say that while social relations connected with hunting activities were dominant in Eskimo summer life, those related to rituals became dominant during the winter months. Paralleling this, we may try to understand North Korean society as a society where political relations define social relations. More concretely, social relations, including kinship relations, workplace relations, romantic relations, school camaraderie, and other forms of interpersonal and intra-group relations, are dominated by political concerns related to how one can be more loyal and dedicated to the Leader. This dominance is precisely why I deem North Korea as having an excess of the political.

On Literature

In North Korea today, the domestic is political and the private is public. We have seen in the preceding chapters that political concerns fully penetrate family life and romantic relations. This does not mean that North Koreans are devoid of feelings of kinship and romance. On the contrary, men and women in North Korea are expected to get married and have children.

The ideal match between prospective spouses is thought to be one based on romantic relations developed in the path to be loyal for the Great Leader, rather than on arranged courtship. In *Yonghaegongdeul* (introduced in Chapter 3 above), Ryeon-A's mother's scheme of marrying her daughter with a physician in Pyongyang is thwarted by Ryeon-A's own choice of Ho-Cheol, an ironworker. Ryeon-A's choice is given an exemplary position in the story, as opposed to certain "good conditions" that her mother proposes, her mother being depicted as insufficiently revolutionary as compared to ironworkers including the protagonist Hyeon Dae-Heung. The top criterion for loving someone in North Korea is, moreover, as I argued in Chapter 1 above, politically determined. That is to say, it is based on the extent to which the other is dedicated and devoted to the Leader. Love that does not contribute to politicization of individuals or more precisely, attainment of political life by individuals, is seen as tainted with bourgeois backward ideology and harmful for both individuals themselves and the nation itself.

On the basis of this, then, how should we view the role of literature in North Korea? In North Korea, as the reader may have perceived, journalism as such does not exist. From the earliest days of the nation's history, North Korean authorities have seriously discouraged the inclusion of negative news in the media. Referred to as *ocherk* or "sketch" (from the Russian эскиз), North Korean journalism is replete with news stories rather than news items. What I mean is that in North Korea, press or media coverage is basically allegorical: it has a clear and distinct purpose of ideological education and as such, news reports are only vehicles for political messages. News can be understood as, shall we say, a series of fables or morality tales in North Korea, which primarily serve to educate the masses — that is, educate them in certain political values. The concept of press objectivity that is often celebrated by the Western media (but that is basically unattainable) is absent from the North Korean media. This is perhaps not news to many: as we understand it, North Korea is full of propaganda.

But, there is one aspect to this propaganda enterprise that needs to be stressed: it is primarily dedicated to the Leader. During the last two decades or so, especially reflecting the influx of consumer electronics from Japan brought or sent by Koreans living there, television sets have become available in North Korea. While these remain difficult to obtain for families and individuals, they are one of the most sought after items. Further, television sets are found in public places in North Korea's urban locales, most prominently in Pyongyang. *Bodo* or news programs, are usually the top item to be broadcast. As in the West, newscasters are formally dressed and well presented, but the way they read out the news items is distinctly different from that of Western newsreaders. North Korean television newsreaders recite the news, rather than read it, and they deliver it item by item, emotively uttering their words with eyes cast upward as if they are kneeling down in front of the Leader.

This politicized and ritual-like aspect of the North Korean media does produce, somewhat paradoxically, one important effect for us to consider when dealing with North Korean literature: it augments literature's instructional role as well as its informative function. Literature provides the vocabulary required for North Koreans to lead a proper political life. And it reminds the people what kind of line they should be taking when participating in self-criticism sessions at their work units or what kind of wording is preferred and accepted as up-to-date when discussing study material in public, for example. In other words, in a society like North Korea's, the difference between the news media and literature is diminished: news presentations are rendered exponentially closer to poetic or artistic recitals, primarily for the Great Leader and only secondarily for the people, while literature is fashioned into a finite resource for the transmission of legitimate words and expressions. As discussed in the previous chapter, since North Korean society has many occasions for individuals to explore their internal selves and present accounts of them in public, the role played by literature and the vocabulary set it offers is crucial in keeping North Korean individuals politically safe and conforming to the norm.

In this kind of setting, we need a new tool to analyze the social role of literature. In the societies with which we are familiar, literature belongs to the liberal arts, considered as education for the sake of education and knowledge for the sake of knowledge. It enriches one's appreciation of life, of beauty, and of humanity. In a society such as North Korea, the social role of literature bears a distinctly practical element. That is to say, it helps citizens to be able to handle the proper words, vocabulary, and discourse to lead one's political life and by extension, to ensure one's political survival. In this sense, literature is no longer a tool for life's enrichment, but rather a tool for survival, a necessary element in helping one to maintain proper political conduct.

In this book, we have seen how literature helped North Koreans shift the nature of their relations with Kim Il Sung. During the 1970s, Kim Il Sung was more like a man—a great man, but nevertheless, a human. During the 1980s, humanly depictions of Kim gradually disappeared and he became more abstract and aloof, this tendency augmenting his sacredness. As I argued in the foregoing pages, this subtle shift prepared North Koreans for the 1990s and the ultimate humanly death of Kim Il Sung, who was then declared to be eternally alive and forever presiding over North Korea as its Eternal President. His saintly immortality would not have been rationally acceptable unless society had pre-structured this vision, and literature played an important role in this mission. At the same time, while it has functioned as a constitutive part of such a vision, literature has also reflected the discursive fabric in North Korea where Kim Il Sung is positioned as a sacred being in the innermost terrain of one's self-reflections and self-contemplation.

Postscript

North Korea has acquired myriad labels, having been variously referred to as a rogue state (Triplett 2004), the Hermit Kingdom (Lerner 2008), or the Kim Dynasty (Martin 2004), to cite only a few examples. It has been counted as one of the world's two remaining examples of totalitarian states alongside Turkmenistan (Dewi 2008) and its form of government has been called "National Stalinism," along with Romania under Nicolae Ceauşescu (Chen and Lee 2007). In today's globalizing world, the contemporary conscience would insist that we take a moral responsibility to engage with regimes such as that of North Korea. And, this certainly does not mean simply name-calling or labeling it or speculating that its regime is "close to its dead end" (Chen and Lee 2007, 473). Rather, we might first look at this nation, and look at it again *(re-specere)* as a society inhabited by humans. People there may be placed under a radically unique form of cultural logic, or values that are far removed from those found in the so-called West, as I have shown in this book. Nevertheless, as banal as this may be to state, one point is clear: they are fellow humans and, as such, are deserving of serious attention—academic, humanitarian, political, economic, or otherwise. While at this time North Korea may be the last remaining citadel of humanity that anthropologists have yet to enter, this may not be the case for too much longer. In the meantime, our imagination, intellectual astuteness, and compassion will help us to humanize what has otherwise been imagined and portrayed as an arid and decrepit nation.

So far, so good. Granting humanity to this last-remaining social scientific enigma would seem the right thing to do, at least for any fair-minded individual. But, in order to do this, we must first recognize the difference (and hence, challenge) that North Korean society presents to the rest of the world. Without this recognition, we will not be able to humanize this society. And, paradoxically, this recognition may be predicated upon the prior admission that this society may not be so human after all.

By 2011, we are told, over 20,000 North Korean refugees had settled in South Korea. Already, South Korean anthropologists and other researchers are "studying" them, resorting to the Mead-esque "culture at a distance" method, asking them questions about North Korea and trying to figure out what North Korean society is like. No doubt, this body of research will allow us to learn more about North Korea, and we will hear more demands to humanize these North Koreans. Indeed, they will be humanized by way of linking them directly with some research questions, hypotheses, critiques, and other paraphernalia of modern social science. By so doing, we will be able to tame their "radical strangeness" through this process, making them more like ourselves. Indeed, upon their arrival in South Korea, North Koreans are firstly housed in a government-operated camp-like institution, where they are given educational courses to familiarize themselves with South Korean social convention. In other words, they are *rehabilitated*—I would even say rehabilitated to what we consider to be humanity (see Ryang forthcoming, Chapter 3). For, regardless of whether North Korean political indoctrination is successful or not, these individuals come from a society where the dominant public discourse bears radically different values from our own: there, death for the Leader is not feared, instead deemed as the utmost honor, the supreme form of happiness that a human can attain.

In humanizing North Koreans, in accepting them as members of our own humanity, to what extent is North Korea's fundamental difference recognized in South Korea and the world at large beyond the superficial level of negotiating behavior at the Six-Party Talks or in the presentation of its public face, for example? Such recognition requires a radical alteration of our own values as well. After all, when do North Koreans become human (again) in our view? When they start owning private property? When they start going to the House of God? When they start calculating profit over loss? When they start taking advantage of a welfare system? Or when they start realizing that to be successful is to become rich? On one level, they have already done all these in North Korea, but according to a radically alternative logic. Yet, this does not mean that we can therefore simply replace the apparatus and suddenly, a new human being is born, a human that is fit to survive in a capitalist environment.

Humanizing North Koreans is perhaps the easy part of our dealings with North Korea, since it can be done on a purely discursive level. A more difficult question needs to be asked by momentarily stepping into the domain of morality: is the humanity of North Koreans so different that it lies beyond or outside of our repertoire of humanity? In other words, could North Korean society be inhuman and by extension, could North Koreans be non-human? This is a terrifying question to ask our conscience, because, for want of a better choice of words, we feel sorry — sorry for North Koreans that are subjected to illogical dictatorship, totalitarian madness, and extreme forms of poverty. And, of course, there is nothing wrong in recognizing a tragedy in the misfortune of others if indeed, those others recognize it as such as well. And here, I gravely hesitate in making a facile and optimistic conclusion about our capability to humanize North Korean society or any other society deemed to be so fundamentally different from our own. The answer is not clear to me. For, it seems that we are still drowning in an abyss, a bottomless sea, trying to figure out the limits of our own moral capability.

I began this book by setting out my position as a non-apologetic one that sought neither to advocate for nor to demonize North Korea. In closing, I would like to re-invoke that position. In doing so, I would also like to add a renewed emphasis that any endeavor to understand a society such as North Korea represents a challenge, for the Right, the Left, and the watered-down versions thereof: conservatives and liberals. Liberal democracy faces a more profound challenge in dealing with North Korea, as the latter's cultural logic is fundamentally alien (*not* opposed) to the values that the former cherishes, including individual freedom, tolerance, and diversity. My modest hope is that this book has helped the reader to gain some points of reference to use when looking — and looking again — at North Korea.

Reference Matter

References

Agamben, Giorgio. 1998. *Homo Sacer: Sovereign Power and Bare Life.* Stanford, CA: Stanford University Press.

———. 2000. *Means Without End: Notes on Politics.* Minneapolis, MN: University of Minnesota Press.

Anderson, Perry. 1974. *Lineages of the Absolutist State.* London: New Left Books.

Arendt, Hannah. 1974. *The Origins of Totalitarianism.* New York: Harcourt and Brace.

Armstrong, Charles. 2004. *The North Korean Revolution, 1945–1950.* Ithaca, NY: Cornell University Press.

———. 2009. "Socialism, Sovereignty, and the North Korean Exception." In *North Korea: Toward a Better Understanding,* ed. S. Ryang, 41–56. Lanham, MD: Lexington Books.

Banner, Lois. 2003. *Intertwined Lives: Margaret Mead, Ruth Benedict, and Their Circle.* New York: Knopf.

Bataille, Georges. 1993. *The Accursed Share, Volume II and III,* New York: Zone Books.

Beeman, William. 2000. "Introduction: Margaret Mead, Cultural Studies, and International Understanding." In *The Study of Culture at a Distance,* ed. M. Mead and R. Métraux, xiv–xxxi. New York: Berghahn Books.

Berlin, Isaiah. 1958. *Four Essays on Liberty.* Oxford, UK: Oxford University Press.

Chen, Chen, and Ji-Yong Lee. 2007. "Making Sense of North Korea: 'National Stalinism' in Comparative-Historical Perspective." *Communist and Post-Communist Studies* 40(4): 459–75.

Cheung, Seong-Chang. 2000. "Stalinism and Kimilsungism: A Comparative Analysis of Ideology and Power." *Asian Perspective* 24(1): 133–61.

Choe Eun-Hui and Sin Sang-ok. 1988. *Jogugeun jeo haneul jeo meolli* (The fatherland is under that sky so far away). Pacific Palisades, CA: Pacific Artist Corporation.

Choe Hak-Su. 1970. "Keun simjang" (A big heart). In *Binnaneun jauk* (Brilliant footsteps), 28–57. Pyongyang: Munye chulpansa.

Choe Sang-Sun. 1974. "Uri hakkyo" (Our school). In *Jeolmeun sedae* (Young generations), 5–24. Pyongyang: Munye chulpansa.

Chung, Steve. 2009. "The Split Screen: Sin Sang-ok in North Korea." In *North Korea: Toward a Better Understanding*, ed. S. Ryang, 85–109. Lanham, MD: Lexington Books.

Clifford, James. 1988. *The Predicament of Culture: Twentieth-Century Ethnography*. Cambridge, MA: Harvard University Press.

Clifford, James, and George Marcus, eds. 1986. *Writing Culture: The Poetics and Politics of Ethnography*. Berkeley, CA: University of California Press.

Cumings, Bruce. 1981. *The Origins of the Korean War, Volume I: Liberation and the Emergence of Separate Regimes, 1945–1947*. Princeton, NJ: Princeton University Press.

———. 1990. *The Origins of the Korean War, Volume II: The Roaring of the Cataract, 1948–1950*. Princeton, NJ: Princeton University Press.

———. 1994. *War and Television*. London: Verso.

———. 2004. *North Korea: Another Country*. New York: New Press.

Demick, Barbara. 2009. *Nothing to Envy: Ordinary Lives in North Korea*. New York: Spiegel and Grau.

Dewi, Kezia. 2008. "North Korea and Turkmenistan, Totalitarian States in the World," *Associated Content* August 1, 2008. http:// www.associatedcontent.com/article/911711/north_korea_and_ turkmenistan_totalitarian.html (accessed September 29, 2009).

Drucker, Peter. 1995. *The End of Economic Man: The Origins of Totalitarianism*. New York: Transaction Publishers.

Evans-Pritchard, E. P. 1969. *The Nuer: A Description of the Modes of Livelihood and Political Institutions of a Nilotic People*. Oxford, UK: Oxford University Press.

———. 1971. *Nuer Religion*. Oxford, UK: Oxford University Press.

Fisher, Helen. 1993. *Anatomy of Love: A Natural History of Marriage, Mating, and Why We Stray*. New York: Quill.

Foucault, Michel. 1986. *The History of Sexuality, Volume Three: The Care of the Self.* New York: Penguin.

———. 1988. "Technologies of the Self." In *Technologies of the Self: A Seminar with Michel Foucault,* ed. L. Martin, H. Gutman, and P. Hutton, 16–49. Amherst, MA: University of Massachusetts Press.

Frier, Bruce, Thomas McGinn, and Joel Lidov. 2003. *A Casebook on Roman Family Law.* Washington, DC: American Philosophical Association.

Gluck, Carol. 1987. *Japan's Modern Myths.* Princeton, NJ: Princeton University Press.

Godelier, Maurice. 1996. *The Mental and the Material: Thought, Economy, and Society.* London: Verso.

Gorer, Geoffrey. 1942. *Japanese Character Structure and Propaganda.* New Haven, CT: Institute of Human Relations, Yale University.

Gordon, Daniel. 2007. *Crossing the Line.* Documentary. DVD. London: Kino International.

Haboush, Ja Hyun. 1996. *The Memoires of Lady Hyegyong: The Autobiographical Writings of a Crown Princess of Eighteenth Century Korea.* Berkeley, CA: University of California Press.

Han Jung-Mo and Jeong Seong-Mu. 1983. *Jucheui munye riron yeongu* (A study of *juche* literary art theory). Pyongyang: Sahoekwahak chulpansa.

Harada Katsumasa. 2007. *Mantetsu* (The South Manchurian Railway Company). Tokyo: Nihon hyōronsha.

Harris, Mark. 2007. *Inside North Korea.* San Francisco, CA: Chronicle Books.

Jeong Chang-Yun. 1983. *Meon kil* (The long road). Pyongyang: Munye chulpansa.

Kang, Chol-hwan. 2005. *The Aquariums of Pyongyang: Ten Years in the North Korean Gulag.* New York: Basic Books.

Kang, Hyok. 2004. *Ici, c'est le paradis: une enfance en Corée du Nord.* Neuilly-sur-Seine: M. Lafon.

Kang Jin-ung. 2001. "Bukhanui kajokgukkachejeui hyeongseong" (The formation of North Korea's family state system). *Tongilmunje yeongu* (Reunification studies) 13(2): 323–46.

Kantorowicz, Ernst. 1957. *The King's Two Bodies: A Study in Mediaeval Political Theology,* Princeton, NJ: Princeton University Press.

Katō Yōko. 2007. *Manshūjihen kara nitchūsensō made* (From the establishment of Manchukuo to the Sino-Japanese War). Tokyo: Iwanami shoten.

"Keullodanchedeureseo kyeongchukhaengsa" (Celebrations held by labor organizations). *Rodong shinmun*, February 12, 2009. http://www .kcna.co.jp/today-rodong/rodong.htm (accessed June 25, 2009).

Kim Dong-Ho. 1983. "Haeppicheun kkeudeopsi" (Sunshine forever). In *Inminui hanmaeum* (One heart of the people), 180–202. Pyongyang: Munye chulpansa.

Kim Jong Il. 1982. *On the Juche Idea.* Pyongyang: Foreign Languages Publishing House.

———. 1984. *On Correctly Understanding the Originality of Kimilsungism: Talk to Theoretical Propagandaists of the Party, October 2, 1976.* Pyongyang: Foreign Languages Publishing House.

———. 1985. *On the Juche Idea of Our Party.* Pyongyang: Foreign Languages Publishing House.

———. 1992. *Eumak yesullon* (Musical art theory). Pyongyang: Choseon rodongdang chulpansa.

"Kim Jong Il's Mistress, Secret Daughter Revealed." 2009. *Seoul Times*, June 18, 2009. http://theseoultimes.com/ST/?url=/ST/db/read .php?idx=1643 (accessed June 25, 2009).

Kim Sam-Bok. 1982. *Seongjangui bom* (A spring of growth). Pyongyang: Munye chulpansa.

———. 1983. "Mirubeol jeonseol" (The legend of Miru Plain). In *Inminui hanmaeum* (One heart of the people), 252–78. Pyongyang: Munye chulpansa.

Ko Byeong-Sam. 1970. "Malgeun achim" (Pure morning). In *Binnaneun jauk* (Brilliant footsteps), 5–27. Pyongyang: Munye chulpansa.

———. 1976. "Pyongyangeun noraehanda" (Pyongyang is singing). In *Seungrijadeul* (The victors), 3–36. Pyongyang: Munye chulpansa.

Kwon, Heonik. 2010. "North Korea's Politics of Longing." *Critical Asian Studies* 42(1): 3–24.

Lankov, Andrei. 2007. *North of the DMZ: Essays on Daily Life in North Korea.* Jefferson, NC: McFarland.

Lapsley, Hilary. 2001. *Margaret Mead and Ruth Benedict: The Kinship of Women.* Boston, MA: University of Massachusetts Press.

Lebacqz, Karen. 2001. "On the Elusive Nature of Respect." In *The Human Embryonic Stem Cell Debate: Science, Ethics, and Public Policy*, ed. S. Holland, K. Lebacqz, and L. Zoloth, 149–62. Cambridge, MA: MIT Press.

Lerner, Mitchell. 2008. "Making Sense of the 'Hermit Kingdom': North Korea in the Nuclear Age," *Origins* 2 (3). http://ehistory

.osu.edu/osu/origins/print.cfm?articleid=21 (accessed September 29, 2009).

Lewis, C. S. (Clive Staples). 1960. *The Four Loves*. London: Bles.

Li Jin-U. 1981a. *Ireumeomneun yeongungdeul* (Unsung heroes). Vol. 1. Pyongyang: Munye chulpansa.

———. 1981b. *Ireumeomneun yeongungdeul* (Unsung heroes). Vol. 2. Pyongyang: Munye chulpansa.

Li Jong-Ryeol. 1961 [1976]. "Bultaneun bam" (Burning night). In *Seungrijadeul* (The victors), 258–76. Pyongyang: Munye chulpansa.

Li Taek-Jin. 1982. *Yonghaegongdeul* (The ironworkers). Pyongyang: Munye chulpansa.

Lindholm, Charles. 1993. *Charisma*. New York: Blackwell.

Lummis, C. Douglas. 2007. "Ruth Benedict's Obituary of Japanese Culture." *Japan Focus*, July 19, 2007. http://www.japanfocus.org/-C_Douglas-Lummis/2474 (accessed on June 22, 2010).

Malinowski, Bronisław. 1961. *Argonauts of the Western Pacific: An Account of Native Enterprise and Adventure in the Archipelagoes of Melanesian New Guinea*. London: E. P. Dutton.

———. 1987. *The Sexual Life of Savages*. Boston, MA: Beacon Press.

———. 1992. *Magic, Science and Religion and Other Essays*. Long Grove, IL: Waveland Press.

Marcus, George, and Michael Fischer. 1994. *Anthropology as Cultural Critique: An Experimental Moment in the Human Sciences*. Chicago, IL: University of Chicago Press.

Martin, Bradley. 2004. *Under the Loving Care of the Fatherly Leader: North Korea and the Kim Dynasty*. New York: St. Martin's Press.

Matsubara, Hiroshi, and Mayuko Tokita. 2007. "Japan's Korean Residents Caught in the Japan-North Korea Crossfire," *Japan Focus*, January 20, 2007. http://www.japanfocus.org/-John-Feffer/2327 (accessed August 6, 2010).

Mauss, Marcel. 1979. *Seasonal Variations of the Eskimo: A Study in Social Morphology*. London: Routledge and Kegan Paul.

Morris-Suzuki, Tessa. 2007. *The Exodus to North Korea: In the Shadows of Japan's Cold War*. Lanham, MD: Rowman and Littlefield.

Oh, Kongdan, and Ralph Hassig. 2000. *North Korea through the Looking Glass*. Washington, DC: Brookings Institution Press.

Orwell, George. 1949. *Nineteen Eighty-four, A Novel*. New York: Harcourt Brace.

Paek Hyeon-U. 1966 [1976]. "Byeoldeuri heureunda" (The stars are flowing). In *Seungrijadeul* (The victors), 136–63. Pyongyang: Munye chulpansa.

Park, Hyun Ok. 2005. *Two Dreams in One Bed: Empire, Social Life, and the Origins of the North Korean Revolution in Manchuria.* Durham, NC: Duke University Press.

Pettigrew, Thomas. 1834. *A History of Egyptian Mummies and an Account of the Worship and Embalming of the Sacred Animals by the Egyptians,* London: Longman, Reese, Orme, Brown, Green, and Longman.

Poivert, Michel, Jonathan Fenby, and Philippe Chancel. 2007. *North Korea.* London: Thames and Hudson.

Ryang, Sonia. 1997. *North Koreans in Japan: Language, Ideology, and Identity.* Boulder, CO: Westview Press.

———. 2000. "The North Korean Homeland of Koreans in Japan." In *Koreans in Japan: Critical Voices from the Margin,* ed. S. Ryang, 32–54. London: Routledge.

———. 2004. *Japan and National Anthropology: A Critique.* London: Routledge.

———. 2006. *Love in Modern Japan: Its Estrangement from Self, Sex, and Society,* London: Routledge.

———. 2008. "A Letter from Afar: Totalitarianism, Neoliberalism, and Self-Reference." In *Writing Selves in Diaspora: Ethnography of Autobiographics of Korean Women in Japan and the United States,* ed. S. Ryang, 63–100. Lanham, MD: Lexington Books.

———. 2009. "Biopolitics, or, the Logic of Sovereign Love—Love's Whereabouts in North Korea." In *North Korea: Toward a Better Understanding,* ed. S. Ryang, 57–84. Lanham, MD: Lexington Books.

———. Forthcoming. *Reading South Korea: Humanity in the Digital Age.* Unpublished manuscript.

Ryu Man and Kim Jeong-Ung. 1983. *Jucheui changjak riron yeongu* (A study of *juche* literary creation theory). Pyongyang: Sahoekwahak chulpansa.

Saint Augustine. 1998. *Confessions.* New York: Oxford University Press.

Suh, Dae-Sook. 1995. *Kim Il Sung: The North Korean Leader.* New York: Columbia University Press.

Triplett, William. 2004. *Rogue State: How a Nuclear North Korea Threatens America.* New York: Regnery Publishing.

Yun Se-Jung. 1952 [1976]. "Kudaewongwa sindaewon" (An old soldier and a young soldier). In *Seungrijadeul* (The victors), 82–108. Pyongyang: Munye chulpansa.

———. 1974. *Yonggwangroneun sumswinda* (The steel furnace is breathing). Pyongyang: Munye chulpansa.

Wada Haruki. 1992. *Kin Nissei to Manshū kōnichi sensō* (Kim Il Sung and the anti-Japanese guerrilla war in Manchuria). Tokyo: Heibonsha.

Weil, Simone. 1951. *Waiting for God*. New York: Perennial.

———. 1952a. *The Need for Roots*. London: Routledge.

———. 1952b. *Gravity and Grace*. London: Routledge.

———. 1986. *Simone Weil: An Anthology*. Ed. S. Miles. New York: Grove Books.

Whyte, Martin King. 1983. *Small Groups and Political Rituals in China*. Berkeley, CA: University of California Press.

"Widaehan tangui ryeongdottara pugangjogugui challanhan raeireul wihayeo himchage ssawonagaja" (Let us fight forward vigorously for the sake of the brilliant future of our strong and prosperous fatherland, under the guidance of our great party). 2009. *Rodong shinmun*, February 16, 2009. http://www.kcna.co.jp/today-rodong/rodong.htm (accessed June 25, 2009).

Žižek, Slavoj. 2002. *Welcome to the Desert of the Real: Five Essays on September 11 and Related Dates*. London: Verso.

———. 2008. *In Defense of Lost Causes*. London: Verso.

———. 2010. *Living in the End Times*. London: Verso.

Index

Abductions, 32–33, 108, 129–30
Abyss, 39, 210
Adorno, Theodor, 200
Agamben, Giorgio, 86, 135
Agriculture, 45, 55–60, 154, 155. See also *Seongjangui bom*
Albright, Madeleine, 133
Ancestors, 24, 191
Anthropo-ization, 4–5, 8
Anthropology: British Social, 5, 10; Culture and Personality School, 9–11; "culture at a distance" approach, 10–11, 208–9; enemy studies, 6, 8, 10–11, 194; study of "primitive" peoples, 4–6. *See also* Ethnographic fieldwork
Arendt, Hannah, 38, 198
Arirang mass games, 22
Augustine, Saint, *Confessions*, 143

Bataille, Georges, 20, 61, 77
Bateson, Gregory, 10
Benedict, Ruth, 6, 8, 10–11, 13, 194

Berlin, Isaiah, 83–84
Binnaneun jauk (Brilliant Footsteps), 44
Biopolitics, 188
Bipangwa jagibipan (criticism and self-criticism), 142, 184
Boas, Franz, 9–10
Bodies: infatuation symptoms, 76–77; of Kim Il Sung, on display, 21–22, 34, 35–36, 191; of leaders, on display, 34–36; of monarchs, 34, 35, 80; mummification, 35; souls and, 34–35
Bongwan (lineages), 192
Britain, *see* United Kingdom
British Social Anthropology, 5, 10
Buddhism, Tibetan, 34
Bultaneun bam (Burning Night; Li Jong-Ryeol), 87–91, 105
Bush administration, 137, 202–3
"Byeoldeuri heureunda" (The Stars Are Flowing; Paek Hyeon-U), 92, 93, 94–100, 105

Camp societies, 86, 135–38. *See also* State of emergency
Capitalism, 201, 203–4, 209–10
Carter, Jimmy, 21
Charisma, 76, 82, 83–84
Cheollima movement, 132
Children: indoctrination, 18; military games, 51–52, 53–54; Young Pioneers, 184. *See also* Fathers
China: Cultural Revolution, 154; Korean War and, 44, 105–6; Maoism, 199; Mao's body, 34; Qing emperors, 14
Choe Eun-Hui, 32, 33, 129
Choe Hak-Su, *Keun simjang* (A Big Heart), 45–48, 81
Choe Sang-Sun, *Uri hakkyo* (Our School), 42–43, 81–82
Choe Yong-Gon, 16, 17
Chonghwa (self-review), 141–42
Chongryun (General Association of Korean Residents in Japan), xi, 28, 30–31
Christianity: ascetic movement, 141; confession, 142–43; differences from North Korean ideas, 195–96; Eastern Orthodox, 143; of Kim family, 14–15; Pietà, 194–95; Protestantism, 19
Church of England, 19
CNN, 138
Cold War, 7, 10–11, 83
Colonial period, 13–16, 142
Comfort women, 135–36
Concentration camps, 202

Confession, Christian, 142–43
Confucianism, 21, 24, 191, 192, 193–94
Crossing the Line, 108
Cultural relativism, 5
Culture and Personality School, 9–10

Dalai Lama, 34
Dear Leader, *see* Kim Jong Il
Death rituals, 21–22, 34–35, 191
Dehumanization of other, 5–8
Demick, Barbara, 18
Democratic People's Republic of Korea, *see* North Korea
Dresnok, James Joseph, 108
Drucker, Peter, 197, 200, 201, 202, 203

Eastern Orthodox Christianity, 143
Economic plans, 45, 200
Egypt, mummification, 35
Elizabeth II, Queen, 19
Emotions: human, 48, 50, 54, 98, 99; politicization, 185. *See also* Love
Enemy: images, 133–34; in Korean War, 107; United States as, 51–52, 132, 133–34, 135, 137
Enemy studies, 6, 8, 10–11, 194
England, *see* United Kingdom
Eobeoi suryeongnim (Father/Mother Leader), 80–81
Eskimo life, 23, 190, 204
Espionage, 129–30. See also *Ireumeomneun yeongungdeul*

Eternal President, Kim Il Sung as, 22, 32, 33–34, 35–36, 137, 195, 207

Ethnographic fieldwork, 3, 8–10

Ethnology: data sources, 3, 4, 8–9, 10–11; dehumanization of subjects, 5–7; meaning, 3; study of North Korea, 1–2, 3–4, 208–9

Evans-Pritchard, E. E., 5–6

Expatriates, *see* Koreans in Japan

Families, *see* Fathers; Kinship

Fascism, 197, 201

Fatherland, 29, 33, 59, 75, 131

Fathers: Japanese emperor as, 191–92; Kim Il Sung seen as, 24, 80–81, 192–93, 194, 195; leaders addressed as, 24; love of, 60; missing, 79–80, 88–89, 101; relationships with sons, 144–54, 179–80, 181–83, 193; in traditional Korean kinship system, 192

Films: abductions of South Korean director and star, 32, 33, 129; *Crossing the Line*, 108; Kim Jong Il's involvement, 32, 33, 129; in 1980s, 26, 27, 32, 33; performing songs from, 27. See also *Ireumeomneun yeongungdeul*

Foucault, Michel, 140–41, 142

Free will, *see* Liberty

Friendships, 104, 130–31, 180–81

Functionalism, 5, 10

Gender: portrayals of Kim Il Sung as gender-free, 51, 80–81; of protagonists of novels, 80. *See also* Men; Women

Gender relations, 180–81. *See also* Love, romantic; Marriage

Generational differences, 179–80

Germany, Nazism, 197, 198, 201

Geumsusan Memorial Palace, 21, 191, 201

Godelier, Maurice, 204

Goodwill, 40–41

Gorer, Geoffrey, 10–11

Great Leader (*suryeong*), 2, 22, 187. *See also* Kim Il Sung

Guerrillas, anti-Japanese, 14, 15–17, 134

Guerrilla state, North Korea as, 16–17

Haeppicheun kkeudeopsi (Sunshine Forever; Kim Dong-Ho), 50, 51–55

Humanization of North Koreans, xiv, 8, 208–10

Humans: dehumanization of other, 5–8; emotions, 48, 50, 54, 98, 99; Kim Il Sung depicted as, 48, 50, 81–82, 207; North Koreans as, xiv, 8, 208–10

Hyeongmyeongjeontong (revolutionary tradition), 134

Hyeonjijido ("on-the-spot" guidance meetings), 45–48, 51, 52–55, 72–74

Ideological education, 25, 27, 134, 144, 205

Ideology: *hyeongmyeongjeontong* (revolutionary tradition), 134; Marxism-Leninism, 199; news media as vehicles, 205; origins of North Korean, 13–14. See also *Juche*

Immortality, *see* Eternal President

Imperialism, U.S. (*mije*), 7–8, 133–34

Inca society, 204

Inminui hanmaeum (One Heart of the People), 50

International Committee of the Red Cross, 28

Ireumeomneun yeongungdeul (Unsung Heroes): American characters, 108, 110–11, 114–15, 117, 118, 119–21, 122, 123–26, 133–34; characterizations, 127–28; hotel screenings, 134–35; popularity, 135; screenplay publication, 108, 131–32; significance, 126–31; volume 1, 107–19; volume 2, 119–26; Western cultural references, 108–9, 126

Ironworkers, see *Yonghaegongdeul*

Italian fascism, 197, 201

Japan: abductions by North Korea, 32–33, 108, 129–30; colonial rule of Korea, 13–16, 142; comfort stations for military, 135–36; death rituals, 34–35; emperors, 14, 136, 191–92, 194, 195, 196; enemy studies, 6, 8, 10–11, 194; Meiji Restoration, 191–92, 197; military, 194; as nation, 196. *See also* Koreans in Japan

Jenkins, Charles Robert, 108

Jeong Chang-Yun, *Meonkil* (The Long Road), 61, 62–80, 81, 82, 84, 131

Journalism, 205–6

Juche ("self-reliance"): differences from Marxism, 199–200; elements of, 25, 186; Kim Jong Il's writings on, 32; slogans, 132; study of, 25, 27

Jungpyeon soseol (medium-length novels), 144

Kang Ban-Seok, 14, 15

Keun simjang (A Big Heart; Choe Hak-Su), 45–48, 81

Kidnappings, *see* Abductions

Kim Chaek, 16

Kim Dong-Ho, *Haeppicheun kkeudeopsi* (Sunshine Forever), 50, 51–55

Kim Hyeong-Jik, 14–15

Kim Il Sung: as anti-Japanese guerrilla, 14, 15–17; birth, 14; death, 20, 21, 137, 194–95, 207; display of body and relics, 21–22, 34, 35–36, 191; early life and education, 15, 31; as Eternal President, 22, 32, 33–34, 35–36, 137, 195, 207; family, 14–15; Korean nation and, 196; portraits, 19; sanitization, 107; as sovereign, 17–21, 188, 193–94, 197; in Soviet Union, 16; speeches and writings, 25, 26, 185;

titles, 2, 24, 80–81, 192–93, 195, 196

Kim Il Sung, fictional images of: as benevolent old man, 42–43, 44, 48, 82; as gender-free, 51, 80–81; as human being, 48, 50, 81–82, 207; during Korean War, 42–45, 55–57, 91–92, 107; love, 43–44, 45, 48, 49–50, 54, 60, 76–77, 81, 83; as non-aging, 51, 80, 82; relations with individuals, 42–43, 46–48, 49, 52–53, 55–59, 72–75, 145–46; as sacred being, 134, 207; significance, 11; suprahuman capacities, 50–55, 66–67; workplace visits, 45–48, 51, 52–55, 72–74, 145

Kim Il Sung, relationship to people: after death, 20, 21–24, 35–36, 191; birthday gifts, 30–31; commitment, 202; as Father, 24, 80–81, 192–93, 194, 195; identification with Leader, 17–18, 187–89; individualized, 186; logocentric, 25, 26, 27; love, 18, 26, 41–42, 48, 50, 54, 61–62, 77, 200; loyalty, 35, 80, 186, 187, 188, 196; obedience, 41; pilgrimages, 172–73, 201; religiosity, 19–20; respect, 20; rewards, 200–201; as role model, 19; as sacred being, 17–19, 24, 67, 131, 185, 195–96, 198, 207; self-criticism sessions, 142–43, 184–85; sensory, 26–27, 32; shift in 1970s and 1980s, 17–18, 20, 25–27, 32, 207; as sovereign, 17–21, 188, 193–94, 197; state of emergency and, 87; ubiquity, 18–19

Kim Jong Il: artistic proclivity, 26, 32, 33; birth, 16, 31, 201; descriptions of, 33; differences from father, 31–32, 36; early life and education, 31–32; Eternal Presidency of father and, 33–34, 36, 137, 195; film productions, 32, 33, 129; future replacement, 36; as heir, 32; meeting with Koizumi, 129–30; as military leader, 132–33; political emergence, 32; positionality, 33–34, 36; succession of father, 2, 36, 137; titles, 2, 24, 36, 195

Kim Jong Suk, 16

Kim Jong Un, 36

Kim Sam-Bok: *Mirubeol jeonseol*(The Legend of Miru Plain), 50, 55–60, 87, 90, 91, 107; *Seongjangui bom* (A Spring of Growth), 144, 154–69, 174–78, 180, 181, 183

Kinship: Confucian system, 193–94; in Japan, 191–92; Korean system, 192; lineages (*bongwan*), 192; patriarchies, 193–94

Ko Byeong-Sam: *Malgeun achim* (Pure Morning), 44–45; "Pyongyangeun noraehanda" (Pyongyang Is Singing), 48–49, 81, 91–92, 107; stories, 49–50

Ko Yeong-Hui, 36

Koizumi Jun'ichirō, 129–30

Korea: colonial period, 13–16, 142; dehumanization, 7; kinship relations, 24; partition, 27, 28, 74, 133, 196, 197–98; royal family, 14, 24, 193. *See also* North Korea; South Korea

Korean Air Lines bombing, 33

Korean Revolutionary People's Army, 14

Koreans in Japan: legal status, 28, 29; organizations, xi, 28, 30–31; relationship with North Korea, xi-xiii, xiv, 27, 28–31; repatriations, xii-xiii, xiv, 27–30, 36; schools, xiii, xiv, 28; supporters of South Korea, 28; visits to North Korea, 29–30, 134–35

Korean War: American occupation of north, 92, 104, 105–6, 133; contacts between Northerners and Southerners, 106, 107; cultural construction of, 132; effects in North Korea, 198; fiction set in, 42–45, 49, 55–57, 87–92, 93–105, 107; fiction written during, 86–87, 94, 100–105; Incheon landing, 44, 92–93; liberation of Seoul, 95; media coverage, 6; as ongoing war, 86, 106, 132–33, 135, 137–39; personal relationships during, 106; prisoners of war, 121; reconstruction period, 45–47, 51, 132; truce, 44, 86; U.S. and Chinese involvement, 44, 105–6, 133; Wolmi Island battle, 92–93. *See also* War stories

"Kudaewongwa sindaewon" (An Old Soldier and A Young Soldier; Yun Se-Jung), 93–94, 100–105

Kwon, Heonik, 22, 194

Language: of self, 144–45, 181; of self-criticism sessions, 184–85, 206

Leaders: charismatic, 76, 82, 83–84; embalmed bodies on display, 34–36; totalitarian, 82, 83–84. *See also* Kim Il Sung

Lebacqz, Karen, 9

Levinas, Emmanuel, 199

Lewis, C. S., 104

Li Jin-U, 108. See also *Ireumeomneun yeongungdeul*

Li Jong-Ryeol, *Bultaneun bam* (Burning Night), 87–91, 105

Li Taek-Jin, *Yonghaegongdeul* (The Ironworkers), 143–54, 169–74, 178–80, 181–83, 201, 205

Liberal democracy, 85, 203, 210

Liberty, 40–41, 82, 83–84

Lindholm, Charles, 84

Lineages (*bongwan*), 192

Literature: changes in 1990s and later, 48; collective production, 12, 144; commissioned, 94; educative purpose, 12, 13; extra-textual information, 13; key texts, 12; in 1950s and 1960s, 26, 86–87; novels, 26, 144; readers, 13, 144; social role, 205, 206–7; as source, 4, 11–13; state production, 12–13, 144; technical details, 185–86; writers, 12–13

Living standards, urban-rural differences, 170–71, 178

Love: fatherly, 60; in fictional images of Leader, 43–44, 45, 48, 49–50, 54, 60, 76–77, 81, 83; of God, 41, 61, 77, 83; in Leader's relationship to people, 18, 26, 41–42, 48, 50, 54, 61–62, 77, 200; location in North Korea, 61–62; physical manifestations, 76–77; politicization, 185, 205; social role, 60–61; sovereign, 61–62, 77; triangles, 61, 77, 80, 84; Weil on, 41–42, 60–61, 77, 82–83, 84

Love, romantic: charisma and, 84; in fiction, 69, 70–72, 76, 98, 100, 147–51, 169–80; in *Ireumeomneun yeongungdeul*, 110, 111–12, 130–31; political life and, 204–5; secondary to Leader relationship, 78–79, 80. *See also* Marriage

Love stories: mundane, 169–70, 177–79; as secondary stories, 169–70, 180–81

Loyalty: fake, 78; to Great Leader, 35, 80, 186, 187, 188, 196; in totalitarian regimes, 198; of veterans, 134

Malgeun achim (Pure Morning; Ko Byeong-Sam), 44–45

Malinowski, Bronisław, 5

Manchukuo, 14

Manchuria, 13–14, 15, 16–17, 134

Mao Zedong, 34, 199

Marriage: arranged, 170–71, 176, 205; between members of same lineage, 192; in North Korea, 204–5. *See also* Love, romantic

Marxism-Leninism, 199

Mass entertainment, 22, 23, 26, 27, 135, 138–39. *See also* Films

Mauss, Marcel, 23, 190, 204

Mead, Margaret, 9–10, 11

Media, *see* Films; News media; Television

Men: male bonds, 100–105; relationships with Leader, 77–78. *See also* Fathers; Gender

Meon kil (The Long Road; Jeong Chang-Yun), 61, 62–80, 81, 82, 84, 131

Mije (U.S. imperialism), 7–8, 133–34

Military: American, 128–29; Japanese, 194

Military, North Korean, *see* North Korean People's Army

Military games, 51–52, 53–54

Mirubeol jeonseol (The Legend of Miru Plain; Kim Sam-Bok), 50, 55–60, 87, 90, 91, 107

Mourning, *see* Death rituals

Movies, *see* Films

Mummification, 35

Munye chulpansa, 144

Nationalism, 197–98

National security, 132–33, 136. *See also* State of emergency

National Security Agency, U.S., 203

Nazism, 197, 198, 201
Neo-Confucian state, North
    Korea as, 21, 24, 191
Neoliberal states, 202–3
News media, 6, 205–6
Nineteen Eighty-Four (Orwell),
    50
NKPA, *see* North Korean
    People's Army
North Korea: ethnological study
    of, 1–2, 3–4, 208–9; founding
    of state, 16, 197–98, 199;
    as guerrilla state, 16–17;
    historiography, 14, 15; ideo-
    logical origins, 13–14, 199;
    imports from Japan, 30, 134,
    206; as nation, 196; nuclear
    weapons program, 133, 135;
    outsiders' views of, xiii–xiv,
    7, 8, 207–8, 209, 210; previous
    works on, 2–3; propaganda,
    7–8; reunification goal, 196,
    197, 199
North Korean People's Army
    (NKPA): fictional soldiers,
    45, 88–89, 94–105; liberation
    of Seoul, 95; retreat, 44, 92,
    105; Supreme Commander,
    2; Wolmi Island battle,
    92–93. *See also* Korean
    War
North Koreans: compulsory
    Friday labor, 30; defectors,
    18; humanization, xiv, 8, 208–
    10
Nuclear weapons program, 133,
    135
Nuer people, 5–6

Obedience, 41, 82, 83

"On-the-spot" guidance meet-
    ings (*hyeonjijido*), 45–48, 51,
    52–55, 72–74
Orwell, George, *Nineteen Eighty-
    Four*, 50

Pacific War, *see* World War II
Paek Hyeon-U, "Byeoldeuri
    heureunda" (The Stars Are
    Flowing), 92, 93, 94–100,
    105
Patriarchies, 193–94
Performances, *see* Mass enter-
    tainment; Rituals
Perpetual ritual state, 21–24
Pietà, 194–95
Pilgrimage tours, 172–73, 201
Political life: dominance in
    North Korea, 4, 140, 186–88,
    190–91, 204; role of literature,
    206–7; self and, 140, 181, 184,
    185–87
Propaganda, 3, 9, 13, 133, 134,
    205–6
Protestantism, 19. *See also* Chris-
    tianity
Puyi, 14
Pyongyang: fall of, 44; Geum-
    susan Memorial Palace, 21,
    191, 201; Kim Il Sung statue,
    191; living standards,
    170–71; underground theater,
    44, 49
"Pyongyangeun noraehanda"
    (Pyongyang Is Singing;
    Ko Byeong-Sam), 48–49, 81,
    91–92, 107

Red Cross, 28
Refugees, 208–9

Republic of Korea, *see* South Korea
Respect, 9, 20
Revolutionary pilgrimage tours, 172–73, 201
Rhee, Syngman, 111, 112
Rituals: death, 34–35, 191; in Eskimo life, 23, 190; Inca, 204; perpetual ritual state, 21–24
Romantic love, *see* Love, romantic
Rome, ancient, 193
Ryeongdoja, 2

Sado, Prince, 193
Sarang (love), 98, 130–31
Self: language of, 144–45, 181; political aspects, 140, 181, 184, 185–87; public existence, 141, 144, 181, 184–85; purification, correction, and transformation, 141, 181; relationship to Great Leader, 187–89, 197; role in North Korean society, 140–41, 186, 188–89; sacrifice of, 140, 188
Self-criticism sessions: language, 184–85, 206; mandatory, 184; in novels, 159–60, 169, 206; relationship with Great Leader, 142–43, 184–85
Self-cultivation, 183–84, 185
Self-examination, 141, 152, 161–62, 182–84
Self-review (*chonghwa*), 141–42
Seongjangui bom (A Spring of Growth; Kim Sam-Bok), 144, 154–69, 174–78, 180, 181, 183

Seungrijadeul (The Victors), 91–92
Sexual slavery, 135–36
Sin Sang-ok, 32, 33, 129
Socialist Youth League, 184
Social relations: complexity, 180–81; dominated by political, 204, 205; Great Leader and, 18–19, 24; hierarchical, 67. *See also* Friendships; Kinship; Love
Souls, 40
South Korea: abductions by North Korea, 32, 33, 129; refugees from North Korea, 208–9; terrorist attacks on, 33. *See also* Korean War
South Manchurian Railway Company, 14
Sovereign love, 61–62, 77
Sovereigns: Japanese emperor as, 194; Kim Il Sung as, 17–21, 188, 193–94, 197
Soviet Union: influences in North Korea, 45, 142, 199, 200; Lenin's body, 34; Marxism-Leninism, 199
Spies, *see* Espionage
State of emergency: continuous, 85–86, 106, 132–33, 135, 136, 137–39; effects on individual lives, 85–86; in United States, 85, 136–37. *See also* Camp societies
Suh, Dae-Sook, 16
Suryeong (Great Leader), 2, 22, 187. *See also* Kim Il Sung

Television, 206
Terrorism, 33, 202–3

Three Revolutions program, 154–55, 156, 160–61. See also *Seongjangui bom*
Tibetan Buddhism, 34
Totalitarianism: differences from North Korean regime, 198, 199; German and Italian, 197, 198, 201; leaders, 82, 83–84; non-economic rewards, 201–2; in North Korea, 199, 200, 202, 208
Transgression, 39
Trobriand Islanders, 5

United Kingdom: British Social Anthropology, 5, 10; MI5 agents, 115, 117, 126; monarchy, 19, 34, 35, 48, 80
United Nations, 6
United States: as enemy, 51–52, 132, 133–34, 135, 137; imperialism, 7–8, 133–34, 137; North Korean relations with, 133; Office of War Information, 11; state of emergency, 85, 136–37; war on terror, 136–37, 202–3. *See also* Korean War
Unsung Heroes, see *Ireumeomneun yeongungdeul*
Uri hakkyo (Our School; Choe Sang-Sun), 42–43, 81–82

Visual media, 26, 32, 206. *See also* Films

Wada Haruki, 16–17, 20
War, *see* Korean War; State of emergency; World War II
War on terror, 136–37, 202–3

War stories: enemy images, 133–34; in 1950s and 1960s, 86–87. See also *Ireumeomneun yeongungdeul*
Weil, Simone, 40–42, 60–61, 77, 82–83, 84
Women: comfort women, 135–36; in U.S. military, 128–29. *See also* Gender
Workers' Party of Korea, 16–17, 25, 32, 184
World War II: anti-Japanese guerrillas, 14, 15–17, 134; comfort women, 135–36; enemy studies by anthropologists, 6, 8, 11, 194; Japanese atrocities, 194; Korean expatriates in Japan, 27

Yeongjo, King, 193
Yonggwangroneun sumswinda (The Steel Furnace Is Breathing; Yun Se-Jung), 61, 93–94, 103, 104
Yonghaegongdeul (The Ironworkers; Li Taek-Jin), 143–54, 169–74, 178–80, 181–83, 201, 205
Young Pioneers, 184
Yun Se-Jung: "Kudaewongwa sindaewon" (An Old Soldier and A Young Soldier), 93–94, 100–105; *Yonggwangroneun sumswinda* (The Steel Furnace Is Breathing), 61, 93–94, 103, 104

Žižek, Slavoj, 199, 200, 203

Harvard East Asian Monographs
(*out-of-print)

*1.   Liang Fang-chung, *The Single-Whip Method of Taxation in China*
*2.   Harold C. Hinton, *The Grain Tribute System of China, 1845–1911*
 3.   Ellsworth C. Carlson, *The Kaiping Mines, 1877–1912*
*4.   Chao Kuo-chün, *Agrarian Policies of Mainland China: A Documentary Study, 1949–1956*
*5.   Edgar Snow, *Random Notes on Red China, 1936–1945*
*6.   Edwin George Beal, Jr., *The Origin of Likin, 1835–1864*
 7.   Chao Kuo-chün, *Economic Planning and Organization in Mainland China: A Documentary Study, 1949–1957*
*8.   John K. Fairbank, *Ching Documents: An Introductory Syllabus*
*9.   Helen Yin and Yi-chang Yin, *Economic Statistics of Mainland China, 1949–1957*
10.   Wolfgang Franke, *The Reform and Abolition of the Traditional Chinese Examination System*
11.   Albert Feuerwerker and S. Cheng, *Chinese Communist Studies of Modern Chinese History*
12.   C. John Stanley, *Late Ching Finance: Hu Kuang-yung as an Innovator*
13.   S. M. Meng, *The Tsungli Yamen: Its Organization and Functions*
*14.   Ssu-yü Teng, *Historiography of the Taiping Rebellion*
15.   Chun-Jo Liu, *Controversies in Modern Chinese Intellectual History: An Analytic Bibliography of Periodical Articles, Mainly of the May Fourth and Post-May Fourth Era*
*16.   Edward J. M. Rhoads, *The Chinese Red Army, 1927–1963: An Annotated Bibliography*
*17.   Andrew J. Nathan, *A History of the China International Famine Relief Commission*
*18.   Frank H. H. King (ed.) and Prescott Clarke, *A Research Guide to China-Coast Newspapers, 1822–1911*
*19.   Ellis Joffe, *Party and Army: Professionalism and Political Control in the Chinese Officer Corps, 1949–1964*
*20.   Toshio G. Tsukahira, *Feudal Control in Tokugawa Japan: The Sankin Kōtai System*
*21.   Kwang-Ching Liu, ed., *American Missionaries in China: Papers from Harvard Seminars*
*22.   George Moseley, *A Sino-Soviet Cultural Frontier: The Ili Kazakh Autonomous Chou*

23. Carl F. Nathan, *Plague Prevention and Politics in Manchuria, 1910–1931*

*24. Adrian Arthur Bennett, *John Fryer: The Introduction of Western Science and Technology into Nineteenth-Century China*

*25. Donald J. Friedman, *The Road from Isolation: The Campaign of the American Committee for Non-Participation in Japanese Aggression, 1938–1941*

*26. Edward LeFevour, *Western Enterprise in Late Ching China: A Selective Survey of Jardine, Matheson and Company's Operations, 1842–1895*

27. Charles Neuhauser, *Third World Politics: China and the Afro-Asian People's Solidarity Organization, 1957–1967*

*28. Kungtu C. Sun, assisted by Ralph W. Huenemann, *The Economic Development of Manchuria in the First Half of the Twentieth Century*

*29. Shahid Javed Burki, *A Study of Chinese Communes, 1965*

30. John Carter Vincent, *The Extraterritorial System in China: Final Phase*

31. Madeleine Chi, *China Diplomacy, 1914–1918*

*32. Clifton Jackson Phillips, *Protestant America and the Pagan World: The First Half Century of the American Board of Commissioners for Foreign Missions, 1810–1860*

*33. James Pusey, *Wu Han: Attacking the Present Through the Past*

*34. Ying-wan Cheng, *Postal Communication in China and Its Modernization, 1860–1896*

35. Tuvia Blumenthal, *Saving in Postwar Japan*

36. Peter Frost, *The Bakumatsu Currency Crisis*

37. Stephen C. Lockwood, *Augustine Heard and Company, 1858–1862*

38. Robert R. Campbell, *James Duncan Campbell: A Memoir by His Son*

39. Jerome Alan Cohen, ed., *The Dynamics of China's Foreign Relations*

40. V. V. Vishnyakova-Akimova, *Two Years in Revolutionary China, 1925–1927*, trans. Steven L. Levine

41. Meron Medzini, *French Policy in Japan During the Closing Years of the Tokugawa Regime*

42. Ezra Vogel, Margie Sargent, Vivienne B. Shue, Thomas Jay Mathews, and Deborah S. Davis, *The Cultural Revolution in the Provinces*

43. Sidney A. Forsythe, *An American Missionary Community in China, 1895–1905*

*44. Benjamin I. Schwartz, ed., *Reflections on the May Fourth Movement.: A Symposium*

*45. Ching Young Choe, *The Rule of the Taewŏngun, 1864–1873: Restoration in Yi Korea*

46. W. P. J. Hall, *A Bibliographical Guide to Japanese Research on the Chinese Economy, 1958–1970*

47. Jack J. Gerson, *Horatio Nelson Lay and Sino-British Relations, 1854–1864*

48. Paul Richard Bohr, *Famine and the Missionary: Timothy Richard as Relief Administrator and Advocate of National Reform*

49. Endymion Wilkinson, *The History of Imperial China: A Research Guide*

50. Britten Dean, *China and Great Britain: The Diplomacy of Commercial Relations, 1860–1864*

51. Ellsworth C. Carlson, *The Foochow Missionaries, 1847–1880*

52. Yeh-chien Wang, *An Estimate of the Land-Tax Collection in China, 1753 and 1908*

53. Richard M. Pfeffer, *Understanding Business Contracts in China, 1949–1963*

Harvard East Asian Monographs

*54. Han-sheng Chuan and Richard Kraus, *Mid-Ching Rice Markets and Trade: An Essay in Price History*

55. Ranbir Vohra, *Lao She and the Chinese Revolution*

56. Liang-lin Hsiao, *China's Foreign Trade Statistics, 1864–1949*

*57. Lee-hsia Hsu Ting, *Government Control of the Press in Modern China, 1900–1949*

*58. Edward W. Wagner, *The Literati Purges: Political Conflict in Early Yi Korea*

*59. Joungwon A. Kim, *Divided Korea: The Politics of Development, 1945–1972*

60. Noriko Kamachi, John K. Fairbank, and Chūzō Ichiko, *Japanese Studies of Modern China Since 1953: A Bibliographical Guide to Historical and Social-Science Research on the Nineteenth and Twentieth Centuries, Supplementary Volume for 1953–1969*

61. Donald A. Gibbs and Yun-chen Li, *A Bibliography of Studies and Translations of Modern Chinese Literature, 1918–1942*

62. Robert H. Silin, *Leadership and Values: The Organization of Large-Scale Taiwanese Enterprises*

63. David Pong, *A Critical Guide to the Kwangtung Provincial Archives Deposited at the Public Record Office of London*

*64. Fred W. Drake, *China Charts the World: Hsu Chi-yü and His Geography of 1848*

*65. William A. Brown and Urgrunge Onon, translators and annotators, *History of the Mongolian People's Republic*

66. Edward L. Farmer, *Early Ming Government: The Evolution of Dual Capitals*

*67. Ralph C. Croizier, *Koxinga and Chinese Nationalism: History, Myth, and the Hero*

*68. William J. Tyler, tr., *The Psychological World of Natsume Sōseki,* by Doi Takeo

69. Eric Widmer, *The Russian Ecclesiastical Mission in Peking During the Eighteenth Century*

*70. Charlton M. Lewis, *Prologue to the Chinese Revolution: The Transformation of Ideas and Institutions in Hunan Province, 1891–1907*

71. Preston Torbert, *The Ching Imperial Household Department: A Study of Its Organization and Principal Functions, 1662–1796*

72. Paul A. Cohen and John E. Schrecker, eds., *Reform in Nineteenth-Century China*

73. Jon Sigurdson, *Rural Industrialism in China*

74. Kang Chao, *The Development of Cotton Textile Production in China*

75. Valentin Rabe, *The Home Base of American China Missions, 1880–1920*

*76. Sarasin Viraphol, *Tribute and Profit: Sino-Siamese Trade, 1652–1853*

77. Ch'i-ch'ing Hsiao, *The Military Establishment of the Yuan Dynasty*

78. Meishi Tsai, *Contemporary Chinese Novels and Short Stories, 1949–1974: An Annotated Bibliography*

*79. Wellington K. K. Chan, *Merchants, Mandarins and Modern Enterprise in Late Ching China*

80. Endymion Wilkinson, *Landlord and Labor in Late Imperial China: Case Studies from Shandong by Jing Su and Luo Lun*

*81. Barry Keenan, *The Dewey Experiment in China: Educational Reform and Political Power in the Early Republic*

*82. George A. Hayden, *Crime and Punishment in Medieval Chinese Drama: Three Judge Pao Plays*

*83. Sang-Chul Suh, *Growth and Structural Changes in the Korean Economy, 1910–1940*

84. J. W. Dower, *Empire and Aftermath: Yoshida Shigeru and the Japanese Experience, 1878–1954*

85. Martin Collcutt, *Five Mountains: The Rinzai Zen Monastic Institution in Medieval Japan*

86. Kwang Suk Kim and Michael Roemer, *Growth and Structural Transformation*

87. Anne O. Krueger, *The Developmental Role of the Foreign Sector and Aid*

*88. Edwin S. Mills and Byung-Nak Song, *Urbanization and Urban Problems*

89. Sung Hwan Ban, Pal Yong Moon, and Dwight H. Perkins, *Rural Development*

*90. Noel F. McGinn, Donald R. Snodgrass, Yung Bong Kim, Shin-Bok Kim, and Quee-Young Kim, *Education and Development in Korea*

*91. Leroy P. Jones and Il SaKong, *Government, Business, and Entrepreneurship in Economic Development: The Korean Case*

92. Edward S. Mason, Dwight H. Perkins, Kwang Suk Kim, David C. Cole, Mahn Je Kim et al., *The Economic and Social Modernization of the Republic of Korea*

93. Robert Repetto, Tai Hwan Kwon, Son-Ung Kim, Dae Young Kim, John E. Sloboda, and Peter J. Donaldson, *Economic Development, Population Policy, and Demographic Transition in the Republic of Korea*

94. Parks M. Coble, Jr., *The Shanghai Capitalists and the Nationalist Government, 1927–1937*

95. Noriko Kamachi, *Reform in China: Huang Tsun-hsien and the Japanese Model*

96. Richard Wich, *Sino-Soviet Crisis Politics: A Study of Political Change and Communication*

97. Lillian M. Li, *China's Silk Trade: Traditional Industry in the Modern World, 1842–1937*

98. R. David Arkush, *Fei Xiaotong and Sociology in Revolutionary China*

*99. Kenneth Alan Grossberg, *Japan's Renaissance: The Politics of the Muromachi Bakufu*

100. James Reeve Pusey, *China and Charles Darwin*

101. Hoyt Cleveland Tillman, *Utilitarian Confucianism: Chen Liang's Challenge to Chu Hsi*

102. Thomas A. Stanley, *Ōsugi Sakae, Anarchist in Taishō Japan: The Creativity of the Ego*

103. Jonathan K. Ocko, *Bureaucratic Reform in Provincial China: Ting Jih-ch'ang in Restoration Kiangsu, 1867–1870*

104. James Reed, *The Missionary Mind and American East Asia Policy, 1911–1915*

105. Neil L. Waters, *Japan's Local Pragmatists: The Transition from Bakumatsu to Meiji in the Kawasaki Region*

106. David C. Cole and Yung Chul Park, *Financial Development in Korea, 1945–1978*

107. Roy Bahl, Chuk Kyo Kim, and Chong Kee Park, *Public Finances During the Korean Modernization Process*

108. William D. Wray, *Mitsubishi and the N.Y.K, 1870–1914: Business Strategy in the Japanese Shipping Industry*

109. Ralph William Huenemann, *The Dragon and the Iron Horse: The Economics of Railroads in China, 1876–1937*

*110. Benjamin A. Elman, *From Philosophy to Philology: Intellectual and Social Aspects of Change in Late Imperial China*

111. Jane Kate Leonard, *Wei Yüan and China's Rediscovery of the Maritime World*

Harvard East Asian Monographs

112. Luke S. K. Kwong, *A Mosaic of the Hundred Days:. Personalities, Politics, and Ideas of 1898*

*113. John E. Wills, Jr., *Embassies and Illusions: Dutch and Portuguese Envoys to K'ang-hsi, 1666–1687*

*114. Joshua A. Fogel, *Politics and Sinology: The Case of Naitō Konan (1866–1934)*

*115. Jeffrey C. Kinkley, ed., *After Mao: Chinese Literature and Society, 1978–1981*

116. C. Andrew Gerstle, *Circles of Fantasy: Convention in the Plays of Chikamatsu*

117. Andrew Gordon, *The Evolution of Labor Relations in Japan: Heavy Industry, 1853–1955*

*118. Daniel K. Gardner, *Chu Hsi and the "Ta Hsueh": Neo-Confucian Reflection on the Confucian Canon*

119. Christine Guth Kanda, *Shinzō: Hachiman Imagery and Its Development*

*120. Robert Borgen, *Sugawara no Michizane and the Early Heian Court*

121. Chang-tai Hung, *Going to the People: Chinese Intellectual and Folk Literature, 1918–1937*

*122. Michael A. Cusumano, *The Japanese Automobile Industry: Technology and Management at Nissan and Toyota*

123. Richard von Glahn, *The Country of Streams and Grottoes: Expansion, Settlement, and the Civilizing of the Sichuan Frontier in Song Times*

124. Steven D. Carter, *The Road to Komatsubara: A Classical Reading of the Renga Hyakuin*

125. Katherine F. Bruner, John K. Fairbank, and Richard T. Smith, *Entering China's Service: Robert Hart's Journals, 1854–1863*

126. Bob Tadashi Wakabayashi, *Anti-Foreignism and Western Learning in Early-Modern Japan: The "New Theses" of 1825*

127. Atsuko Hirai, *Individualism and Socialism: The Life and Thought of Kawai Eijirō (1891–1944)*

128. Ellen Widmer, *The Margins of Utopia: "Shui-hu hou-chuan" and the Literature of Ming Loyalism*

129. R. Kent Guy, *The Emperor's Four Treasuries: Scholars and the State in the Late Chien-lung Era*

130. Peter C. Perdue, *Exhausting the Earth: State and Peasant in Hunan, 1500–1850*

131. Susan Chan Egan, *A Latterday Confucian: Reminiscences of William Hung (1893–1980)*

132. James T. C. Liu, *China Turning Inward: Intellectual-Political Changes in the Early Twelfth Century*

*133. Paul A. Cohen, *Between Tradition and Modernity: Wang T'ao and Reform in Late Ching China*

134. Kate Wildman Nakai, *Shogunal Politics: Arai Hakuseki and the Premises of Tokugawa Rule*

*135. Parks M. Coble, *Facing Japan: Chinese Politics and Japanese Imperialism, 1931–1937*

*136. Jon L. Saari, *Legacies of Childhood: Growing Up Chinese in a Time of Crisis, 1890–1920*

137. Susan Downing Videen, *Tales of Heichū*

138. Heinz Morioka and Miyoko Sasaki, *Rakugo: The Popular Narrative Art of Japan*

139. Joshua A. Fogel, *Nakae Ushikichi in China: The Mourning of Spirit*

Harvard East Asian Monographs

140. Alexander Barton Woodside, *Vietnam and the Chinese Model: A Comparative Study of Vietnamese and Chinese Government in the First Half of the Nineteenth Century*
*141. George Elison, *Deus Destroyed: The Image of Christianity in Early Modern Japan*
142. William D. Wray, ed., *Managing Industrial Enterprise: Cases from Japan's Prewar Experience*
*143. T'ung-tsu Ch'ü, *Local Government in China Under the Ching*
144. Marie Anchordoguy, *Computers, Inc.: Japan's Challenge to IBM*
145. Barbara Molony, *Technology and Investment: The Prewar Japanese Chemical Industry*
146. Mary Elizabeth Berry, *Hideyoshi*
147. Laura E. Hein, *Fueling Growth: The Energy Revolution and Economic Policy in Postwar Japan*
148. Wen-hsin Yeh, *The Alienated Academy: Culture and Politics in Republican China, 1919–1937*
149. Dru C. Gladney, *Muslim Chinese: Ethnic Nationalism in the People's Republic*
150. Merle Goldman and Paul A. Cohen, eds., *Ideas Across Cultures: Essays on Chinese Thought in Honor of Benjamin I. Schwartz*
151. James M. Polachek, *The Inner Opium War*
152. Gail Lee Bernstein, *Japanese Marxist: A Portrait of Kawakami Hajime, 1879–1946*
*153. Lloyd E. Eastman, *The Abortive Revolution: China Under Nationalist Rule, 1927–1937*
154. Mark Mason, *American Multinationals and Japan: The Political Economy of Japanese Capital Controls, 1899–1980*
155. Richard J. Smith, John K. Fairbank, and Katherine F. Bruner, *Robert Hart and China's Early Modernization: His Journals, 1863–1866*
156. George J. Tanabe, Jr., *Myōe the Dreamkeeper: Fantasy and Knowledge in Kamakura Buddhism*
157. William Wayne Farris, *Heavenly Warriors: The Evolution of Japan's Military, 500–1300*
158. Yu-ming Shaw, *An American Missionary in China: John Leighton Stuart and Chinese-American Relations*
159. James B. Palais, *Politics and Policy in Traditional Korea*
*160. Douglas Reynolds, *China, 1898–1912: The Xinzheng Revolution and Japan*
161. Roger R. Thompson, *China's Local Councils in the Age of Constitutional Reform, 1898–1911*
162. William Johnston, *The Modern Epidemic: History of Tuberculosis in Japan*
163. Constantine Nomikos Vaporis, *Breaking Barriers: Travel and the State in Early Modern Japan*
164. Irmela Hijiya-Kirschnereit, *Rituals of Self-Revelation: Shishōsetsu as Literary Genre and Socio-Cultural Phenomenon*
165. James C. Baxter, *The Meiji Unification Through the Lens of Ishikawa Prefecture*
166. Thomas R. H. Havens, *Architects of Affluence: The Tsutsumi Family and the Seibu-Saison Enterprises in Twentieth-Century Japan*
167. Anthony Hood Chambers, *The Secret Window: Ideal Worlds in Tanizaki's Fiction*
168. Steven J. Ericson, *The Sound of the Whistle: Railroads and the State in Meiji Japan*
169. Andrew Edmund Goble, *Kenmu: Go-Daigo's Revolution*

170. Denise Potrzeba Lett, *In Pursuit of Status: The Making of South Korea's "New" Urban Middle Class*

171. Mimi Hall Yiengpruksawan, *Hiraizumi: Buddhist Art and Regional Politics in Twelfth-Century Japan*

172. Charles Shirō Inouye, *The Similitude of Blossoms: A Critical Biography of Izumi Kyōka (1873–1939), Japanese Novelist and Playwright*

173. Aviad E. Raz, *Riding the Black Ship: Japan and Tokyo Disneyland*

174. Deborah J. Milly, *Poverty, Equality, and Growth: The Politics of Economic Need in Postwar Japan*

175. See Heng Teow, *Japan's Cultural Policy Toward China, 1918–1931: A Comparative Perspective*

176. Michael A. Fuller, *An Introduction to Literary Chinese*

177. Frederick R. Dickinson, *War and National Reinvention: Japan in the Great War, 1914–1919*

178. John Solt, *Shredding the Tapestry of Meaning: The Poetry and Poetics of Kitasono Katue (1902–1978)*

179. Edward Pratt, *Japan's Protoindustrial Elite: The Economic Foundations of the Gōnō*

180. Atsuko Sakaki, *Recontextualizing Texts: Narrative Performance in Modern Japanese Fiction*

181. Soon-Won Park, *Colonial Industrialization and Labor in Korea: The Onoda Cement Factory*

182. JaHyun Kim Haboush and Martina Deuchler, *Culture and the State in Late Chosŏn Korea*

183. John W. Chaffee, *Branches of Heaven: A History of the Imperial Clan of Sung China*

184. Gi-Wook Shin and Michael Robinson, eds., *Colonial Modernity in Korea*

185. Nam-lin Hur, *Prayer and Play in Late Tokugawa Japan: Asakusa Sensōji and Edo Society*

186. Kristin Stapleton, *Civilizing Chengdu: Chinese Urban Reform, 1895–1937*

187. Hyung Il Pai, *Constructing "Korean" Origins: A Critical Review of Archaeology, Historiography, and Racial Myth in Korean State-Formation Theories*

188. Brian D. Ruppert, *Jewel in the Ashes: Buddha Relics and Power in Early Medieval Japan*

189. Susan Daruvala, *Zhou Zuoren and an Alternative Chinese Response to Modernity*

*190. James Z. Lee, *The Political Economy of a Frontier: Southwest China, 1250–1850*

191. Kerry Smith, *A Time of Crisis: Japan, the Great Depression, and Rural Revitalization*

192. Michael Lewis, *Becoming Apart: National Power and Local Politics in Toyama, 1868–1945*

193. William C. Kirby, Man-houng Lin, James Chin Shih, and David A. Pietz, eds., *State and Economy in Republican China: A Handbook for Scholars*

194. Timothy S. George, *Minamata: Pollution and the Struggle for Democracy in Postwar Japan*

195. Billy K. L. So, *Prosperity, Region, and Institutions in Maritime China: The South Fukien Pattern, 946–1368*

196. Yoshihisa Tak Matsusaka, *The Making of Japanese Manchuria, 1904–1932*

Harvard East Asian Monographs

197. Maram Epstein, *Competing Discourses: Orthodoxy, Authenticity, and Engendered Meanings in Late Imperial Chinese Fiction*
198. Curtis J. Milhaupt, J. Mark Ramseyer, and Michael K. Young, eds. and comps., *Japanese Law in Context: Readings in Society, the Economy, and Politics*
199. Haruo Iguchi, *Unfinished Business: Ayukawa Yoshisuke and U.S.-Japan Relations, 1937–1952*
200. Scott Pearce, Audrey Spiro, and Patricia Ebrey, *Culture and Power in the Reconstitution of the Chinese Realm, 200–600*
201. Terry Kawashima, *Writing Margins: The Textual Construction of Gender in Heian and Kamakura Japan*
202. Martin W. Huang, *Desire and Fictional Narrative in Late Imperial China*
203. Robert S. Ross and Jiang Changbin, eds., *Re-examining the Cold War: U.S.-China Diplomacy, 1954–1973*
204. Guanhua Wang, *In Search of Justice: The 1905–1906 Chinese Anti-American Boycott*
205. David Schaberg, *A Patterned Past: Form and Thought in Early Chinese Historiography*
206. Christine Yano, *Tears of Longing: Nostalgia and the Nation in Japanese Popular Song*
207. Milena Doleželová-Velingerová and Oldřich Král, with Graham Sanders, eds., *The Appropriation of Cultural Capital: China's May Fourth Project*
208. Robert N. Huey, *The Making of 'Shinkokinshū'*
209. Lee Butler, *Emperor and Aristocracy in Japan, 1467–1680: Resilience and Renewal*
210. Suzanne Ogden, *Inklings of Democracy in China*
211. Kenneth J. Ruoff, *The People's Emperor: Democracy and the Japanese Monarchy, 1945–1995*
212. Haun Saussy, *Great Walls of Discourse and Other Adventures in Cultural China*
213. Aviad E. Raz, *Emotions at Work: Normative Control, Organizations, and Culture in Japan and America*
214. Rebecca E. Karl and Peter Zarrow, eds., *Rethinking the 1898 Reform Period: Political and Cultural Change in Late Qing China*
215. Kevin O'Rourke, *The Book of Korean Shijo*
216. Ezra F. Vogel, ed., *The Golden Age of the U.S.-China-Japan Triangle, 1972–1989*
217. Thomas A. Wilson, ed., *On Sacred Grounds: Culture, Society, Politics, and the Formation of the Cult of Confucius*
218. Donald S. Sutton, *Steps of Perfection: Exorcistic Performers and Chinese Religion in Twentieth-Century Taiwan*
219. Daqing Yang, *Technology of Empire: Telecommunications and Japanese Expansionism in Asia, 1883–1945*
220. Qianshen Bai, *Fu Shan's World: The Transformation of Chinese Calligraphy in the Seventeenth Century*
221. Paul Jakov Smith and Richard von Glahn, eds., *The Song-Yuan-Ming Transition in Chinese History*
222. Rania Huntington, *Alien Kind: Foxes and Late Imperial Chinese Narrative*
223. Jordan Sand, *House and Home in Modern Japan: Architecture, Domestic Space, and Bourgeois Culture, 1880–1930*

224. Karl Gerth, *China Made: Consumer Culture and the Creation of the Nation*
225. Xiaoshan Yang, *Metamorphosis of the Private Sphere: Gardens and Objects in Tang-Song Poetry*
226. Barbara Mittler, *A Newspaper for China? Power, Identity, and Change in Shanghai's News Media, 1872–1912*
227. Joyce A. Madancy, *The Troublesome Legacy of Commissioner Lin: The Opium Trade and Opium Suppression in Fujian Province, 1820s to 1920s*
228. John Makeham, *Transmitters and Creators: Chinese Commentators and Commentaries on the Analects*
229. Elisabeth Köll, *From Cotton Mill to Business Empire: The Emergence of Regional Enterprises in Modern China*
230. Emma Teng, *Taiwan's Imagined Geography: Chinese Colonial Travel Writing and Pictures, 1683–1895*
231. Wilt Idema and Beata Grant, *The Red Brush: Writing Women of Imperial China*
232. Eric C. Rath, *The Ethos of Noh: Actors and Their Art*
233. Elizabeth Remick, *Building Local States: China During the Republican and Post-Mao Eras*
234. Lynn Struve, ed., *The Qing Formation in World-Historical Time*
235. D. Max Moerman, *Localizing Paradise: Kumano Pilgrimage and the Religious Landscape of Premodern Japan*
236. Antonia Finnane, *Speaking of Yangzhou: A Chinese City, 1550–1850*
237. Brian Platt, *Burning and Building: Schooling and State Formation in Japan, 1750–1890*
238. Gail Bernstein, Andrew Gordon, and Kate Wildman Nakai, eds., *Public Spheres, Private Lives in Modern Japan, 1600–1950: Essays in Honor of Albert Craig*
239. Wu Hung and Katherine R. Tsiang, *Body and Face in Chinese Visual Culture*
240. Stephen Dodd, *Writing Home: Representations of the Native Place in Modern Japanese Literature*
241. David Anthony Bello, *Opium and the Limits of Empire: Drug Prohibition in the Chinese Interior, 1729–1850*
242. Hosea Hirata, *Discourses of Seduction: History, Evil, Desire, and Modern Japanese Literature*
243. Kyung Moon Hwang, *Beyond Birth: Social Status in the Emergence of Modern Korea*
244. Brian R. Dott, *Identity Reflections: Pilgrimages to Mount Tai in Late Imperial China*
245. Mark McNally, *Proving the Way: Conflict and Practice in the History of Japanese Nativism*
246. Yongping Wu, *A Political Explanation of Economic Growth: State Survival, Bureaucratic Politics, and Private Enterprises in the Making of Taiwan's Economy, 1950–1985*
247. Kyu Hyun Kim, *The Age of Visions and Arguments: Parliamentarianism and the National Public Sphere in Early Meiji Japan*
248. Zvi Ben-Dor Benite, *The Dao of Muhammad: A Cultural History of Muslims in Late Imperial China*
249. David Der-wei Wang and Shang Wei, eds., *Dynastic Crisis and Cultural Innovation: From the Late Ming to the Late Qing and Beyond*

Harvard East Asian Monographs

250. Wilt L. Idema, Wai-yee Li, and Ellen Widmer, eds., *Trauma and Transcendence in Early Qing Literature*
251. Barbara Molony and Kathleen Uno, eds., *Gendering Modern Japanese History*
252. Hiroshi Aoyagi, *Islands of Eight Million Smiles: Idol Performance and Symbolic Production in Contemporary Japan*
253. Wai-yee Li, *The Readability of the Past in Early Chinese Historiography*
254. William C. Kirby, Robert S. Ross, and Gong Li, eds., *Normalization of U.S.-China Relations: An International History*
255. Ellen Gardner Nakamura, *Practical Pursuits: Takano Chōei, Takahashi Keisaku, and Western Medicine in Nineteenth-Century Japan*
256. Jonathan W. Best, *A History of the Early Korean Kingdom of Paekche, together with an annotated translation of* The Paekche Annals *of the* Samguk sagi
257. Liang Pan, *The United Nations in Japan's Foreign and Security Policymaking, 1945–1992: National Security, Party Politics, and International Status*
258. Richard Belsky, *Localities at the Center: Native Place, Space, and Power in Late Imperial Beijing*
259. Zwia Lipkin, *"Useless to the State": "Social Problems" and Social Engineering in Nationalist Nanjing, 1927–1937*
260. William O. Gardner, *Advertising Tower: Japanese Modernism and Modernity in the 1920s*
261. Stephen Owen, *The Making of Early Chinese Classical Poetry*
262. Martin J. Powers, *Pattern and Person: Ornament, Society, and Self in Classical China*
263. Anna M. Shields, *Crafting a Collection: The Cultural Contexts and Poetic Practice of the* Huajian ji 花間集 (*Collection from Among the Flowers*)
264. Stephen Owen, *The Late Tang: Chinese Poetry of the Mid-Ninth Century (827–860)*
265. Sara L. Friedman, *Intimate Politics: Marriage, the Market, and State Power in Southeastern China*
266. Patricia Buckley Ebrey and Maggie Bickford, *Emperor Huizong and Late Northern Song China: The Politics of Culture and the Culture of Politics*
267. Sophie Volpp, *Worldly Stage: Theatricality in Seventeenth-Century China*
268. Ellen Widmer, *The Beauty and the Book: Women and Fiction in Nineteenth-Century China*
269. Steven B. Miles, *The Sea of Learning: Mobility and Identity in Nineteenth-Century Guangzhou*
270. Lin Man-houng, *China Upside Down: Currency, Society, and Ideologies, 1808–1856*
271. Ronald Egan, *The Problem of Beauty: Aesthetic Thought and Pursuits in Northern Song Dynasty China*
272. Mark Halperin, *Out of the Cloister: Literati Perspectives on Buddhism in Sung China, 960–1279*
273. Helen Dunstan, *State or Merchant? Political Economy and Political Process in 1740s China*
274. Sabina Knight, *The Heart of Time: Moral Agency in Twentieth-Century Chinese Fiction*
275. Timothy J. Van Compernolle, *The Uses of Memory: The Critique of Modernity in the Fiction of Higuchi Ichiyō*

Harvard East Asian Monographs

276. Paul Rouzer, *A New Practical Primer of Literary Chinese*
277. Jonathan Zwicker, *Practices of the Sentimental Imagination: Melodrama, the Novel, and the Social Imaginary in Nineteenth-Century Japan*
278. Franziska Seraphim, *War Memory and Social Politics in Japan, 1945–2005*
279. Adam L. Kern, *Manga from the Floating World: Comicbook Culture and the* Kibyōshi *of Edo Japan*
280. Cynthia J. Brokaw, *Commerce in Culture: The Sibao Book Trade in the Qing and Republican Periods*
281. Eugene Y. Park, *Between Dreams and Reality: The Military Examination in Late Chosŏn Korea, 1600–1894*
282. Nam-lin Hur, *Death and Social Order in Tokugawa Japan: Buddhism, Anti-Christianity, and the* Danka *System*
283. Patricia M. Thornton, *Disciplining the State: Virtue, Violence, and State-Making in Modern China*
284. Vincent Goossaert, *The Taoists of Peking, 1800–1949: A Social History of Urban Clerics*
285. Peter Nickerson, *Taoism, Bureaucracy, and Popular Religion in Early Medieval China*
286. Charo B. D'Etcheverry, *Love After* The Tale of Genji: *Rewriting the World of the Shining Prince*
287. Michael G. Chang, *A Court on Horseback: Imperial Touring & the Construction of Qing Rule, 1680–1785*
288. Carol Richmond Tsang, *War and Faith:* Ikkō Ikki *in Late Muromachi Japan*
289. Hilde De Weerdt, *Competition over Content: Negotiating Standards for the Civil Service Examinations in Imperial China (1127–1279)*
290. Eve Zimmerman, *Out of the Alleyway: Nakagami Kenji and the Poetics of Outcaste Fiction*
291. Robert Culp, *Articulating Citizenship: Civic Education and Student Politics in Southeastern China, 1912–1940*
292. Richard J. Smethurst, *From Foot Soldier to Finance Minister: Takahashi Korekiyo, Japan's Keynes*
293. John E. Herman, *Amid the Clouds and Mist: China's Colonization of Guizhou, 1200–1700*
294. Tomoko Shiroyama, *China During the Great Depression: Market, State, and the World Economy, 1929–1937*
295. Kirk W. Larsen, *Tradition, Treaties and Trade: Qing Imperialism and Chosŏn Korea, 1850–1910*
296. Gregory Golley, *When Our Eyes No Longer See: Realism, Science, and Ecology in Japanese Literary Modernism*
297. Barbara Ambros, *Emplacing a Pilgrimage: The Ōyama Cult and Regional Religion in Early Modern Japan*
298. Rebecca Suter, *The Japanization of Modernity: Murakami Haruki between Japan and the United States*
299. Yuma Totani, *The Tokyo War Crimes Trial: The Pursuit of Justice in the Wake of World War II*

300. Linda Isako Angst, *In a Dark Time: Memory, Community, and Gendered Nationalism in Postwar Okinawa*

301. David M. Robinson, ed., *Culture, Courtiers, and Competition: The Ming Court (1368–1644)*

302. Calvin Chen, *Some Assembly Required: Work, Community, and Politics in China's Rural Enterprises*

303. Sem Vermeersch, *The Power of the Buddhas: The Politics of Buddhism During the Koryŏ Dynasty (918–1392)*

304. Tina Lu, *Accidental Incest, Filial Cannibalism, and Other Peculiar Encounters in Late Imperial Chinese Literature*

305. Chang Woei Ong, *Men of Letters Within the Passes: Guanzhong Literati in Chinese History, 907–1911*

306. Wendy Swartz, *Reading Tao Yuanming: Shifting Paradigms of Historical Reception (427–1900)*

307. Peter K. Bol, *Neo-Confucianism in History*

308. Carlos Rojas, *The Naked Gaze: Reflections on Chinese Modernity*

309. Kelly H. Chong, *Deliverance and Submission: Evangelical Women and the Negotiation of Patriarchy in South Korea*

310. Rachel DiNitto, *Uchida Hyakken: A Critique of Modernity and Militarism in Prewar Japan*

311. Jeffrey Snyder-Reinke, *Dry Spells: State Rainmaking and Local Governance in Late Imperial China*

312. Jay Dautcher, *Down a Narrow Road: Identity and Masculinity in a Uyghur Community in Xinjiang China*

313. Xun Liu, *Daoist Modern: Innovation, Lay Practice, and the Community of Inner Alchemy in Republican Shanghai*

314. Jacob Eyferth, *Eating Rice from Bamboo Roots: The Social History of a Community of Handicraft Papermakers in Rural Sichuan, 1920–2000*

315. David Johnson, *Spectacle and Sacrifice: The Ritual Foundations of Village Life in North China*

316. James Robson, *Power of Place: The Religious Landscape of the Southern Sacred Peak (Nanyue 南嶽) in Medieval China*

317. Lori Watt, *When Empire Comes Home: Repatriation and Reintegration in Postwar Japan*

318. James Dorsey, *Critical Aesthetics: Kobayashi Hideo, Modernity, and Wartime Japan*

319. Christopher Bolton, *Sublime Voices: The Fictional Science and Scientific Fiction of Abe Kōbō*

320. Si-yen Fei, *Negotiating Urban Space: Urbanization and Late Ming Nanjing*

321. Christopher Gerteis, *Gender Struggles: Wage-Earning Women and Male-Dominated Unions in Postwar Japan*

322. Rebecca Nedostup, *Superstitious Regimes: Religion and the Politics of Chinese Modernity*

323. Lucien Bianco, *Wretched Rebels: Rural Disturbances on the Eve of the Chinese Revolution*

324. Cathryn H. Clayton, *Sovereignty at the Edge: Macau and the Question of Chineseness*

325. Micah S. Muscolino, *Fishing Wars and Environmental Change in Late Imperial and Modern China*

326. Robert I. Hellyer, *Defining Engagement: Japan and Global Contexts, 1750–1868*

327. Robert Ashmore, *The Transport of Reading: Text and Understanding in the World of Tao Qian (365–427)*

328. Mark A. Jones, *Children as Treasures: Childhood and the Middle Class in Early Twentieth Century Japan*

329. Miryam Sas, *Experimental Arts in Postwar Japan: Moments of Encounter, Engagement, and Imagined Return*

330. H. Mack Horton, *Traversing the Frontier: The* Man'yōshū *Account of a Japanese Mission to Silla in 736–737*

331. Dennis J. Frost, *Seeing Stars: Sports Celebrity, Identity, and Body Culture in Modern Japan*

332. Marnie S. Anderson, *A Place in Public: Women's Rights in Meiji Japan*

333. Peter Mauch, *Sailor Diplomat: Nomura Kichisaburō and the Japanese-American War*

334. Ethan Isaac Segal, *Coins, Trade, and the State: Economic Growth in Early Medieval Japan*

335. David B. Lurie, *Realms of Literacy: Early Japan and the History of Writing*

336. Lillian Lan-ying Tseng, *Picturing Heaven in Early China*

337. Jun Uchida, *Brokers of Empire: Japanese Settler Colonialism in Korea, 1876–1945*

338. Patricia L. Maclachlan, *The People's Post Office: The History and Politics of the Japanese Postal System, 1871–2010*

339. Michael Schiltz, *The Money Doctors from Japan: Finance, Imperialism, and the Building of the Yen Bloc, 1895–1937*

340. Daqing Yang, Jie Liu, Hiroshi Mitani, and Andrew Gordon, eds., *Toward a History Beyond Borders: Contentious Issues in Sino-Japanese Relations*

341. Sonia Ryang, *Reading North Korea: An Ethnological Inquiry*